C000253478

COPS
AND
HORRORS

COPS AND HORRORS

Secret Tales From The Front Line

MATT CALVELEY

MIRROR BOOKS

mß

MIRROR BOOKS

© Matt Calveley

1

Published in Great Britain and Ireland in 2022 by
Mirror Books, a Reach PLC business,
5 St Paul's Square, Liverpool, L3 9SJ.

www.mirrorbooks.co.uk
@TheMirrorBooks

Print ISBN 9781913406967
eBook ISBN 9781913406974

Edited by Simon Monk.
Additional production by Harri Aston.
Page design and typesetting by Danny Lyle.

Photos: Matt Calveley personal collection.

Printed and bound in Great Britain by
CPI Group (UK) Ltd, Croydon, CR0 4YY.

This book is dedicated to the families of police officers. The unsung heroes who put up with shifts, disruption to family life, missed Christmas parties, dinners and school performances, and living with the uncertainty of not knowing when – or even if – their serving loved one is coming home.

PROLOGUE

East Acton, 1986

'*Just put down the knife and let the boy go,*' *I say. My voice is surprisingly level, optimistic even, but I'm thinking,* 'I might die tonight.'

I'm standing before a man called Dwayne, who's six-feet-six and built like an American footballer. He's holding his son Tyler, lifting him off the kitchen floor by his curly hair, yanking his head backwards while pressing a twelve-inch blade against the boy's throat. Between juddered gasps and screams, Tyler calls,'Mummy, Mummy. Help me. Mummy. Please.' Tears stream over his upturned chin, down his neck. He is no older than ten.

Dwayne tightens his grip on the boy and the knife, eyes blazing. '*Get the fuck out of my house, or I'll cut his fucking throat,*' *he yells.*

I inch forwards in the hallway, clenching my pathetic truncheon aloft. Beneath my woollen tunic, my back is wet with sweat. '*Let the boy go. Don't do anything stupid. Put the knife down,*' *I repeat. I take another tentative step, so as I'm on the threshold of the hall and the kitchen. Dark thoughts whirl:* What if Dwayne slits his son's throat? I can't let that happen. No way. But Dwayne's at least three inches taller and four stone heavier than me. His weight is all muscle. Will he stab me? Will it be a quick death? I'm just a few months into the Job, yet I could die right here. In this maisonette on a housing estate in East Acton.

'Put the knife down.' That's Constable Fiona. She's behind me in the hall, my backup until the armed response unit arrives. But we can't afford to wait for them. Frantic screams from the front garden, where Tyler's mum Sandra waits with my other colleague, Constable Graham.

'I said, get the fuck out of my house,' Dwayne warns me again, his tone now low and demonic. 'Or I will slice his throat.' He shuffles towards me, still gripping his son. The blade, slick with Tyler's tears, glistens in the fluorescent lighting. As Dwayne advances, a reflection of his back appears in the glass door that gives way to the rear garden. He has another knife stashed in the left back pocket of his jeans. A taste of bile fills my mouth.

An hour earlier I'd been on foot patrol, the Housemartins' *Happy Hour* looping in my mind as I plodded along nearby Old Oak Common Lane. There wasn't much doing. *I need a big incident,* I'd thought and, just then the police radio cut in: 'Domestic disturbance in progress. The caller says her boyfriend is being aggressive and has threatened to assault her. There is a young child on the premises. Graded immediate response.' I was at the scene in less than five minutes, well within the recommended twelve-minute response time. A minute later, Constables Graham and Fiona hurtled into the street in their Rover 2600 Area car, twos and blues (sirens and lights) screaming and flashing.

Sandra had answered the door, visibly distressed, her partner Dwayne effing and blinding in the background. At this point, Tyler was sitting on the stairs, sobbing. Once inside

I took Sandra into the lounge while Fiona and Graham spoke to Dwayne in the kitchen. And what happened next happened fast. Fiona screamed, 'Knife!' and torpedoed out of the house with Graham. When I crept into the hall seconds later, Dwayne was dragging the screaming Tyler into the kitchen. Under my cover, Sandra escaped through the front door, and that's how I ended up here, confronting a maniac who's threatening to slice open his kid's throat.

I open my mouth to speak but no words form. My heart thrums in my ears. I'm trying to maintain eye contact with Dwayne, whose face is wild and feral. His breath a rumbling growl. Tyler's hysterical, hyperventilating. But my attention shifts; I see a figure in the back garden, on the other side of the glass door behind Dwayne. A man in dark clothing, holding what looks to be a brick above his head: Constable Graham. I swallow hard. 'Put the knife down and let the boy go,' I say once more as Graham's silhouette fills the doorframe.

'Fuck you, get the fuck out of…'

Crash. The glass door explodes, sending a shower of shards over Dwayne and Tyler. I power into the kitchen, where Dwayne is bent over, shaking glass from his dreadlocks. One, two, three steps, and I'm there, smashing my truncheon into Dwayne's head. It makes a sickening sound, like a sledgehammer to a peach. At the same time, Fiona steams in, grabs the knife from Dwayne's hand, and the one in his pocket, and throws them into the hall. Tyler breaks free and runs to his mum. Blood pours from Dwayne's head. As he slumps to the glass carpet he mumbles, 'Oh no.'

While Dwayne's down I drop to my knees and, handcuffing him, read him his rights. 'You're nicked for knives and fighting and stuff,' I begin. It's not the correct terminology, but in adrenaline-fuelled moments such as these, official language goes out of the window. 'You do not have to say anything, but it'll look pretty bad for you if you don't.'

Dwayne is semi-conscious, his head split open. As my adrenaline rush subsides, panic creeps in. I look at Dwayne, at his bloody head and think, I could've killed him. If I were armed, I would have been within my rights to shoot him. Likewise, Dwayne could have killed his son, or killed me.

I breathe in, exhale, slip my bloodied truncheon into its pocket on my outer trouser leg, and suddenly realise: This is my job for the next thirty years.

CHAPTER ONE
ARRESTING MOMENTS

Lytham, Lancashire 1978

I was with my mate Kevin and thigh-deep in foxgloves when the copper bustled through the garden gate. 'Oi, you boys, stop what you're doing,' he shouted, cheeks like lumps of sweaty raw beef in the August heat. 'Get away from those flowers. You are *trespassing*.' He thumped towards us in his shiny shoes, making a stop signal with his right hand. A rotund figure who'd pass for the Laughing Policeman were he in a jolly mood. Although, now I thought about it, most cops who patrolled this seaside town looked like him. Kevin snorted into the neck of his *Happy Days* T-shirt, which set me off laughing too, and the PC's blood pressure visibly skyrocketed as he neared the flower bed. 'Poor Mrs Jamieson's nerves are shot. Do your parents know you're here? You two are coming with me to…'

I didn't catch the end of that sentence. Kevin and I took one look at one another and legged it, beheading Mrs Jamieson's perennials as we ripped through the flowerbed and vaulted a wall, into the lane where the cop had parked his Panda car. Silence. Followed by the sound of wrought iron smashing brick, heavy footsteps, a crackle of radio and, 'Oi, police, stop!' The chase was on.

We sprinted down the narrow lane, laughing and panting, the plod a few metres behind, wheezing, 'Police, stop, come back here.' Over a fence and into another garden, through a gate, up an alley, into a further garden, trampling more flower beds, knocking over bins and scrambling army-style over compost heaps. Kevin, who looked ablaze with his shoulder-length orange hair streaming behind him, brought down a few pairs of Y-fronts as he zipped past a rotary washing line. I had a near miss with a kid on a space hopper. We tore through many of the gardens and alleys that linked rows of terraced houses in Lytham.

The overweight copper didn't stand a chance; we outran him, left him huffing and puffing somewhere around garden two or three, and a part of me felt let down by his poor pursuit. Admittedly, our 'trespassing' offence was not the crime of the century. We hadn't set out to deliberately wreck Mrs Jamieson's blooms. Kevin and I had been searching for our football, which I'd accidentally kicked over the wall into Mrs Jamieson's garden. But I couldn't help thinking, *If I were that cop, I wouldn't have let Kevin or me get away.*

Being slow on his feet was not the only mistake the PC made that day. Returning to our so-called crime scene some 40 minutes later, we were surprised to see the plod's Panda car – a blue Austin Allegro – still parked in the same spot in the lane. The motor was empty, its engine running, but the copper was nowhere to be seen. Even then, as a lad of 13, I thought, *what self-respecting cop abandons his car, unlocked, with the keys in the ignition and the engine running?*

'We could nick that,' Kevin said, throwing a freckled arm in the direction of the Panda.

'Yeah,' I said, admiring the car, a gleaming vision in Tic Tac blue. 'We could take it for a quick spin around town. My heart disco-danced at the idea. Me, behind the wheel of a police car? I'd lived this fantasy in my head so many times. Arms outstretched, I gripped an imaginary steering wheel and mimed taking a corner at speed.

Kevin laughed briefly then straightened his face. 'We should probably split – before that copper comes back to nick us,' he said. I nodded, and, without further deliberation, we made our getaway, accelerating to breakneck speed along the lane, on foot, away from the Panda car. We never found our football.

Ever since I was a kid, I'd wanted to be a cop. I grew up watching police series on television – *CHiPs, Juliet Bravo, Kojak* and, much later, *The Bill*. But *Starsky & Hutch* were my ultimate cop heroes. Every Saturday evening, I'd be glued to the TV, my adrenal glands on overdrive as I watched the duo's full-throttle car chases in their bright red Ford Gran Torino. God, I wanted that car. I also wanted to be just like Starsky, the handsome dark-haired cop played by Paul Glaser. He was my favourite of the two. I loved how he was so accident-prone and reckless. Starsky had it all; he even looked cool in a chunky knit cardigan.

I can still see Kevin and me, after our run-in with PC Plod, clutching our bellies as we jiggled over the freezer in the sweetshop, barely able to talk for laughing while considering our options: Zoom, Screwball or Jubbly? Likewise, the copper's angry red face remains a vivid snapshot in my mind. OK, our chase scene was hardly a *Starsky & Hutch*-inspired event. No burning rubber fumes filled the air – just a blend of mown grass and creosote over the familiar smell of seaweed. The local cop's feeble Allegro was no competition for the TV duo's Gran Torino. And being an underweight teenager – my body like sticks and bolts wrapped in filo pastry – I looked nothing like Starsky. A chunky knit cardi would have been incongruous on such a sweltering day. But I had experienced the thrill of the chase – and from that moment, I was hooked. You see, such excitement was rare in this quaint, Victorian Lancashire town, where I came screaming into the world one windy Saturday evening in October 1964.

I went to Arnold School in Blackpool, a posh acade-my whose alumni includes former Conservative MP Sir Walter Clegg, Blue Peter presenter Peter Purves, Pet Shop Boys singer Chris Lowe and electronic musician David Ball, who played in the band Soft Cell. But in my day, unless you were Einstein-bright, good at sports, or a bully, you'd struggle to thrive at Arnold. Aside from being an OK sprinter – an ability I'd utilised well when being chased by the cop – I had no special talents. Academia wasn't my thing, so I was often bottom of the class. Being a bully didn't appeal.

Arnold felt like a prison camp. I'd spend lunch breaks alone in the playground, counting the hours until the final bell rang at 3.30pm, when I could escape to Lytham and be among people who *were* my friends. Lads like Kevin, and my two mates, Dave and Paul. Park Street Youth Club became my sanctuary, with activities held on most weekend evenings, either at the club itself or at members' houses, where we'd play snooker or watch videos. Normal kids' stuff. Years later I would become the leader of the Youth Club.

Days, terms and years at Arnold moved at a glacial pace and, by the time I reached sixth form, it was obvious I wouldn't be splitting the atom any time soon. I'd achieved nothing remarkable academically, even though I'd signed up for four A-levels – including maths and physics, which I might have been OK at given the right encouragement. But my physics teacher, I'll call him Mr Joyce, preferred mocking me in class. Whenever I asked a question, he would laugh, then turn to one of the brainbox boys destined for places like Oxbridge or astronaut school, and say, 'Do you want to tell dim Calveley here the answer?' Now, should Joyce have had the foresight to say, 'Calveley, I'd like to explain to you, in an accessible form, Newton's equations of motion. They'll be useful in a few years' time when you've qualified as a forensic collision investigator for the Metropolitan Police and you are trying to establish what speed a young drunk driver was travelling at before he crashed his BMW and died at the scene...' that would have almost certainly have grabbed my attention. In the end, I stopped asking questions, lost interest in the subject, and subsequently failed my A-level physics.

I failed maths too, and left Arnold school having scraped an E-grade pass in computer science and a D in general studies, which wasn't even enough to get me into North Staffordshire Polytechnic, where, bizarrely, I'd applied to study computer science. It was summer 1982, my prospects were grim, and I couldn't go anywhere without hearing Irene Cara's chart-topping hit *Fame*.

Truth was, I had zero interest in pursuing a career in computers – or being stuck behind a desk all day. I wanted an adrenaline-fuelled job – one where no two days were the same. Having passed my second driving test at 17, I was happiest when speeding along the country lanes in my Ford Escort, with Pink Floyd or Dire Straits blaring from the cassette player. That car, registration plate EFR 254S, was my prized possession. Canary yellow, I pimped it up with four extra headlights and a red stripe running over the bonnet and roof. My youth club mates, Dave and Paul, had similar pimped-up cars and, together, we became stereotypical boy-racers, tearing along country lanes and performing lethal manoeuvres. We'd race each other around Lytham – on roads and pavements – at night, sometimes with our headlights switched off to add to the buzz.

I had no fear. My appetite for fast and dangerous driving was insatiable. I started to think of which jobs involved driving like a maniac, and that's when I returned to my childhood aspirations. *I'll join the police force*, I thought, *Then I'll be able to drive fast cars every day, on wailing twos and blues. Chase villains, be a crime-buster, make a difference… drive fast cars.* It was a no-brainer. Alas, my journey from boy racer to one of the boys in blue would not be so straightforward.

I felt under pressure to get a job fast. The only paid work I'd done so far was a summer job the previous year, working on a construction site.

I still wanted to become a cop, but there were no

vacancies for trainee Constables at Lancashire Police at that time. So, I shelved my policing dreams and instead, after a few months working as an 'office junior' at my dad's legal firm (a role hastily created to keep me off the dole queue) I managed to get a job as a clerk at the county court in Blackpool. I enjoyed the job, even though it involved sitting in court or the office all day, dealing with civil cases involving debts between people. The court building was next door to Blackpool Central Police Station, and often, I'd find myself staring out of the window, watching police officers coming and going in their cars, thinking, *If only*.

I spent three years at the county court – then I spotted an advert in *The Sunday Times*. The Metropolitan Police were looking for recruits. Until now, I hadn't thought about moving to London. My eye had long been on joining Lancashire Constabulary. I'd applied to Lancashire a year ago, only to be knocked back for being two years underage. In my haste I'd neglected to notice that the force's entry age was 21. But the Met's advert clearly stated: 'Applicants must be 18 or over.'

I read the advert about three times, picturing life as a PC in crime-ridden London. The Big Smoke, where cops risked their lives dealing with robberies, shootings, knife attacks and riots. Months earlier, Met police officer Yvonne Fletcher was shot dead outside the Libyan embassy while monitoring a demo against Colonel Gaddafi. Did I really want to leave sleepy Lytham to police London? I grabbed my dad's best Parker ballpoint and filled in the form, which asked for basic details such as my name, address, qualifications and my vital statistics (height and weight). An hour later, my application was in the post. London was calling – with twos and blues.

The next few weeks were nail-bitingly tense. Initially, I received a card saying my application was being processed, which I thought was a good sign. But, days later, another letter from the Met's Careers Information Selection Centre landed on the doormat at Lodore Villa. I turned hot all over when I read it. The Met was questioning my height-weight ratio. At six feet three, I tipped the scales at a scrawny ten-stone-nine. The selection centre now wanted me to be measured and weighed at my local police station to 'certify' my statistics.

Just as I'd failed to observe the age limit in my Lancashire Constabulary application, I hadn't paused to consider the Met's then strict entry rule that recruits must be of proportional weight and height. Gutted is too tame a word to describe my mood as I shuffled into my local nick to be weighed and measured. What was the point even? There was no way I could have gained an extra half stone in the last week. Then, just when I thought my policing dream was over, somebody came to my rescue. His name was Sergeant Steel.

As expected, my weight had not changed, but fortunately, Steel was a generous soul. 'You're underweight,' he said, dunking a chocolate digestive in his tea. 'I'd better give you some extra pounds or you'll have no chance, lad.'

'Really?' I said, unsure whether Steel's comment was some kind of joke. 'That would be much appreciated. I really, really want to be a cop – more than anything else in the world.'

Steel laughed. 'Don't mention it, lad. Just make sure you get some pies down your neck before the interview.'

'Absolutely,' I said.

Flash forward nine months and the InterCity coughed me, in my ill-fitting grey C&A suit, into the smoggy chaos of Euston station, London. Thanks to Steel's creativity, I had been invited to attend a two-day Metropolitan Police 'selection process'.

The force put me up in a bed and breakfast on Praed Street, close to its recruitment centre at Paddington Green Police Station, which was known by its then call sign, Delta Delta. For a big operation such as the Met, I had expected to stay in a plush hotel room. The Hilton perhaps? No such luck. Inside, this B&B dormitory was like a grotty, flea-ridden youth hostel, with a threadbare, stained carpet the colour of oxtail soup. Picture it: one small room, four bunkbeds and eight wannabe cops, the air dense with sweat and testosterone and inflated egos. An occasional whiff of beef and tomato Pot Noodle, Brut and Old Spice. I walked into the room, claimed a top bunk and had just started unpacking when a voice boomed over my shoulder. 'Alright to take this bunk?' I turned and came face to face with a lad in a burnt orange velvet suit and a shoulder-length shaggy perm.

'Sam,' he said, and his hair danced. 'The Metropolitan Police's next rising star.' As we shook hands, he looked me up and down, then, sniggering, added: 'Ha, you've got no chance, mate. Did you not read about the weight restrictions?' *Bastard*. Sam had hit a nerve. Despite a shedload of pies, I'd put on only a pound or two. I thought about a witty retort – asking Sam whether he'd come as Michael Bolton auditioning for the part of Hendrix, for example, but I thought better of it. I dropped my hand.

'Yeah, that bunk's free,' I said.

On day two of the selection process, after sailing through the first day's written and real-life policing exercises, I faced the dreaded medical. In a cold, TCP-scented room I stepped onto the column scales and came eye to eye socket with a hanging human skeleton, darting me a freakish grin that cried, 'You and I are two of a kind, baby.' The nurse fiddled with the sliding weights. My mouth went bone dry. I could hear my heart banging over the sound of rush hour traffic on the A40 outside. The nurse could probably hear it too.

In line with Sergeant Steel's thinking, I had come prepared with a few tricks to cheat the system. My suit jacket and trouser pockets were loaded with coins. The nurse scribbled on her clipboard. 'Ten-stone-eight,' she announced. *Shit, ten-stone-eight.* Sergeant Steel had 'fixed' my weight to eleven-stone-six. In seconds, my dreams of becoming a cop could be over. The nurse reached for the headboard on the vertical ruler. *Think Matt, think.* Instinctively, I slowly bent my knees, now grateful that my trousers were too big for me. 'Keep nice and still for me,' added the nurse, as I strained to hold my pose while trying to avoid the skeleton's gaze. 'Six feet one,' the nurse said, 'Surprisingly, you're just within the required measurements.' I thanked the nurse and hurried out of the room before she suggested a re-measure.

Compared to the medical tests – during which I was

also made to strip naked before three male doctors, one of whom, for reasons unknown, instructed me to turn around and touch my toes – the final interview part of the selection process was a breeze. Walking along the corridor to the interview room, I spotted Sam. He was stomping back and forth, hands in his hair. I gave him a nod. 'Everything OK, Sam?'

'No,' he said. 'The Met doesn't want me. Can you believe it? Idiots told me to try again next year. Fuck that.'

I placed my hand on his velvet shoulder. 'Bad luck, mate.'

My interview took place in a meeting room at Paddington Green Police station with two women – Superintendent Moss, and a personnel manager whose name escapes me. The interview was informal, more of a chat. After a few minutes, just as I was about to start on my list of prepared questions, Superintendent Moss stood up, walked around the desk and proffered her hand. 'Congratulations, Matthew,' she said, her shake warm and firm and police-like. 'Welcome to the Metropolitan Police. Any questions?'

I wanted to throw my stringy arms around her. For a moment I was lost for words. Then I heard sirens outside, the sound bending and warping as it flew past the building.

Yes,' I said, 'Just the one... when do I start?'

CHAPTER TWO
PASSING OUT

Wanstead Flats, east London, January 1986

'On your feet, Calveley, now.' Our PT instructor's voice clattered, loud as gunfire through the blizzard, 'I mean it, Bambi, you've got five seconds… One –'

He had a knack for telling it as it is, did PC Davies. I'd hit the ground like a newborn deer. Slip, slosh, thud as my legs buckled under the weight of wood on my shoulder, and I fell on my coccyx into a mixture of snow and mud. Now I was on my back in the freezing slush, winded and pinioned at my left armpit and shoulder by a 65-kilogram log, snow filling my mouth as I gasped for air.

It was 6.30am, zero degrees, and raven dark.

'C'mon Matt, get up, for fuck's sake.' That was my class-mate Nigel, still standing and holding the other end of the log. We were supposed to be running while shouldering the trunk. Nigel at the front, me at the back, but I'd slipped after only a few yards into this one-and-a-half-mile endurance exercise.

I looked up at Nigel, a fuzzy grey shape behind the falling snow. Like a figure on an untuned black and white telly. 'Just lift the log – it's not heavy, I've got the other end.'

Breathing hard, I clamped my iced palms on either side of the log and tried to heave it skywards while also trying to push up from my feet. But my trainers skidded south, and my legs spraddled east and west and, my God, it was baltic. Tongue-sticking-to-the-lamppost cold.

'... Two. This should be a piece of piss for you, Calveley.'

'I'm trying my best.' The words wheezed out of me. Fine for PC Davies to call this task easy. He was fit as an Olympic hurdler, with cartoonish ripped muscles to boot. One of those types who does the Ironman Triathlon, just for a laugh. But, as you know, I weighed only a couple of kilos more than the log itself and, like my twenty colleagues running around Wanstead Flats on this polar morning, I was frozen to the bone.

'Three. On your feet.'

As I tried once more to lever myself from the ground, another duo ferrying a second log pounded past, splattering me in slush and grit in their wake

'For fuck's sake, they've overtaken us now. What's wrong with you? Move it,' Nigel shouted down the log. He was lifting it higher and subsequently ramming the back end harder into my armpit.

'Four. C'mon, Bambi.'

Humiliation fuelled my determination in that moment. *C'mon Matt, you can do this. Prove Davies wrong.* With all the strength in my spindly, frozen body, I pushed the wet log with the front of my shoulder and hands and managed to manoeuvre myself into a seated position. Then I drew in my legs and let out a sound somewhere between a grunt and sob as I rose to my feet.

'Now move it, Calveley,' yelled PC Davies.

The snow was turning to sleet, a brisk wind blowing it horizontally into my face. I felt a sharp tug from the front of the log as Nigel powered forth and, energised, I called into the wet air, 'I've got this. Let's go.' I followed Nigel for a few rickety paces before my Bambi legs gave way again and, splat, down I went.

Now I know why they call this the Beast Run.

They hit us with our first Beast Run – or beasting as it was also known – on day three of police training. At the end of it, I was sweating and shivering at once. I couldn't decide whether my legs were burning hot or cold. My feet did not belong to me, and I was sure I'd seriously injured my shoulder. We would endure the Beast Run every Wednesday morning as part of our fitness regime. Although running through snow with a heavy tree on your shoulder felt more like army training to me. There were several logs that were passed around the group, and PC Davies would bark and bark and bark at the two teams of two, busting their guts to run a mile-and-a-half in less than twelve minutes. Even when it wasn't your turn with the log, you still had to run the distance, which was eventually raised to two-and-a-half miles. Those sessions were lethal. It seemed all my colleagues were far better distance runners than me, much to their frustration. People must have dreaded being partnered with me as I was forever falling over. Sprinting was more my thing.

I was one of a hundred students sent to the Police Training Centre in east London during that arctic winter of January 1986. I'd expected to train at the world-famous cop school, Hendon Police College, in northwest London, but that facility could not accommodate our excessive intake. And so, I found myself in the overspill group based in Wanstead, a leafier part of the Big Smoke, close to Epping Forest and on the Hainault via Newbury Park loop of the Central Line. However, being separated from the Hendon lot didn't bother me or my colleagues. From the outset we Wanstead trainees decided we were at an "elite college" for recruits identified as having great potential. That's what we kept telling ourselves, anyway.

At first sight, the Wanstead institution – a toothy-white, post-modernist high-rise – scared the living daylights out of me with its bony facade and serried prison-block-style windows. It loomed incongruously amid streets lined with period houses and the sprawling greenery of Wanstead Flats.

I arrived at the centre one Sunday evening, pulled up outside the eleven-storeyed monstrosity in my Metro, with Pink Floyd's *Dark Side of The Moon* album playing on the stereo. The track was *Brain Damage*, and the sound was a bit warped where the cassette ribbon had stretched, as I recall. Glancing up at the building through the windscreen, I shuddered as a chill squeezed my scalp then shot down my spine. Oh, but I was excited too. Here was I, Matt Calveley, skinny boy-racer from small-town Lytham, embarking on a five-month course in London that would, all being well, lead to my dream job on London's frontline. Four months had passed since I'd cheated the Metropolitan Police medical, but it felt like yesterday that I was staring at that hanging skeleton, fearing I'd be InterCity-ing it back to Lytham with another failure under my belt. Now, I could not quite believe I was here – all ten-stone-eight of me. I switched off the stereo and engine, grabbed my suitcase and guitar from the boot, then hurried up the swirl of frosted steps and through the door to my new life.

On the Monday morning, I met my fellow trainee Constables and our instructors as the boss, Chief Inspector McCrory, split us into five groups of twenty and gave us a tour of the building, which was equally eerie inside as its exterior. The first four floors gave way to offices and cold, lino-floored classrooms furnished with Formica-top tables, plastic chairs and whiteboards holding ghostly remnants of previous lessons in policing. The ground floor also housed the gym, which was much like a school gymnasium with its climbing bars and ropes and wooden vaulting boxes. I flinched just thinking about the feats expected of us within those four walls.

The top seven floors were where we trainee Constables lived in rooms not even the size of police cells. My room was on the seventh floor and was basic to say the least. A composition of worn-out wood furniture upon a dark brown carpet: single bed, chest of drawers that doubled as a desk, and a mustard armchair from the Seventies. A utilitarian white sink clung for dear life to the wall, and the curtains were the colour and texture of Bourbon biscuits. Down the corridor another door led to the shared toilets and showers. But the view of Wanstead Park out of the boxy window was not too shabby, and at least I didn't have to pay rent. My £104-a-week training salary would go a long way if I was canny.

In the basement of that imposing block was the canteen and bar, which smelled of fry-ups and reminded me of a working men's club lounge. We assembled around McCrory in the canteen. 'You can help yourselves to as much food and drink as you like,' McCrory began, rocking back and forth in his shoes as his eyes swung from one hungry recruit to the next. Then he fixed his gaze on me. 'On one condition – you *must* eat and drink everything you take. We don't tolerate waste here.'

The atmosphere in our group was subdued at first. I think everybody was on edge, a little untrusting or too afraid to speak for fear of making a tit of themselves. This would all change as the days, weeks and months slipped by and we got to know one another. But you always get one, don't you, who's cocky from the outset. In our group, that person was Keith, a rugby player with a quiff channelling Morten Harket from A-ha. Loudest one in our group. After McCrory's comment in the canteen, Keith rubbed his hands together and piped up, 'Right, lads, let's get the pints in,' then laughed a laugh that matched his six-foot-five-frame. Unbeknownst to any one of us then, Keith's career in the Met would be short-lived.

Beast Run aside, I thoroughly enjoyed my first week at training school. We east London recruits bussed it to Hendon College, where we collected our uniforms and appointments. Incidentally, the term 'appointments' means truncheon, handcuffs and incident notebooks in police talk. The uniform consisted of two pairs of navy wool trousers, two tunics, six long-sleeved shirts and three with short sleeves, a rain mac, flat cap, and traditional bobby-on-the-beat helmet. We were also issued our warrant numbers. Mine was 184713, which meant 184,712 male officers had joined the Met before me since the force started in 1829. (Female officers had a different numbering system.)

Standing proud in the gym with my ninety-nine class-mates, I took my oath.

I still remember the words:

I, Matt Calveley, of the Metropolitan Police, do solemnly and sincerely declare and affirm that I will well and truly serve the Queen in the office of Constable, with fairness, integrity, diligence and impartiality, upholding fundamental human rights and according equal respect to all people; and that I will, to the best of my power, cause the peace to be kept and preserved and prevent all offences against people and property; and that while I continue to hold the said office I will to the best of my skill and knowledge discharge all the duties thereof faithfully according to law.

I meant every single word. Now all I had to do was put those words into practice, which would be a challenging affair marked with injuries, competitiveness, and mortify-ing moments, sprinkled with a generous amount of light to dark humour.

Living in east London, in the E11 postcode area, I had expected to be surrounded by Kray twins-level gangster-ism – you know, shootings, stabbings, and extortion rackets galore. This was the picture I'd formed in my head, further enhanced by the Pet Shop Boys' hit *West End Girls*, whose lyrics paint a bleak picture of inner-city life. The song was number one in the charts at that point. I remember watching the video just days before I left Lytham and thinking, *That Chris Lowe bloke went to my school*, then, *Who are these east end lads he's singing about? They sound dangerous.* But Wanstead seemed neither deprived nor steeped in crime. On the contrary, this pocket of east London felt affluent and villagey – although, thinking like a cop, I suspected some shady, nefarious activities rumbled on behind the scenes.

The training was intense and demanding, our days crammed with classes led by serving Constables and Sergeants. We studied first aid, attended officer safety classes, threw each other around in self-defence classes, and challenged one another during role-play sessions. We also sat two to three law and police procedure multiple choice exams per week and attended daily exercises and inspections in the parade square outside the training centre.

We were taught early on how to use our handcuffs and truncheons. 'Be realistic but careful,' warned our officer safety tutor, Sergeant Peters, at the start of our handcuffing session, 'or you'll be spending the day down A&E at Whipps Cross Hospital. You don't want to know how many broken wrists I've seen over the years.' Then in pairs, we took turns to play roles of police officer and prisoner to practise the technique. Fortunately, nobody in our group ended up down A&E, but we all walked away with red raw wrists and slightly scraped arms.

The idea of whacking somebody with a truncheon in real life terrified me. Again, there's a technique involved when using this weapon. You lift the truncheon upon your shoulder, then strike, aiming for specific points on the arms and legs. 'I highly recommend you don't hit anyone over the head with your truncheon – because there's a good chance that you'll kill them,' was Sergeant Peters' advice, said like he was telling us not to sling a red towel in the wash with your whites. 'Then again, no action is off limits if you can justify the level of force.'

Suddenly, a silent film played in my head. The scene showed a man, flat on his back, blood gushing from his head. Then I appeared, hovering over him in my navy uniform, staring into his dead eyes while checking for a pulse – because I had just hit this guy over the head with my truncheon. I quickly erased that visual from my mind but from that moment onwards, I could not stop asking myself, *What if I kill somebody while doing the Job?* Unaware that, months later, I would be thwacking Dwayne over the head with my truncheon in a maisonette in East Acton.

Of course, married with thoughts of accidentally killing somebody was the fear that I could be killed on duty – or at training school for that matter. Just four months earlier Constable Keith Blakelock had been hacked to death during riots on the Broadwater Farm estate in nearby Tottenham. Beast Runs alone were a killer, not to mention the hundreds upon hundreds of sit-ups and press-ups we were forced to do during our gym sessions.

Ironically, I suffered my first injury during the one physical activity I was good at – the north, south, east, and west game. This was a sprinting exercise in the gym, a chance to make up for my poor Beast Run performances. PC Davies would shout a compass point and we would all sprint in that direction, then a few seconds later, he'd call out another location, and so on. On this occasion, I was sprinting north when I heard Davies shout, 'south'. I whizzed around like the Looney Tunes Tasmanian Devil and barrelled into my colleague Mike. My face slammed into the back of his head with a heavy thud, and my incisor speared my bottom lip. Mike stumbled forwards a few steps as a metallic taste flooded my mouth and the gym seesawed right, left, left, right. 'Matt, you alright mate?' Mike said, holding the back of his head.

Blood poured from my throbbing lip. 'Yeah, I'm fine,' I said, wiping red stuff from my chin. I sounded like a man with no teeth, but at least the room had stopped jolting. PC Davies came over, did the how-many-fingers-am-I-holding-up test on me, diagnosed 'split lip, no concussion', then told me to 'crack on'. He hollered, 'northeast', and that was that. With a hole in my lip, I ran northeast in my bloodied t-shirt and shorts. Nowadays I would probably be offered trauma support and a safe space after such an accident. But, this was the Eighties, remember.

The next day, sporting a busted lip resembling a squished crimson slug, I suffered a second injury, although this time it was my pride that took the battering. Our class was outside, practising stop and search routines in a mock street abutting the parade square. The cars used for those scenarios had been seized by the Met in crimes ranging from driving without insurance to murder. For all we knew, the motor in our stop and search role play – a russet Ford Cortina – might once have belonged to a serial killer. This thought crossed my mind as I motioned for the Cortina, with our instructor PC Williams at the wheel, to pull over next to the faux zebra crossing.

Williams did as I instructed. He braked, turned off the engine and wound down his window. I stepped forward, my classmates semi-circled behind me, and nodded at

Williams. 'Morning, sir,' I said, 'you are being detained for stop and search purposes. Please can I see your driving documents?' Williams gave a little smirk and rolled his eyes. *Right, I've got an awkward one here. Williams is going to make this task impossible.*

'Do you have your documents, sir?' I asked again and Williams laughed and cocked his narrow head.

'Do you not know who I am, Calveley?' he said, 'I am a foreign diplomat.' He lifted his eyebrows and dropped his jaw. He looked like the tortured soul in Edvard Munch's *Scream* painting for a second or two, then he continued. 'Let me help you out here, Calveley. Sometimes you will encounter someone claiming diplomatic immunity, at which point, you should proceed with caution...'

Ah, now I understood. *Proceed with caution, easy-peasy. I know this word for word.* I straightened my back and attempted to puff my chest. I spoke slowly, my words firm, if a little distorted through my mangled lip. 'You do not have to say anything. But it may harm your defence if you do not mention when questioned something which you later rely on in court. Anything you do say may be given in evidence.' I finished with a swollen smile. It hurt.

There was a brief silence before the laughter started. Keith laughed the loudest under his A-ha quiff. Williams gave me the *Scream* look again and shook his head. 'What the fuck are you doing, Calveley?'

'Reciting the caution, sir,' I said, and turned to look at my laughing colleagues, hoping one of them would back me.

Keith was doubled over now. 'Oh Matt,' he went between bursts, 'that was fucking priceless.'

'I said proceed *with* caution, you wally,' said Williams. 'as in 'be careful''. I realised my faux pas in that moment. Diplomatic immunity is a status reserved for foreign diplomats, provided they don't have British citizenship. It means they can't be arrested for any crime, or civil case. I had completely misinterpreted the brief.

What a donkey.

Later that day in first aid class, it was Keith's turn to screw up, although his gaffe was deliberate – and offensive too. WPC Johnston taught first aid. Tall, with a serious face, she didn't tolerate laughing and joking in the classroom. Today's lesson was on how to deal with epileptic episodes. 'How would you treat a person who's suffering an epileptic episode?' Johnston asked the class.

'I know,' blurted Keith, 'You'd chuck 'em in the bath with some Persil then throw your washing in.'

I admit, people laughed. Not Johnston though, who threw Keith a look that screamed, *I'm going to kill every member of your family – and then I'll kill you* but instead said: 'See me after class.'

Winter slipped into spring and the months began to whizz by. I got to know a few of my colleagues quite well. There was a former farmer called Tim, from a town just a few miles away from Lytham, as well as Steve, a Liverpudlian nicknamed Rambo – because, being short and scrawny with a ghost-like face, Steve looked nothing like the muscle-bound action film hero. He did, however, speak fluent Italian (with a Scouse accent). Despite his frequent bigoted remarks, I did like Keith – he was always good for a laugh. And, like many fellow trainees, he loved a pint or ten.

Drinking was rife in our team. Especially among the lads, who I'd hear staggering through the corridors after their boozy sessions at the Green Man pub (now O'Neills) in Leytonstone.

One Friday I woke in the middle of the night to the familiar drunken chorus. A group of recruits from another class had been out in west London to celebrate one of the lads' birthdays. I didn't really know this group but a few of them also lived on the seventh floor. In fact, it was their rendition of something resembling *Happy Birthday* that woke me. From my bed a few rooms away from the stairwell, I listened with trepidation.

'Let's give him the bumps', shouted one lad.

'Nah, sod that, let's chuck him out of the window,' called another. Shouts of approval and one lone howl of protest ensued.

'And a one. And a two…' they yelled. I pictured them swinging the lad by his arms and legs. *Surely, they're not going to throw him out of the window*, I thought. Then, on the count of three came the murderous sound of glass smashing. I leapt out of bed, opened my window, and looked out, expecting a scene of carnage. Fortunately, the birthday boy wasn't splattered and dead on the tarmac below, but hanging headfirst from the waist up out of the shattered window to my left, screaming, 'Get me back in,' as several hands desperately trying to pull him back into the stairwell without slicing him to ribbons on the remaining shards of glass.

It seemed after twelve weeks of police training, the four drunken recruits had misjudged their strength, and instead of just swinging their colleague towards the window they had rammed him straight through it. Miraculously, their victim escaped with a few minor cuts (and probably significant mental torture), and his four assailants were summoned to a discipline hearing the following day in front of Chief Inspector McCrory. They each received an informal punishment, though being so close to graduation and with otherwise unblemished records, they were allowed to keep their jobs.

I went to the pub a few times with my classmates but, being a teetotaller, I didn't much enjoy the experience. As a teenager I suffered a bad allergic reaction after sampling cider, hence my abstinence. But not being a drinker meant I had little social life in London. I became terribly homesick for Lytham. I missed my mates – Dave, Paul and Kevin, and Park Street Youth Club. So, most Fridays, as soon as classes finished at 4pm, I'd boost up the M1 to Lytham in my Metro, *Dark Side of The Moon* gargling through the speakers, abuzz with excitement. Then, come Sunday afternoon, my mood would darken like that Pink Floyd album as I began the drive back to London.

But I wanted this career more than anything else in the world. So, I'd endure the weight that ballooned inside my chest every time I thought about Lytham. I studied hard, passed every exam, and put every cell in my body into becoming the best cop ever. That said, I was still hopeless at the Beast Run, but hey-ho, God loves a tryer, right?

Towards the end of the course, we faced our first session on death. This is a crucial area in policing. Officers deal with death every day, from lonely old people dying at home of natural causes to murders, suicides, road deaths, freak accidents and mass fatalities from terrorist activity. Preparing for tragic scenarios is therefore essential.

During the lesson, our instructor Sergeant Lincon, indomitable and nearing retirement, showed us photos depicting death in every conceivable form, a synopsis accompanying each scene. Some images were too gruesome to mention, but there was one that piqued my interest. The shot showed a deceased male hanging by a noose from a bannister. The synopsis said: 'Police were called to this house by a concerned family member after the male occupant had repeatedly threatened suicide. Two Constables attended, and on looking through the letterbox could see the male hanging from the bannister. They immediately forced entry, cut him down and attempted to resuscitate him but to no avail. He was pronounced dead at the scene shortly afterwards.'

Confused, I stuck my hand up. 'So, did they hang him back up again to take the photograph?' I asked. Sergeant Lincoln glared at me, his Freddie Mercury moustache twitching.

'I don't know but I'll endeavour to find out,' he said, although he didn't come back to me on that one.

On June 6, 1986, I stood to attention with my remaining ninety-seven classmates – three had decided policing wasn't for them. Although we were no longer trainees. Today was our passing out parade. We'd done it – we'd survived twenty punishing weeks and were now ready to hit the streets of London as fully-fledged cops. A few days ago, amid much ceremony, we'd each been assigned our operational shoulder numbers and told which police stations we'd been posted to.

Clean-shaven and sharp in my dark blue wool trousers and tunic, pressed and immaculate with my new shoulder number – 292F emblazoned in silver on its epaulettes, and a kilo of helmet upon my head, I'd never felt prouder, even though I was boiling in all that gear.

The reviewing officer, Assistant Commissioner Sir Hugh Annesley, spoke to each recruit. We had to introduce ourselves and state which area we'd been posted to. When my turn came, I held my chin at a perfect right angle to my chest. 'Constable Matthew Calveley, sir,' I said. 'Posted to F District. [Hammersmith, Shepherd's Bush and Fulham].' I squinted in the midday sun. Today was a scorcher, the London air clear as lemonade.

Not a bad day for becoming a cop, I thought.

CHAPTER THREE
FIRST IMPRESSIONS

After a week's leave, I arrived at Shepherd's Bush police station to begin street duties. I could not wait to get started, although that horror thought still inched its way into my mind: *Please don't let me kill or get killed on duty.* Fortunately, my passion for the Job and desire to drive fast police cars would supersede that fear... most of the time.

Shepherd's Bush police station – known by its police radio code, Foxtrot Sierra (FS) – was a Sixties cement block concern in a shade of watery porridge. Unremarkable, you might say, but inside, 252 Uxbridge Road pulsed with activity. From the lager-infused expletives and clangs of steel that echoed in the cells on a Friday night, to tales of death and arrests and comedy moments in the smoky canteen on the top floor, I loved the place from the moment I crossed its municipal threshold.

I was no longer a recruit, but a probie, which in police parlance means probationary Constable. With my mates Rambo and Tim and four other colleagues from Wanstead – Wendy, James, Simon, and Derek, who'd given up a career in accounting to join the frontline – we would spend ten weeks learning how to police London while on the Job, shadowing highly-experienced Met officers, some of whom would rather gargle wasps than deal with wet-behind-the-ears probies. It's a tough job but...

My new home was a poky room on the eleventh floor of Paddington Green Section House, where most single men in the force chose to live, if only for the five-quid-a-month rent. Section Houses are like student digs, with shared bathrooms, kitchens and, in our case, a snooker room too. If I spread my arms wide, I could almost touch the facing walls in my bedroom, which boasted a south-west view above the A40, taking in the Hilton Hotel, St Mary's Hospital and skies loaded with jumbos bound for Heathrow. When I opened my bedroom window, petrol fumes and the roar of eight lanes of traffic flooded in. But a blast of noise and pollution didn't bother me; I was young and happy to be there. The cheap rent also meant I'd be able to save my wages until I could afford to buy a flat or a house. It was a no brainer.

Shepherd's Bush, nicknamed The Bush, was a part of London I previously knew little about but, as postings went, it seemed a varied patch, with a good deal of crime going on. Burglaries, street robberies and car radio thefts were the biggest trends at that time. Of course, The Bush was only one section of F District, which covers five square miles in W12. It's a varied patch incorporating affluent neighbourhoods in Kensington and Notting Hill, to the notorious, crime-ridden White City Estate. F District also covers Chiswick and Acton and is home to Queens Park Rangers football club and the BBC Television Centre.

Two days into our street duties stint and I could hit the beat for the first time. I had been waiting for this seminal moment since day one at police training school. Alas, my excitement was marred somewhat when I learned who'd be accompanying me on my foot patrol shift: Sergeant Alan, our street duties boss, and, from what I'd heard thus far, a slippery bloke renowned for backstabbing.

One of our instructors, PC Danny Owen, a broad cockney and doppelganger for the *Carry On* actor Sid James, warned us about Alan on our first afternoon at Shepherd's Bush police station. Owen had about twenty-five years' service under his belt and was close to retiring. In other words, he was an old sweat – a term of endearment used to describe long-serving, experienced officers. Owen revealed all about his colleague in the canteen, which was where our group meetings took place. We were gathered around a table beside the arcade machines when Owen suddenly jabbed his head and thumb sideways, and with a conspiratorial look on his rubbery face, said, 'Your sarge, Alan, you'll need to watch him. Now, you didn't get this from me, but he can be a bit of a wrong 'un. Watch yer backs. Stitched up one of his own men a few months back.'

Owen rubbed his jaw and laughed to himself. 'Yeah, listen to this one: Alan's on duty, right, and he responds to this big pub fight, somewhere over 'ammersmith way... Anyway, in the thick of it all, Alan sees this pissed-up geezer going for another Constable, his colleague. Geezer punches the Constable, smack, in the back of the head...' Owen slammed his fist into his other palm for effect. 'So, the Constable spins round, decks the geezer and, wallop, he goes down like a sack of Jersey Royals. And what does Alan do?' Owen paused, eyeing us one by one, but we all sat there, wordless.

I was surprised at Owen's openness – and equally shocked to hear this news about Alan, who'd seemed a decent enough bloke to me when he'd given his welcome speech that morning. I felt a heavy wave of disappointment wash over me; I thought we were one big family at the Met, all working together to fight crime and restore order on the streets of London. That's what we were told at training school, anyway.

Owen poured powdered cream into his polystyrene cup, whose contents resembled water collected from a muddy puddle, and laughed again. 'He only goes and arrests the Constable, doesn't he. Oh yeah, your boss man, Alan, stormed in and arrested a uniformed colleague for assault. And that ain't the done thing round 'ere, y'know what I'm saying? If you ask my opinion, that Constable was acting in self-defence.'

I glanced at my mate Rambo, sitting opposite me. He looked terrified. Minutes later, Sergeant Alan entered the canteen, sneering into his beard. Owen clocked him, took a swig of his insipid tea and grimaced. 'And another thing,' he said, 'watch out for the White City Estate. Make an arrest over there… do me a favour and make sure you've got the van waiting nearby for a quick getaway. Can be a bit 'ostile round that neck of the woods.'

We all nodded keenly, although, for me, the term 'housing estate' conjured images of South Park Estate in Lytham – wide, tree-lined avenues occupied by detached houses with gardens and ponds and birdfeeders. I had a lot to learn.

I was apprehensive to be on foot patrol with Sergeant Alan on that sweltering June morning. Being keen, I was dying to bombard him with policing questions, but after Owen's speech in the canteen, I thought it best to keep all dialogue with Alan to a minimum and be on my best behaviour. *Don't say anything that could later be used in evidence against you, Matt.*

As I stepped out into the blazing sunshine with the boss, I wondered what exciting events lay ahead throughout the next eight to ten miles of pounding the streets. *I might even get lucky and make my first arrest, catch a disqualified driver, or disarm a knifeman following a high-octane foot chase. Maybe I'll foil a bank heist or intercept a robbery at Rumbelows? A riot would be good.* Ultimately, however – and apologies if this sounds distasteful – I was secretly hoping a large-scale disaster would happen on my first shift. A plane crash or a terror attack, for example. Not that I would have known how to respond to such catastrophes then.

As it happened, none of the above occurred and my first shift was quite uneventful – aside from being sworn at by two miscreants no taller than a keep left bollard. Within minutes of my striding the beat, the following happened:

We walked out of the station and along Uxbridge Road, directly into the path of a twenty-something woman pushing a pram while smoking a fag. She had on tight stonewashed jeans and a *Desperately Seeking Susan* inspired lace top cropped tight above her doughy midriff. There were purple streaks in her crimped hair. The woman was flanked by a boy and girl, both no older than four. Alan and I stepped to one side to allow her and her kids to pass, but when the baby started screaming, the woman stopped ahead of us and peered into the pram, where I spied a twenty-pack of Benson & Hedges nestled in a crumpled blanket by the infant's pink, kicking feet. As the mum sucked on her fag and shook a rattle into the baby's carriage, the kids squinted up at me and giggled, so I flashed them a friendly bobby–on–the–beat smile. 'Hello there,' I said, nodding.

The kids' faces soured. The girl put her head on one shoulder and scrunched her lips and nose as one as she glowered first at me, then at Alan, while the boy stood there, sniggering. 'Bastard pigs,' they shouted in unison, and the baby wailed harder. I jerked my head back in shock while the woman, still puffing away, smiled at the two kids, and powered past us in a cloud of B & H emissions and scorn. I looked at Alan, who was pushing buttons on the edges of his digital watch, seemingly unperturbed by the kids' foul-mouthed tirade.

'Did you hear that?' I said, 'those kids just called us bastard pigs.'

Alan shrugged, a half-hearted shrug at that. 'Get used to it,' he said. 'Welcome to Shepherd's Bush.'

On we walked, but The Bush was quiet. Where were the criminals? There was no wail of sirens. 'Hopefully it'll stay this way,' said Alan. 'All the villains must be off to the seaside today, sunning themselves.'

'Right, fair enough' I said, but my heart sank to the redundant handcuffs on my hip.

I want some action… now.

It didn't get much better, either. An hour later Alan and I took our first call over the radio, which I recorded in my notebook as 'Assistance to Gas Board on the White

City Estate'. British Gas had obtained warrants to enter flats and disconnect supplies in cases where occupants had repeatedly failed to pay bills. 'Assistance to Gas Board,' I said, and shot Alan a questioning look.

'Yeah, pain in the arse,' he said, removing his helmet and wiping a film of sweat from his brow. 'But these losers who don't pay their bills can get a bit lairy when the gas boys arrive to cut off their supplies. We're there as backup – in case it all kicks off.' My mood brightened at the prospect of 'all kicking off'.

Nothing kicked off. All the flats we went to showed only remnants of human occupation – ashtrays spilling dead spliffs and fag ends; empty lager cans trod into threadbare carpets. Plates and cups furry with mould. The air in those properties was clogged with ammonia and sour milk. White City Estate, I discovered, was nothing like Lytham's South Park housing estate. There were no tree-lined avenues. Not a bird box in sight – just high-rise blocks of flats housing over 7,000 people on land the size of twenty football pitches. 'No Ball Games' signs, the occasional discarded syringe, and concrete steps steeped in urine also featured here.

The guys from British Gas attended with a locksmith, who broke into the properties as I stood guard with Alan. After a while, I got chatting to the locksmith – a chirpy bloke called Ian, who had an impressive box of tools. 'Mind if I watch you,' I asked as Ian set to work on another door.

'Sure,' he said, and talked me through the steps of how to break into the property. I studied the locksmith's handiwork, and, by the end of the day, felt I'd received a masterclass in how to bypass most common door security systems. Which would come in useful later in my career.

Maybe it hadn't been such a bad shift after all.

As the weeks slipped by, I became more familiar with the area and the beat routes, which took in landmarks such as the BBC TV Centre, QPR's stadium and, of course, the aforementioned White City Estate. Another landmark was Bridie, an Irish homeless woman who would stagger around Shepherd's Bush Green, day and night, in wafts of cooking sherry and urine, spluttering incoherent sentences. Cops often nicked her for being drunk and disorderly, although I was yet to do so.

In July, I was placed on foot duty in central London for the wedding of Prince Andrew and Sarah Ferguson. A huge event, overseen by some 2,000 police officers and 1,600 military personnel – there to protect the Royal Family and control the 100,000-strong crowd of well-wishers who mobbed the streets.

Our briefing was minimal. Each officer was assigned a section of the procession route to police – and we were then left to get on with it. I was deployed to The Mall, where I endured my second verbal attack amid a sea of elbowing fans brandishing Union Jacks and banners emblazoned with messages like, "All the nice girls love a sailor". I was at the back of the hoard thronging the barriers and, about twenty minutes before the newlyweds' carriage hit The Mall, excitement mounted.

Everybody jostled for a better view and the crowd became a tangled, agitated mass. I lurched forwards into the crowd, anxious to get to the front to open a barrier before people got crushed. Being skinny meant I could slither through with some ease, but one woman did not want to budge. 'Oi, wait your fucking turn,' she shouted into her right shoulder. 'We've been here since eight o'clock this morning.'

'Yes madam,' I said, my voice raised but calm, 'I understand, but I've been here since five o'clock, and if you let me through, everybody will get a better view, and nobody will be injured.' She turned around then, took one look at me and rolled her bottom lip beneath her top teeth, eyes wide with panic as a woman to her right, possibly her mother, also turned and burst out laughing.

'Oh, shit, sorry,' said the ranting woman, 'I didn't realise you were a… you know…'

'Police officer?' I said, smiling. Unlike those little brats in Uxbridge Road who called me a "bastard pig", this woman had not intended to insult a copper. I managed to safely open the barrier before the procession trundled past, taking the happy couple on to Buckingham Palace following their nuptials at Westminster Abbey.

Happy days.

Competition among us probies was fierce; we were all desperate to impress the bosses and old sweats – and each other – with a show-stopping first arrest or foot chase. Equally, we were all paranoid about screwing up and making donkeys of ourselves in front of the entire force. Once, we screwed-up collectively, insensitively. Although, to be fair, our actions were not deliberate.

I remember the date and the time: August 12, just after 3.15pm. I was in the canteen with my fellow probies, playing on the arcade machines while we waited for our instructors to arrive ahead of the late shift. Rambo and I were immersed in a game of Space Invaders, shooting white aliens as they descended on the black screen. Bright, squeaky balloon sounds erupted from the neighbouring Pac-Man machine as Wendy swore at it, while the others gathered around the cabinets, laughing and jeering.

In our squawking bubble, we didn't notice the canteen had fallen silent around us. 'Oh, piss off Shadow… bastard ghost,' shouted Wendy when her Pac-Man perished, and the words 'Game Over' filled the screen.

'Yes,' cried Rambo as aliens shot me dead.

'Right, I'm playing Rambo next,' said James, slapping the side of the Space Invaders cabinet.

'What? No, fuck off, it's my turn,' said Derek.

'No, it's the best of three,' I said, laughing.

Then came a voice behind us: loud, rumbling, and jagged. A rockslide in a canyon. 'What the fuck do you lot think you're playing at?'

Rambo jumped. It was audible. Heat rose from my stomach to my face, then cascaded down my arms. In slow motion, we all turned around, into the full avalanche of PC Owen's words. 'Have you no respect?' Owen paused. Fury on his Sid James face came in the form of a smirky grimace. But his tone was serious as death. Behind us, the machines emitted tinkling peals of laughter. We exchanged looks of confusion. *What was Owen talking about?* Looking around the canteen I noticed all the other coppers were standing to attention with bent heads. 'Twenty years ago today, to the minute, three of your colleagues were murdered. We're trying to mark the tragic occasion with a minute's silence, but all we can hear is you lot laughing and joking about like clowns in a brewery.'

Horrified, we all mumbled our apologies. Owen breathed hard then turned and walked out of the canteen, his steps sticky over the linoleum.

Had we probies known about the minute's silence for those killed in the Braybrook Street Massacre, we would, of course, have observed it. The force was paying respects to PC Geoffrey Fox, Detective Sergeant Christopher Head and Detective Constable David Wombwell, who were shot in an incident involving Harry Roberts, John Duddy and John Witney in Braybrook Street, East Acton, on August 12, 1966. Decades later I learned that PC Owen was one of the first officers on the scene who faced the horrific task of identifying his dead colleagues. No wonder he reacted so strongly.

James was the first in our group to nail an arrest – and get back into Owen's good books. It was a corker of an arrest too, one he was, quite rightly, quick to share with his peers one lunchtime. 'I caught a Yardie mid-deal on the White City Estate today,' he announced over his steak and kidney pudding. 'He ran, so I chased him – then jumped on his back and smashed him to the ground. Done him for possession with intent to supply.'

My first arrest wasn't as dramatic as James'; it certainly didn't involve a heroic Jason Bourne-style foot chase, but it did lead to a conviction – after an Inspector called Paddy taught me a technique known as the Five Negatives. 'Whenever you pull a car over,' Paddy explained, 'you should ask yourself five questions. If all answers are no, then you arrest the driver. Simple as that.'

The five questions were:

1. Has the car got tax?
2. Can the driver produce his driving licence?
3. Has the driver got any other identification on him?
4. Is the driver's name and address the same as the registered keeper of the vehicle?
5. Can the driver tell you who the registered keeper is?

That day, with Paddy's help, I nicked a driver (I'll call him Evans) for unlawful driving. Back at the station, Evans then confessed: 'OK, fine. I can't get tax because I've got no insurance. I can't get insurance because I've got no licence. I'm on a ban for drink-driving.' What a result. Two weeks later, Evans was jailed for a month and banned from driving for a further year.

Finally, I was policing the streets of London for real, learning most lessons 'on the Job'. But there are some elements of policing that can only be taught indoors, like: what happens during a post-mortem? Throughout my 30-year career in the Met I would attend approximately 60 post-mortems, but, like my debut arrest, I'll never forget my first autopsy experience.

Aside from the horrific pictures shown to us at police college, I had never seen a dead body in real life. Now, in the bleachy confines of Fulham Mortuary, I stared with morbid fascination at three bodies, straight out of the fridge: an elderly man who'd dropped dead at home, a woman in her forties who'd OD'd on heroin, and a tiny cot-death victim, no older than eight months.

The technician started work on the man. 'We need to prepare the body so the pathologist can establish cause of death,' he said, lifting his scalpel. 'So, we must remove all the internal organs and place them in steel bowls.' The technician speared the man's chest and unzipped him with ease. He grabbed his surgical bolt cutters, cracked out the ribs and sternum, then removed the victim's organs one by one. 'Next, we need to remove the brain. But to get to the brain we must first remove the face,' added our tutor. Wendy, standing beside me, drew in her breath and shuddered, but I leaned in closer to get a better look. I was fascinated. The technician cut into the man's scalp at the back of his head, then peeled off his face like a Halloween mask. I took another step forward as the technician explained his next move. 'Using a high-powered circular saw, we shall cut through the skull to reach the brain,' he said.

He switched on the saw and crunching sounds issued as the blade gnawed through bone.

And I was fine – until a hunk of bone-splintered gore propelled from the saw and splattered my cheek, wet and cold and dead. Simon, Derek and James started laughing. Wendy gasped and Rambo's face shaded to the hue of a grubby one-pound note. I ran over to the sink, grabbed a handful of paper towels, and scrubbed my face as though the gore were nuclear fallout. Then I slumped in a chair in the corner of the room, dizzy and nauseous and now fully aware of the horror scenes that awaited me in this Job.

CHAPTER FOUR
THINK LIKE A CRIMINAL

My heart belts, a ticking timebomb jumping in my ribcage. The pulsations wallop warmly in my ears, combined with the cold wet slaps of my shoes on the slippery pavement. Rain falls in ragged sheets, but I've never felt better. Nothing can stop me now.

I'm sprinting along Uxbridge Road, helmet in one hand (can't run in this thing), radio vibrating in the other, and pinballing past – and into – pedestrians while trying not to lose sight of the lad some ten metres ahead. Which isn't difficult – he looks like Halley's Comet in his glow-in-the-dark shell suit. Not the best look for a daylight street robber.

Breathing fast I splutter into my radio. 'Pursuing male handbag theft suspect… about sixteen… white, wearing… a violet… and neon yellow shell suit. Suspect now crossing Uxbridge Road, heading…'

I dart into traffic and a passing bus sends a wave of rainwater my way, soaking me from foot to waist. '… West across Shepherd's Bush Green…'

Across the Green, skidding and sliding on the sloppy grass. A figure with Lucozade hair stumbles towards me, waving a bottle of amber liquid, and momentarily eclipses the running robber. 'Fucking eejit,' *she shouts.* Great, Bridie, just what I need.

'Move,' *I yell as I hurtle on, swerving a left arc to avoid Bridie. Into the road again, I slalom through six lanes of traffic, horns blasting. I see the suspect, shooting through a slim gap between two stationary double decker buses. He skips up the kerb and runs, in a bright streak of neon, towards the BBC Television Theatre where they used to film* Crackerjack.

'Suspect heading towards the BBC place,' I choke, and my target makes a sharp right into the alley alongside the theatre (now the O2 Shepherd's Bush Empire). I follow until I'm one lanky stride behind him. 'Police, stop.' I throw my arms forwards, helmet freefalling, and grab the suspect around his slimy, shell-suited torso.

'Fuck off, get yer fucking hands off me,' he yells. He's slippery in my arms, but I'm not letting go. Tightening my grip, I rugby tackle him, the waistband of his jacket spewing a royal blue ladies clutch bag as we drop to the pavement below a box light declaring, 'STAGE DOOR'.

'Nice handbag,' I comment, still catching my breath as I handcuff him. As I do this, I notice he has pigeon excrement over the shoulder of his jacket. Then, into my radio again: 'Suspect – with handbag – detained in passageway next to the BBC Television Centre.'

'I ain't fucking done nuffink wrong,' growls my prisoner, jerking and writhing like a diseased guppy out of water.

It was early September and, despite my recent wobble after getting splatted with a dead man's gore in mortuary class, I had passed the street duties course. Now in a response team and two hours into a Saturday late shift, I had just nailed my first foot chase – and subsequently became the first probie in my group to chalk up an arrest for street robbery.

I delivered the handbag robber to the custody suite at Shepherd's Bush police station, then began writing my notes over a quick coffee in the canteen, before returning to foot patrol. As I was leaving the canteen, I bumped into James, one of my fellow probationers. 'Alright, Matt, how's it going, mate?' he said, biting into a finger of Twix. 'Bit slow today, isn't it? All I've had is one call out – a neighbour complaining about a barking pit-bull on the White City Estate. Boring or what.'

'Oh, I don't know about that,' I said, smiling. 'I just arrested a guy for street robbery after a foot-chase through The Bush.'

James chewed slowly, thoughtfully. 'Nice one, mate. Good work,' he said to his Twix.

I laughed. 'Cheers, mate,' then put on my slightly battered helmet and returned to the beat, feeling optimistic.

'A good cop thinks like a criminal.' This sage advice came from Constable Bob Daniels, an old sweat from my response team. Bob, in his mid-forties, had been in the Met for over twenty years, yet his enthusiasm for sharp policing had not waned. And his ability to make a police car do exactly what he wanted it to do with inch-perfect precision enthralled me.

Bob had given me the 'think like a criminal' speech on our first shift together in the Area Car. 'You've got to get inside a criminal's head, son,' he said, his words woolly in a plume of Raffles cigarette smoke. 'Think how they think,' he added, circling his glowing fag as he spoke. 'And always, *always* be one step ahead. Yeah, you've gotta think like a criminal, son, you know what I'm saying?'

I nodded enthusiastically, trying not to choke on the fumes (Bob was on his fourth fag of the evening). 'Yeah,

I've already learned a few break and entry skills from doing the gas board jobs.'

Bob laughed. 'That's the spirit, son. I love it when a plan comes together.'

Ever the diligent probationer, I soaked up Bob's advice like a sponge, and I pondered his hypotheses as I pounded the streets that Saturday after my street robbery arrest. But the more I thought about it, I realised thinking like a criminal might not be that easy. *After all, doesn't everybody in this world have some good in them?* Then, around 9pm, an hour before my shift was due to end, I got to play the role of a criminal... kind of.

I was passing White City Tube station, eyeing two skinheads loitering suspiciously by the entrance, when the control room radioed. 'PC 292 [my new shoulder number] needed at the BBC Television Centre car park in Wood Lane. Motorist's locked his keys in his car.'

'On my way,' I radioed back, and hotfooted it to the studios around the corner.

I walked into the BBC car park and surveyed the scene. There were more empty bays than parked vehicles, some cars bathed in the amber glow of perimeter streetlights, others, muddy carapaces in the shadows. I switched on my torch and at once a bright voice issued to my right: northern, squeaky, and instantly recognisable. 'I'm over here.' I turned and angled the beam at the sound and almost did a double take. There he was, tuxedoed and grinning in the spotlight, just one head taller than the Volkswagen next to him. He gave me a wave. 'Ah, good evening, officer,' he said. 'Thank you so much for coming.' Yep, the voice matched the face. It was only the late celebrity magician Paul Daniels.

'Evening, Mr Daniels,' I said, trying to keep a straight face as I approached. I wanted to laugh out loud at the irony of the situation: in front of me was a man famous for pulling rabbits out of hats and making things disappear and reappear, yet he could not 'magic' his keys out of his car.

'Locked your keys in?' I said, with a nod towards the motor. 'Easily done, mate.'

Daniels lifted his shoulders and spread his hands wide in a gesture that said, *I wish I could make myself disappear.*

'Should be able to sort this – mind if I tinker a bit?'

'Please, go ahead,' he said, indicating the car. 'I don't know how I managed to do this.'

I got to work on the magician's motor with the aid of a slim, metal tool I kept in my inside pocket – one I'd seen in Ian the locksmith's toolbox that day on the White City Estate. And for the next ten minutes, Daniels watched with intrigue while I poked and clicked and fiddled away at the driver's door. He asked lots of questions and was extremely good-humoured about his predicament. 'I might learn a new trick here,' he said when, finally, I popped the lock. I opened the door, grabbed Daniels' keys from the passenger seat, and passed them to him with a gratifying jangle. 'Wow, thank you,' he said, laughing. 'How did you manage that – and with no damage to the car, either?'

I smiled at Daniels, and with a tip of my helmet towards the car, said, 'Now, *that's* magic.' Because, quite frankly, no other words would have cut it.

Daniels burst out laughing.

* * *

The weeks seemed to whizz by, and my confidence grew with every day spent on the Job. I hadn't killed anyone either, which was a bonus. I was racking up some good arrests, too, including a few more resulting from foot chases – did I mention I was a good sprinter? But one such chase did not end well – thanks to smug Sergeant Alan.

Walking north along Bloemfontein Road one sunny autumn afternoon, I pulled over a man driving a grubby white Alpine. I recognised the car registration from our database as belonging to a disqualified driver. Reluctantly, he got out of the car, then sent a shower of spittle my way as he gave a false name. So I challenged the driver, told him I knew his real name. And with that, he turned and legged it. I chased him through backstreets, all the way to his flat on the White City Estate, where I managed to barge through the front door before he could slam it. I arrested the driver in his hall. Job done… or so I thought.

Half an hour later, I presented my prisoner to Alan, who had returned to his role of custody Sergeant when our Street Duties course ended. Excited at nabbing my first disqualified driver, I explained my actions to Alan, while my detainee sat there, sniggering, and crackling phlegm in his throat. 'I pulled the suspect over, then arrested him at his home address [I gave the full address] for driving while disqualified,' I finished.

Alan threw me a sarcastic smile over his desk, then put down his pen, folded his arms and shouted, 'Wrong!'

'Sorry, I don't understand,' I said, rage rising in my chest. *How dare Alan humiliate me in front of a prisoner. That's a colossal no-no.* 'The suspect was driving while disqualified, so I arrested him.'

'Yes, Calveley, but the law only allows power of arrest for this offence in immediate pursuit [not losing sight of the suspect between committing the offence and nicking him or her].'

'But I chased him,' I said. 'I chased him from Bloemfontein Road to his flat. I never lost sight of him. Not once.'

'Wrong, wrong, wrong. You didn't include this in your evidence.'

I sat there, face like an inferno, wordless. I couldn't believe it; would Alan let a banged-to-rights offender walk free – just for the warped pleasure of giving me a bollocking for forgetting to mention my foot chase? The prisoner laughed. Sounded like he'd swallowed a cement mixer. Along the corridor, a cell door slammed. Alan picked up his pen. 'Well, I suppose this is a legitimate arrest,' he sighed, and proceeded with the charge. There had been no need for Alan to humiliate me in front of the prisoner. He could instead have asked, 'Did you chase the suspect?' But, Alan being Alan, had to be an arse about the matter.

My run-in with Sergeant Alan aside, I loved my new job. Even a severe bout of flu couldn't keep me away. There were times when I dragged myself into work when I should have been at home in bed. You could say I was married to the Metropolitan Police.

Back then we worked to a four-week roster, which included a combination of early (6am-2pm), late (2pm-10pm) and night (10pm-6am) shifts. This pattern, which is illegal today, included two quick changeovers, with just eight hours between shifts. Most cops found the late to early transition a killer. Poor Wendy, in a state of discombobulation during a run of earlies, once fell asleep at home after finishing at 2pm. Three hours later, she woke on her sofa in a panic, thinking it was 5.30am and bolted into work, oblivious to the setting sun and tailbacks of rush hour traffic heading out of town. In the locker room at the station, Wendy did a swift Wonder Woman change into her uniform and headed to the parade room, expecting a bollocking for being late. Still unaware it was early evening, she stood alone in the parade room. *Where were her colleagues?* Fortunately for Wendy, her response team Inspector, Brian, showed up. 'PC Wendy, you're a bit keen, aren't you?' he said, and laughed when Wendy crossed her brows in confusion. 'You're twelve hours early for your shift.'

Ten minutes later, Wendy joined the rush hour traffic, heading out of town.

Foot patrol could be gruelling, made worse if nothing exciting happened. Some days I could walk ten miles in the pouring rain and not nick one person – not even Bridie. Or Danny, another vagrant I was yet to encounter who haunted Shepherd's Bush Green. (It appeared I was the only Constable in our station who hadn't arrested Danny, who you'll be hearing more about later.) Without doubt, those non-eventful foot patrol shifts were the worst, but still, I lapped it all up. I was young, energetic, and, as I soon discovered, there were some tasty perks to this pounding the beat business: free food.

PC Shane introduced me to the kebab shop on Shepherd's Bush Green, nicknamed One-Eye's by coppers – because apparently the owner, Darius, had a glass eye. Although I can't verify this fact as I never did meet the bloke.

'Order everything on the menu in here, if you like – it's all free for us officers of the law,' said Shane, leading me through the glass door dripping with condensation into the fatty aroma of One Eye's one Friday evening. 'The guvnor likes a police presence, if you know what I mean,' he added under his breath, then beamed at the woman behind the counter wearing oversized gold hoop earrings and a world-weary smile. 'I'll have a donner – but easy on the lettuce – double chips and, while you're at it, you best throw in a cheeseburger as well, please, love. Hungry work, this.'

Now I understood why Shane was known as a skinflint. He insisted we return to One Eye's for 'another quick bite' later in our shift. He was forever 'forgetting' to bring his wallet to work and would go to the canteen at closing time to grab leftover sandwiches for his kids' school packed lunches the following day, so my colleagues told me. More shockingly, however, was the alleged act Shane performed when he was first on the scene of a suicide on the east side of Shepherd's Bush. A jumper had thrown himself from the twelfth floor of a tower block, and, according to the Met gossip mill, the first thing Shane did was to remove the dead man's shoes and try them on.

I preferred working nightshifts because, two nights out of seven, I would partner another Constable in a patrol car, which meant being first on the scene to emergency calls. London is a different beast at night, far grittier than during the day, and racing through the streets on twos and blues, even only as a passenger, thrilled me to the core. Blue lights, bleaching the night sky, the shriek of sirens and crackle of radio announcing the next emergency – I loved it all.

Of course, a nightshift wasn't a nightshift without a burglary or two, especially in the affluent regions of F District. I'll never forget my first arrest for burglary.

I arrived at the property with my colleague Constable Nick at about 3am, just four minutes after receiving the 999 call from a vigilant neighbour. The venue was a partially renovated detached house in Ashchurch Park Villas, a stone's throw away from Ravenscourt Park, and I immediately found the point of entry. The suspect had smashed through a bottom, double-paned window in the back door, so I got on my hands and knees and shone my torch through the jagged-edged rectangle. A cocktail of smells assailed my airwaves: fresh emulsion, sawdust and the peaty whiff of whiskey blended with heavy, foetid notes reminiscent of unwashed skin and stale piss.

I swiped my head over my shoulder, fox-like and confident. 'I'm going in,' I said in a loud whisper to Nick, who was keeping guard behind me. Using the head of my torch, I knocked a few remaining pieces of glass out of the frame. They shattered in short but painful cracks on the bare floorboards. I reached through the hole, patting the floor while shining my light ahead, then, as I extended my search further to the right, I felt an object – damp and leathery with a hint of a pulse. When I turned the torch on this article, I nearly whacked the back of my neck on the top of the window frame. It was a tatty, brown brogue, its right partner neighbouring it. The brogues were occupied.

Without thinking, I dropped my torch, grabbed both shoes, pulled them towards me, and, wham, the suspect, the source of the unwashed skin and whiskey notes, crashed to the floor, sending a row of copper pipes barrelling across the boards. 'Don't hurt me. Please don't hurt me,' he slurred in an Irish accent. I bundled through the window frame and pounced on the drunk man. 'You're nicked for burglary,' I began, handcuffing him.

As burglars went, this one, Patrick, was relatively pleasant. He later explained that he'd targeted the house because it was undergoing renovation and would therefore be empty overnight. 'I was only after a few copper pipes to sell.' I had to admire his honesty, which ultimately landed him a six-month stretch at Her Majesty's Pleasure.

Not all jobs went so well. One night, I was in the Area Car with Bob when the control room radioed through with another burglary – at a huge detached house in Hammersmith. Bob stubbed out his fag and ran a hand over his combover. 'Ready son?' he said.

'Born ready,' I replied. *Think like a criminal, Matt. Think like a criminal.* Bob slammed his foot to the floor and Nigel Mansell-ed it to the house, fronted by six–foot high wooden gates.

'I'm going in,' I said, which had become my catch-phrase of late. I flew out of the police car, sprinted like an Olympian going for gold, a mantra thumping in my head: *Think like a criminal, think like a criminal.* I jumped atop the towering double gates, which, unbeknownst to me, the burglars had unbolted from inside to prepare an escape route. The gates swung inwards, slammed into the concrete backstop, and catapulted me, headfirst, into a bush in the neighbouring garden. As I scrambled around in the thickets, I heard the patter of footsteps. *Great, that'll be the burglars escaping.* Next thing I knew, Bob was standing over me, smoking another Raffles while proffering his free hand to help me out of the foliage, laughing bronchially into the cold night. 'Oh, I do love it when a plan comes together,' he said, still laughing.

OK, maybe it doesn't always pay to think like a criminal.

CHAPTER FIVE
REAL–LIFE DEATH

I first smelled a decaying corpse over breakfast in the canteen one Monday morning.

It was about 9.30am. A flat, gunmetal sky filled the windows as Nick Berry's *Every Loser Wins* played on the radio behind the counter, where two hair-netted women were humming along as they slopped greasy chunks of dead animal onto plates.

Constable Gary, a bloke from my response team, was the source of the stench. I'd never smelled anything like it. Imagine being submerged in a tank filled with rotten raw meat, weeks-old broccoli, and decomposed fruit – then throw in fresh vomit and faeces, a barrel of bad eggs – all sloshing and stewing in stale urine. Feel the mixture flooding your mouth, nostrils and ears, the odour intensifying until it chokes you. That's death. It's more than just a smell. It's physical; it moves, clings to your clothes, skin, and hair. Death gets under your fingernails, seeps through your pores and follicles. You can taste that smell.

Death has a life of its own.

I was sitting with Bob and masticating a mouthful of bacon and beans when Gary lumbered over, yawning a waft of decay. The smell engulfed me before Gary reached the table. Up close, the whiff was suffocating. 'Morning lads, mind if I join you?' said Gary, already dropping into the chair next to Bob. As he sat down, Gary removed his cap, tossed it on the table and gave his crewcut a brisk rub. Bob grimaced but continued knifing and forking away at his breakfast. I gagged on my mushed food and covered my nose and mouth with a handful of scratchy serviettes. But that did nothing to mask the fumes that belched from Gary's upended cap, its peak nudging my plate still holding most of my full English.

'I'm bloody ravenous,' Gary added, then reached across the table and tweezered a slither of wet bacon rind out of the overflowing ashtray with his fingers. I pushed back in my chair and watched with revulsion and shock as Gary then popped the wriggle of ash-coated gristle into his mouth and chomped it down. I gagged again and Gary pulled his head back, regarding me and my plate in turn with confused eyes. 'You OK, Matt? I'll have that breakfast if you're not going to eat it. Pity to waste it, eh?'

I motioned for Gary to help himself, while Bob speared a chunk of sausage and started laughing. 'Jesus Gary, you've had a smelly one,' he said, and forked the meat into his mouth.

'Yeah, another junkie,' said Gary, tucking into my breakfast. 'OD'd on smack and carked it in his flat. Reckon he'd lain there at least two weeks before his neighbours noticed the smell. Not a pretty sight on a Monday morning.'

I stood up. 'I'd better get going,' I said through the layers of serviettes. Nick Berry was still whining on. Bob nudged Gary and they looked up at me, grinning.

'Don't worry, Matt, son,' said Bob, 'you'll get a smelly one soon enough.' Then they both rolled up laughing.

I grabbed another handful of serviettes and boosted out of there.

Gary had just returned from a sudden death – and brought with him the putrid aroma of decomposing flesh and leaked bodily fluids. This distinctive odour had permeated Gary's uniform and saturated his skin, and, as I would later discover, no amount of Vicks VapoRub up the nose, disinfectant, or scrubbing in the shower can eradicate the smell of death. It lingers... and lingers.

As Bob had rightly pointed out, I was yet to 'get a smelly one' – police language to describe a heavily decomposed body. Little did I know, as I stepped out onto Uxbridge Road to continue my early foot patrol shift on that October morning, that I would be responding to several sudden deaths over the next two weeks. And as chance would have it, I attended my first sudden death just hours after Gary ruined my breakfast.

'Apparent fatal domestic accident. Looks like a gentleman has fallen off a roof,' the control room informed me before rattling off the address. Less than ten minutes later, I arrived at the address, a quaint, end terraced Victorian house, with a white picket gate and window boxes sprouting heather and lavender. The front door opened as I pushed through the gate. Clinging to the doorframe was a short, cardiganed woman with tight silver curls. 'He went to fix the tiles,' she said, her face trembling as fresh tears spilled from her rheumy eyes. 'My Norman went to fix the tiles… I saw it happen… he fell… now he's…' The woman shuffled backwards to let me in. 'Thank you for coming, officer,' she choked.

Her name was Jill, and she was in her early eighties. She had been married to Norman for sixty-one years. 'How will I live without Norman?' she sobbed. 'I can't live without my Norman.' I guided Jill into the front lounge, conscious of the tragic evidence I spied through the dining room further along the hall: patio doors, splattered with so much gore you could not see through the glass.

I sat Jill down in an armchair and switched on the gas fire. The poor woman was shivering with shock. Then I explained, as gently and tactfully as I could, that I first needed to 'investigate outside'. 'I'll be straight back,' I said.

As much as I steeled myself, nothing could have prepared me for the ghastly vista in Jill's back garden. Even the images of death we'd viewed at training school didn't come close to this. From what I could fathom, Norman must have fallen backwards off the roof and landed headfirst on the patio two floors below (I later discovered he'd suffered a heart attack while fixing the loose tiles before falling). His injuries were catastrophic, and I apologise in advance for the imminent explicit details, but such are the devastating horrors we cops face every day.

Norman's spine had speared his skull, which had forced his head down into his chest. Blood, fragments of his brain and skull swathed the whole patio area. Glutenous clots of gore slugged slow crimson paths down the glass doors. But the smell did not match the one Gary had brought to the breakfast table that morning. This was sharper, metallic – an explosion of iron, although the scent of decay would soon kick in if Norman's body remained in situ for another twenty-four hours. I jotted some notes in my Incident Report Book (IRB) and headed back inside, closing the dining room door behind me. I did not want Jill to be reunited with the carnage.

I spent the next hour chatting to Jill, making pot after pot of tea while also performing the necessary formalities such as taking her statement, liaising with the coroner, and tracking down next of kin. Jill and Norman had one daughter, Lyn, but she lived outside the capital. An interforce message was sent to the local police force, instructing officers to deliver the tragic news to Lyn in person (police officers should never announce a death to relatives via telephone).

Meanwhile, undertakers arrived at the house and removed Norman's body, but it was not their job to clean the scene, and it suddenly occurred to me that Jill would face that gory mess. Her daughter, already on a train to London, would see it too. That played on my mind as Jill sipped her tea and relived some happy memories of her husband, stretching back to before World War Two. 'I met Norman in the Christmas of 1924,' said Jill, a fleeting, dreamy smile curling her lips. 'And come spring 1925, we were married. Norman's my soulmate. We barely argue, you know, which isn't bad going for sixty-one years of marriage.'

Hearing Jill talk about her dead husband in the present tense was heartbreaking. So, when Jill's neighbour Eileen arrived to comfort her friend, I decided to take matters in the back garden into my own hands. I headed back outside, unravelled the garden hose, turned on the tap, and blasted the patio and garden doors, sluicing the blood and other matter into the adjacent flower beds. Now, I'm no horticulturist, but I guessed it couldn't do much harm. It seemed the right thing to do, given the unfortunate circumstances.

After I'd hosed the garden, I told Jill, 'I've sorted everything outside,' offered my final condolences, and headed back to the station to complete my report in the canteen where I'd inhaled death that morning. Officially, my shift had ended half an hour ago, but it's mandatory to write reports while events are still fresh in your mind.

That evening, sprawled over my skinny bed while half watching *EastEnders*, I thought about the horrific scene I'd witnessed in Jill's garden. And I realised, bizarrely, that, after the initial shock, I had been relatively unaffected by what I'd seen, despite the graphic nature of that tableau. I began to question my morals. The smell of decay on Gary had instantly made me nauseous, yet my stomach hadn't as much as flinched when confronted with Norman's mangled remains. *Is this right? Is this normal?* I had, however, felt Jill's pain and, instinctively, had wanted to do anything in my power to ease her trauma – including washing away all traces of her dead husband in her garden. I had felt helpful at that moment.

Nick Berry as Simon "Wicksy" Wicks in *EastEnders* interrupted my thoughts. He was at the piano in the Queen Vic, performing *Every Loser Wins*. God, I was sick of that song. Then number one in the charts, it was annoyingly ubiquitous. I got up and switched the portable telly to ITV – because, in those days, you had to get up to change the channel.

Coincidentally, *EastEnders* featured when I faced my second sudden death on the Job a few days later. A woman called 999 at 7.31pm, concerned about her elderly neighbour Iris. 'Her windows are open, and I can hear the theme tune for *EastEnders*,' she told the operator. 'Iris hates *EastEnders*. She always watches *Coronation Street* on ITV at half seven.'

Luckily, I was on foot patrol close to the address, a Seventies high-rise called Bush Court, when the control room radioed me. I was there in a few minutes, but Iris lived on the fourteenth floor and, as sod's law would have it, the lift had broken down. I sprinted up the stairs, then, sweating and panting, spoke to the neighbour, Marion, who'd called 999. Sure enough, I could hear the raised voices of Den and Angie Watts' *EastEnders* barney through Iris' front door. I rang the doorbell. Nobody answered. So, with the aid of one of my trusty tools, I forced entry into Iris' home.

I knew when I saw Iris, unmoving on the beige settee, chin on her chest, that she had passed away. I felt her cold, limp wrist for a pulse all the same, but there was no thrum of blood, and Iris had no injuries either. It was obvious to me she had died of natural causes. She had on a pink flannelette dressing gown and quilted slippers, and the life she once knew continued around her: the weighted chrome balls, revolving hypnotically inside the glass dome of her carriage clock upon the sideboard. Framed photographs adorned walls and surfaces; a shot showed a young man in a mortarboard hat, holding a scroll. Another photo showed the same man on his wedding day, clutching his new bride's hand as they laughed through a shower of confetti. Then there were a few pictures of young children whom I presumed were Iris' grandchildren.

EastEnders played on. 'Iris can't stand *EastEnders*,' Marion had told me only a few minutes ago. 'But she never misses an episode of *Corrie*. Never.' Just then, an idea came to mind. It was not yet 7.50pm, according to the carriage clock, which meant *Coronation Street* would still be running on ITV. Without hesitation, I walked over to the television, pressed the button labelled 'ITV', and sat on the settee next to Iris through the last few minutes of *Corrie*. I waited for the last credit to roll before making my calls.

Iris' son Dean, the man in the photographs, arrived an hour later, his eyes pooling with tears. When I told him how I'd watched the end of *Coronation Street* with his mother, he was visibly moved. 'Mum would have loved that,' said Dean, shaking my hand. 'What you did was the ultimate act of kindness. Thank you.'

'Not at all, it was the least I could do,' I said. And I meant every word.

Two days later, in the bedroom of a modest terraced house not far from where Iris had lived, I stepped into one of the saddest scenes I would ever face in my three-decade policing career. The house, a red brick semi, belonged to Mr and Mrs Fairclough, both octogenarians who had not been seen by neighbours in several days.

As expected, nobody answered when I knocked at the Faircloughs' front door. A white mountain of post was visible on the doormat through the frosted glass. A few bottles of milk, their foil tops punctured, presumably pecked by birds, stood on the step. Crouching, I pushed open the letterbox – and recoiled at the smell that assailed me: foetid, unmistakable – a concentrated form of the odour worn by Gary in the canteen.

I gained entry to the house and, shielding my nose and mouth with a handkerchief – we had no PPE in those days – began a systematic search, which led me to the front bedroom upstairs, the smell intensifying as I neared its entrance. My handkerchief smelled of death and I was sweating all over as the heating was on full blast. The door to the bedroom was slightly ajar, a jaundiced glow streaking through the gap. I elbowed the door open and stopped in my tracks, shocked, but unable to gasp for the gases and heat that swamped me.

There on the bed, lit by the early afternoon sun filtering through thin, mustard curtains, were Mr and Mrs Fairclough, locked in a tight embrace but seemingly in an advanced stage of decomposition. The couple, and the bed, was alive with maggots. I powered towards the window. *Air, I need air.* Then, out of the corner of my eye, I noticed a rising movement on the bed. Slow and shaky amid the writhing maggots. I turned fast, dropping my handkerchief, and watched, as Mrs Fairclough lifted her hand, and a brittle voice broke in the fug: 'I couldn't leave him.'

Mr Fairclough died in his sleep four days previously. Overcome with grief, his wife of 65 years had gathered him in her arms and lay with him. Two paramedics arrived, and between the three of us, we gently helped Mrs Fairclough off the bed and carried her to the ambulance. Mrs Fairclough made it to the hospital alive but sadly died the following day. It was devastating to realise that, after such a long and happy marriage, Mrs Fairclough spent her final days watching her husband disintegrate before her eyes.

I was told Mrs Fairclough's cause of death was severe dehydration, but I believe she died of a broken heart.

CHAPTER SIX
INTEGRITY

'So, without further ado, I'll hand you over to Police Commissioner, Sir Peter Imbert, who has recorded this important message for you today,' said Chief Inspector Barry, angling the trolley loaded with a TV and VHS recorder towards his audience of twenty-plus officers.

I sat in the front row, sandwiched between Bob and PC Susan, another Area Car driver in my team, cradling a cuppa and keen to hear the commissioner's speech. I felt grateful to be inside for a training day as it was a horrible wet and windy November morning – the worst weather for foot patrol. Back then, all officers attended such training sessions about four times a year – to learn about new legislation or the latest crime hotspots or priority crimes.

'I trust you'll all listen carefully and heed his wise words,' added Barry. He switched on the television and a blur of black and grey dots trembled on the screen. 'Do make a note of any questions and we'll go through them once you've watched the video.' I heard a few muffled sniggers behind me as Barry pressed play on the VHS recorder. He stood back, arms folded, waiting for Sir Peter Imbert to appear on the box. But when wavy white lines finally gave way to an image, there was no sign of the commissioner – unless some camera trickery had turned the 60-year-old cop boss into a perma-tanned Swedish porn star with plastic pecs and a blond permed mullet. He was engaged in some vigorous, flesh-slapping, heavy-breathing doggy-style sex with a blonde woman sporting a magenta-glossed mouth. They were performing upon a shagpile rug in a log cabin, of course.

The room erupted with laughter. Tears streamed from Bob's eyes. I spilt my tea. Susan rattled in her chair, clutching her stomach. Comments about 'handling swollen goods' and 'taking down particulars' flew around the room. Even Barry laughed. 'All right,' he said, gesturing at the rampant actors, who were becoming louder and more energetic by the second. 'It seems there's been a bit of a deliberate mix-up here.' He fumbled for the stop button on the video player as Scott, our instructor, lurched at the TV and switched it off. There were a few cries of protest, but I thought Barry handled the situation with good humour. Cocking his head, he gave an exaggerated wink. 'Bet you didn't know the commissioner was hung like that, did you?' Then he wished us all a pleasant day and walked out of the room to more roars of laughter.

I can't remember who swapped the commissioner's recording for the mucky tape, but we all had a bloody good hoot – and still completed our training without further interruption. Although, as we unanimously agreed, the commissioner's video was not nearly as entertaining as the Swedish porn clip.

It had felt so good to laugh – a good belly laugh, at that. I didn't do much laughing in the section house, where I spent most of my off-duty hours holed in my grotty bedroom in the sky, watching the planes or television. Not being a drinker, I rarely socialised. I wasn't big on visiting art galleries or museums either, so my life in London outside of work felt lonely at times.

I returned to Lytham whenever my shift pattern allowed, usually once or twice a month. Dave, Paul, Kevin, and all my youth club friends would bombard me with questions, seemingly fascinated by my job. 'Who've you nicked?' 'Seen any dead bodies yet?' 'What's the worst thing you've seen so far?' 'Been attacked yet?' And so on. But I didn't mind; I loved talking about policing and regaling my friends with anecdotes from the frontline. And I spared them no details whenever they asked, 'What does a dead body smell like?'

Being a cop felt like the most natural thing in the world to me. Even during long weekends in Lytham, I would wonder what emergencies were happening in London – what action I might be missing. I was my happiest at work – and put every fibre of my being into the Job.

Officially, Met coppers are only allowed to carry force-issued appointments – truncheon, handcuffs, torch, etc, but I thought this ridiculous. For example, the regulation two-cell torches were as helpful as a glow worm. Every cop I knew, myself included, replaced this equipment with a more powerful Maglite torch. But a torch wasn't enough for me, especially now I'd honed my break and entry skills to the nth degree. Such work requires specific tools – and being a gadget man, I had all the gear.

My 'unofficial' kit earned me my first nickname, Inspector Gadget. Seriously, I was a walking hardware store with the amount of stuff I carried, concealed at various locales in my uniform. Attached to my belt were three or four nylon pouches containing all my bits and pieces for breaking into houses and cars: pieces of metal and plastic, Swiss Army knife, and another item, which I'll not divulge, that enabled me to bypass Yale locks. In the dome of my helmet, concealed above the stretched mesh layer that sits on your head, lived a coiled wire coat hanger, a length of polypropylene tape, and a length of 6mm electrical cable. What can I say? Once a geek, always a geek. But my equipment served me well – and saved a lot of time on jobs. I rarely needed to smash down doors to get into properties, which meant I could just shut the door when I left – instead of hanging around, sometimes for hours on end, for the occupier to return.

As I previously mentioned, burglaries were a quotidian affair in F district. House burglars' modus operandi invariably goes like this: break in via a back door or window, bolt the front door (in case they're disturbed); ransack the place at lightning speed; forage for cash, jewellery, and any electrical goods worth flogging on and, finally, escape with said haul before the fuzz arrives. However, one callout to a suspected burglary in a basement flat baffled me – chiefly because it looked like a break-in without a physical 'break-in'.

I was on an early turn one Friday, the day after the Swedish porn tape concern. Walking the beat in Shepherd's Bush that morning, I kept giggling to myself as images of that tape played a dodgy slideshow in my head. Then my radio kicked in and pulled the plug on that montage.

The 'burgled' property was a basement flat in Greenside Road, at the far southwest corner of Shepherd's Bush where it borders Hammersmith. The first odd thing that struck me was that there were no signs of forced entry to the flat. The front door was ajar, but its frame and lock were undamaged. There wasn't even a scratch on the door itself. A man in the flat above had raised the alarm, said he'd noticed the open door long after his neighbour left for work that morning. 'Strange,' the neighbour said, 'I didn't hear a thing.' It crossed my mind: *Maybe the malefactor had used one of my break-in techniques?* But wait a second, opportunist burglars don't have a reputation for being expert lock–pickers, do they?

I went inside to investigate.

The magnolia hall smelled of fruity air freshener. There were no footprints on the parquet flooring – and it was a dirty wet day out, too – pavements carpeted with soggy leaves and decaying conker shells and such. The kitchen looked untouched, but the lounge and bedroom displayed all the classic signs of a burglary: empty television cabinet, tipped-out drawers, clothes and various other items littering the floors. Stranger still was the wad of cash fanned atop a tangle of women's underwear and tights on the bedroom floor. About four hundred quid – a combination of fifty, twenty and ten-pound notes. *No self-respecting burglar would have missed this, surely?* Still, I noted relevant details for my crime report, arranged for a Scenes of Crime Officer (SOCO) to check the place for fingerprints, secured the flat – that was easy, I just had to shut the front door – and left. Following protocol, I took the cash and booked it into the safe at the police station – pending it being returned to its rightful owner.

I heard no more about the burglary until I checked the property transit book a week later. There it was, staring at me in black and white. The cash I'd found at the scene of the 'burglary' had been collected and signed for by a senior officer from some unknown department at Scotland Yard. In that moment it dawned on me: I had been subjected to – and passed – a Metropolitan Police "integrity test", a random method designed to identify and boot out corrupt officers within its ranks. Crafty top brass had staged the entire burglary. If I had pocketed that cash, I would have faced a misconduct hearing, a judge, and time at Her Majesty's Pleasure.

In those early days I would question my every action in the Job. Soon after my integrity test, I attended the 'domestic disturbance' in East Acton – the one where Dwayne held his ten-year-old son Tyler at knifepoint and threatened to slit the boy's throat.

Had I been right to smash Dwayne over the head with my truncheon? It had all happened so fast. After I'd handcuffed and cautioned Dwayne, I slowly got up and stepped backwards, glass shards crunching beneath my feet. A part of me wanted Dwayne to kick off again – to confirm that he wasn't on the brink of death. But he just lay there, eyes disappearing into his head, drifting towards the gash leaking more blood into the crushed glass. Wiping sweat from my brow, I stood for a moment, watching, thinking. Tyler's raw sobs sounded from the lounge, eerie and echoey, like I was hearing his cries through deep water. At the same time, I recalled Sergeant Peter's advice during truncheon training at Wanstead: *I highly recommend you don't hit anyone over the head with your truncheon – because there's a good chance that you'll kill them.* Likewise, I remembered the vision I'd had at the time, of me standing over a dead-eyed man after I'd hit him over the head with my truncheon. *Had that been a premonition?* All these thoughts came to me in a matter of seconds, then Dwayne groaned and rolled his head right and left.

Yeah, he'll live.

Our backup officers, including a dog-handler arrived and, surprisingly, Dwayne didn't give us much grief from then on. We took him to Hammersmith Hospital, got his head stitched, then I accompanied him back to the custody suite at Shepherd's Bush police station, where I finished my crime report. As I did so, I realised, again, *Tyler could have died tonight. Dwayne might have killed me too.* Question was, would top brass consider my actions justified? I had to present my truncheon to the custody Sergeant for inspection. Satisfied there were no nails or bits of glass stuck to it, the Sergeant returned my appointment. That wouldn't happen today; my truncheon would be placed in a sealed bag and sent to the forensics lab for testing, possibly amid a misconduct inquiry.

Once I'd submitted my crime report, I had no further dealings with Dwayne. CID officers took over and subsequently charged Dwayne with various offences including threats to kill and affray. Dwayne pleaded guilty to all charges, which meant I didn't have to give evidence at court, and, a few months later, Dwayne would be jailed for two years. I laughed when I heard what he said in mitigation: 'I make no complaint about the officer who hit me over the head. I deserved everything I got.' But did Dwayne get what he deserved? I was happy with his sentence. In retrospect, he was the only one hurt after threatening to kill his ten-year-old son – and I wasn't injured. So, a whack over the head *and* two years in the Big House for Dwayne? Yeah, I'll take that.

Domestic violence cases did not attract much sympathy from the Metropolitan Police in the Eighties. Fortunately, this attitude would change over time, especially once Scotland Yard launched a Domestic Violence Unit (DVU) on every one of London's thirty-two boroughs. But, back in those Margaret Thatcher days, it was common to hear officers and control room staff say, 'Oh, it's just a domestic,' whenever such cases arose.

The festive season is a peak time for reports of family disturbances and domestic violence – as I witnessed when I worked my first of many Christmas Day late shifts. As much of the country tucked into their roast turkey dinners, I paced the quiet streets of Shepherd's Bush in the freezing drizzle, waiting for the crime of the century to happen. It didn't. Instead, early into my shift the control room dispatched me to a 'disturbance' at a terraced house in Percy Road. 'Looks like it's just a domestic,' said the male operator.

'Right, I'm on my way,' I said, thinking, *I hope there are no knives involved this time.*

I arrived at the house to hear a man and woman, swearing and shouting at each other over the velvet strains of Elvis' *Lonely This Christmas*. The living room window had been smashed, and a cooked turkey, still in its roasting tin and swimming in hot oil, sat on a bed of broken glass in the front garden. I walked up the path, my sigh visible in the cold winter air. I rang the bell, but the couple couldn't have heard it above Elvis and their voices.

'If you want a divorce, you can have a fucking divorce,' screamed the woman.

And the man laughed a demonic laugh. 'You're a fucking headcase. All of this over a frigging turkey?'

I pressed the bell again, then looked at my watch. It had just gone 3pm.

I guess this is going to be a long night, then.

CHAPTER SEVEN
MONKEY BUSINESS

By spring 1987, although still a probie, I felt more established within the force, my confidence building with
every passing day – and those days, and weeks and months
passed like bullets. No two days were the same, ever. That's
what I loved most about being a cop. Every day was a journey into the unknown.

Getting to know my colleagues better also made me feel
at home in the Met – and London. Aside from bent cops
(I would encounter a few) – and backstabbers like Sergeant
Alan – my fellow officers were decent people. There was
a strong camaraderie among us coppers; we worked hard
and looked out for one another. Finally, I felt part of the big
Met crime-busting 'family' our tutors had told us about at
training school. And when we weren't busy restoring order
on the streets of London, we enjoyed a good laugh, usually
at a colleague's expense – but it was all harmless, friendly
banter... most of the time.

Back then, police officers employed a unique vocabu-
lary for describing their co-workers. I'm talking derogatory,
un-PC terms, invented in-house. Over time, I got to know

those expressions, but initially, I had no idea what people were talking about. For example, sitting with Bob and Gary one lunch time, I listened with confused ears to their bizarre exchange, which went something like this:

Gary: 'D'you hear the latest about that blister, Terry?'

Bob: 'You mean Constable Terry Walters – geezer who did nothing at that supermarket robbery?'

Gary: 'Yeah, court case is on just now. Terry gave evidence this morning. Complete jigsaw by all accounts.'

Bob: 'I'm surprised he [Terry] made it to the robbery even. I had him down as an Olympic flame.'

Gary [grinning]: 'He was – but now he's a bungalow.'

Bob [acknowledging me with a wink]: 'What d'you reckon son?'

Me [trying to pull an insouciant face]: 'Why is Terry a bungalow?'

Bob [laughing]: 'Ah, stick with me, Matt, my son. I'll teach you everything you need to know.'

True to his word, a few days later, on a quiet morning in the Area Car with Bob, he explained all about his conversation with Gary – and taught me some more police words to boot. Blister, said Bob, referred to a cop renowned for turning up once all the hard work is done. I nodded keenly. 'And what does jigsaw mean?'

Bob lit another Raffles fag. 'A jigsaw is a copper who falls to pieces in the box – the witness box that is, son.'

I laughed. 'How did I not know that? And Olympic flame?'

'Easy – that's a copper who never goes out [of the police station]'.

'Bungalow?'

'Copper who only has one story to tell. In other words, a bit of a boring git.'

I nodded sagely. 'Yeah, I guess that makes sense,' I said.

'Know what a Chi Chi is?' added Bob. I unwound my window an inch to let in some fresh air, conjuring images of the giant, cuddly female panda who was the star attraction at London Zoo before her demise in 1972.

'Go on, then.'

'A Chi Chi is a cop who has a lot of polcolls [a portmanteau of police and collisions, meaning crashes involving police vehicles]. Or, as we like to say, somebody who fucks Panda cars,' said Bob, laughing his infectious, throaty laugh again.

'Bloody hell, Bob,' I said. 'That's taking it a bit far.'

Bob shrugged. 'I didn't make that one up. But, hey, plenty more where that came from, son.'

I learned several more nicknames from Bob that morning, including: Ghurka (a cop who 'takes no prisoners'); Opium (a slow-acting dope); Awl (a boring tool); Harpic (clean around the bend) and Boils (boring, obnoxious, insignificant little shit). 'Oh, and another one,' finished Bob as we pulled into the White City Estate. 'Kipper – it means two-faced and gutless. But I wouldn't call your colleagues these names to their faces, son. That'll get you in a lot of bother.'

Armed robbery in progress on Uxbridge Road...

I switched on the twos and blues and watched with a mixture of admiration and frustration as Bob executed a Starsky and Hutch-style J-turn. 'Right, here we go,' he

74

said, stamping on the accelerator. 'I love it when a plan comes together.'

I wish I was in Bob's seat right now.

Still a boy racer at heart, I couldn't wait to get behind the wheel of one of the Met's high-performance motors and tear through the city on twos and blues – primarily in the name of chasing criminals and protecting you, the public, of course. Alas, I would not be performing J-turns like Bob overnight. To become an Area Car driver, I would first need to pass the Met's three-week Standard Driving Course, followed by the force's six-week Advanced Driving Course, which is fiercely competitive. Only one or two places on the Advanced Driving Course are allocated per police station a year. I could be waiting years for my chance.

'If you want to be a driver, you'll need to get yourself noticed by the big wigs, son,' Bob told me. 'And the way to do so is to volunteer for every job going – even if it's something you're not sure of. Main thing is, you'll be heard over the radio – and the bosses will see how keen you are. Volunteer for all the big emergency jobs, but also be first to say yes to all the boring gigs and smelly deaths. Oh, and arrest as many villains as you can.'

That was the best advice Bob ever gave me. From then on, I made it my mission to be heard. '292, I'll do it,' I'd blurt into my radio whenever the control room announced an incident – even if I was on foot and miles away from the scene. I would do anything that might fast-track me onto the driving course.

Saying yes to more jobs also increased my chances of arresting criminals. At that time, I averaged around ten to fifteen arrests per month for offences ranging from shoplifting, credit card fraud, cannabis-related crimes (dealing, possession or possession with intent to supply), to drink-driving, affray, public order, and burglary. And I finally arrested Danny Crampsey, the Irish homeless guy who roamed Shepherd's Bush Green.

Like Bridie, Danny spent his days boozing to oblivion – and often threatening passers-by in his drunken stupors. A stocky chap in his early fifties, what I knew of Danny's backstory saddened me. Once an accomplished boxer in Ireland, he descended into alcoholism and his life fell apart from there. Danny had a love-hate relationship with the police. Mostly, he'd want to fight us, but occasionally, we'd see glimpses of chirpy, humble Danny. Compliant, and grateful, especially when we chucked a bag of chips his way after collecting our takeaways from One Eye's on nightshifts.

One Danny story that amuses me to this day was when he prompted repeated 999 calls from disgruntled passers-by during a frantically busy early shift. Two Constables, patrolling in the police van, found Danny, drunk, shadow boxing and lashing out at anybody who dared go near him. Weary of his games, the officers managed to restrain Danny – then bundled him into the cage in the back of the van. But rather than take him to the station, they instead took Danny on a twenty-five-mile road trip to a remote park in Surrey. They dragged him out of the van, uncuffed him, then left him there while they drove through heavy traffic back to London. The Constables got as far as Chiswick, about a mile away from Shepherd's Bush, when the police control room called on the radio. 'Another 999 complaint regarding Danny Crampsey – he's causing a disturbance on Shepherd's Bush Green again.' Incredibly, somehow, like a drunken homing pigeon, Danny had beaten the van back to The Bush, ready for round two.

When I arrested Danny, he was, again, blinding drunk. I also found him staggering around the Green after 999 complaints from the public. In his habitual toffee corduroy trousers, belted with string, his legs moved like wobbling skittles. He was trying to shadow-box, but his arms were windmilling more than punching. He dribbled a combination of swear words between repeated shouts of 'on the ropes.' But surprisingly, when I appeared, he calmed down and, apologising, placed his hands behind his back for me to cuff him. I took Danny to the custody suite and booked him into a cell. We kept him in for seven hours until he sobered up then released him with a warning. Danny caused no trouble in the cells – and he couldn't thank me enough when he left the station. 'I'm so very sorry for putting you out,' he added. 'I can assure you, officer, this will not happen again. I'll be no trouble from now on.'

'Good stuff. Cheerio, Danny,' I said as he shambled out of the custody suite with his head bowed.

Danny and I would meet again.

I relished the variety of my job. I could attend a sudden death, burglary, and armed siege in one shift alone. In March 1987, while on crowd control at Queens Park Rangers, Liverpool striker Ian Rush knocked my helmet clean off my head with a wayward shot that cleared the crossbar. Imagine: eighteen thousand fans chanting, 'On the 'ead, on the ead.' Yeah, I found that funny too.

Mostly, once a job was done and dusted, I'd quickly forget about it and move on to the next incident. Occasionally, however, a job from the past would return to haunt – or amuse – me. That would happen whenever I gave evidence in court, for example. Or occasionally, I'd read about an incident I'd attended in a newspaper. One afternoon, as I sat flicking through a local newspaper in the locker room, I stumbled across an article that made me look twice. The headline grabbed me first: 'Widow finds dead husband's false teeth in flower bed.' (Or something very similar.) I read on and discovered that the widow, 'Jill, 82, of Shepherd's Bush', had discovered her husband Norman's gnashers while watering her hydrangeas. My heart jumped. Jill and Norman? *Shit, that's the garden I hosed down last year – after Norman fell from the roof of the couple's house. I didn't see a set of teeth at the time – there was too much gore.* And briefly, I wondered, *will I get into trouble for this?* But Jill's quotes were good-humoured and, once the initial shock passed, I had a little laugh to myself.

Things were about to get weirder.

Plodding the beat could be frustrating, especially when exciting 999 calls happened outside my walking or running range. Sick of missing out on such action, I started hitching lifts from random motorists. One of the first times I did this, I flagged down a stretched limo. I thought, *Might as well travel in style to this RTA (Road Traffic Accident).* The chauffeur, smart in his cap and driving gloves, could not be more obliging. 'Jump in, officer,' he said with a smile and a wink. 'Plenty of room in the back.'

'Nice one, thanks,' I said, then opened the back door to reveal a tableau most men would give anything to join: five tipsy women, in their twenties, all wearing skimpy outfits – spangled miniskirts and dresses, accessorised with fishnet stockings and bottles of Asti Spumante. One had a net curtain on her head and L-plates pinned haphazardly on her Ra-Ra skirt. A hen do, complete with a blaring soundtrack of Cyndi Lauper's *Girls Just Want to Have Fun*. I hesitated for a moment, but the bride-to-be pulled me into the car. The next ten minutes were like an extended scene from *The Benny Hill Show*: me, a uniformed cop, surrounded by scantily dressed women making remarks such as, 'Show us your truncheon' and 'That's a big, shiny helmet you've got, officer.' What's a man to do?

When the limo pulled up at the crash scene, the hens tumbled out so I could exit, while the two male drivers involved in the RTA watched from the kerb, laughing. I straightened my helmet and marched up to the men. 'Right, this isn't how it looks,' I said, trying to invoke an air of authority. 'I am *not* a stripper.'

'Yeah, right,' the drivers said in unison, 'not heard that one before.'

My next lift whisked me to the scene of a Saturday night pub brawl. It was dark when I flagged down the Ford Fiesta, so I didn't see who was behind the wheel until the car screeched to a halt. The driver was a dear woman called Mrs Keeble, in her eighties, with a blue rinse hairdo. I barely had time to pull on my seatbelt before she hit the gas and wheel-spun away. She did a mile through west London in a little over a minute, speeding through at least three red lights. 'I've always wanted to do this,' she shrieked as I gripped the dashboard.

The fight was over quickly, with a few men arrested, and as I left the pub, Mrs Keeble was waiting in her Fiesta. She unwound her window. 'Where to next, officer?' she said, grinning.

Catching lifts from the public was fun, but I felt safer in an Area Car. Although not all calls involved racing to the scene on twos and blues.

I was on patrol with Bob one Sunday morning when the control room radioed this bizarre message: 'Female occupier reports a green and yellow monkey has climbed through her kitchen window.' Suspecting a prank (quiet Sundays were prime time for practical jokes), Bob and I initially declined the call. But the control room insisted this was a genuine scenario reported by a 'Mrs Jones'. 'This is definitely a wind-up,' said Bob as we headed to the address.

'Yeah,' I said, 'Least they could do is come up with an original name. I mean, Jones?'

Ten minutes later, in a Victorian terraced house near Chiswick...

'Where on earth did that come from?' I say, staring at the squirrel monkey perched on the kitchen worktop. The monkey's eating a hard-boiled egg, mushy yolk crumbs collecting in its yellowy green fur. Mrs Jones, the homeowner, is equally bemused.

'I've no idea. I was doing the washing-up and...' she gestures at the animal with a Marigold-clad hand. 'It just appeared at the window – and climbed in.'

'Is it tame?' I ask as Bob goes outside to radio the control room.

'Yes, it's been playing with the kids. Seems friendly enough,' says Mrs Jones. I proffer my hand to the primate, who emits a few excitable screams and scurries up my arm. Then it sits on my shoulder, still eating the egg. Then Mr Jones enters the kitchen, carrying a cardboard box.

'Let's stick the monkey in here till we know what to do with it,' he says, so I reach for the creature.

'C'mon then, down you come,' I say in a cooing voice reserved for cute animals and babies. But as I go to lift the monkey, it suddenly drops the egg and clamps its teeth around my left thumb. I rip the monkey's head away from my hand and blood spurts from my digit. When I look down, I see my left thumb is partially detached at the knuckle. There's blood everywhere. I hear screaming, then my vision turns muddy. The terracotta tiled floor jumps to meet me – as I fade into blackness.

The next thing I hear is the wail of sirens.

CHAPTER EIGHT
NEVER START A FIGHT YOU CAN'T POSSIBLY WIN

I came to in the Area Car, sprawled like a broken deckchair over the back seat. I was facing the roof, with a window winder embedding my skull. My left knee skewed the gap between the front seats, while my other leg held a position only achievable by a contortionist. A fiery, needly pain coursed through my left thumb. Was it ablaze? When I looked down at my injured hand, I glimpsed my thumb bandaged to five times its natural size in layers of blook-soaked kitchen roll. Urgent blue light washed over me through the window as Bob floored it at maniacal speed, shouting, 'Hang in there, son, we're nearly there.' I bit down on my bottom lip and scrunched my eyes shut, but still cobalt light flooded my retinas – through which emerged the yellowy face of a squirrel monkey.

I hobbled into Hammersmith Hospital, helped along by Bob. 'The lad's been bitten by a monkey,' he told the receptionist in Accident and Emergency, and honestly, I would have laughed my head off were it not for the accelerating pain in my bloody thumb.

Fortunately, the Met had a great relationship with A&E staff at Hammersmith Hospital, so injured cops would be whisked into a side room and treated within minutes. Today, it was my turn. 'Right, son, I'll leave you to it,' said Bob, patting my shoulder as he steered me towards the room. 'I'll get the paperwork done and we'll be out of here faster than you can say "monkey's uncle".'

'Thanks Bob, I really appreciate all this,' I said, and lumbered into the room, where a male doctor wearing a serious, 'I'm sorry, we did everything we could' expression, waited in his starchy white coat. He was flanked by two female nurses who looked to be around my age. One wore Deidre Barlow-inspired glasses. Both looked as though they were about to burst into giggles.

'Drop your trousers – you need a tetanus shot,' said the doctor when I explained how the monkey had sunk its teeth into my thumb. I got onto the couch, fumbled with my trousers with my good hand. As I did so, I noticed crusty white and yellow crumbs clinging to my tunic – remains of the monkey's boiled egg feast. *Damn that monkey*. 'You might feel a small prick,' added the doctor. I heard the nurses' muffled laughter from behind the screen as the needle speared my arse cheek. 'Right, let's look at this wound, then.'

The next few minutes were excruciating. While the doctor examined my thumb, which looked like a Halloween prop from a joke shop, the nurses took the piss out of me. 'So how big was the monkey?' asked the one in the Deidre Barlow specs.

'About a foot tall,' I said. Cue more laughing.

'Well, well, well. Would you believe it?' said the second nurse, nudging her colleague. 'A big man like yourself, an officer of the law, attacked by a twelve-inch cuddly monkey. What kind of message is that sending out?'

I tried to think of a funny retort, but I still felt disorientated – and my thumb throbbed like hell. Although I now had a vague memory of Bob dragging me from the Jones' house to the Area Car. I looked up at the nurses. 'It's the little ones you need to watch,' I croaked. 'That said, I think the monkey came off worse than me.' More waves of pain shot through my digit and wrist. Saliva clicked in my mouth as I flinched and sucked in my breath.

'Ooh, you look deathly white, PC Calveley,' said the bespectacled nurse.

Bandaging my thumb, the doctor advised me to take a month off work for the wound to heal.

'What? I can't take a whole month off,' I said.

'Well, at least take a week off – and no public-facing roles for another three weeks.'

'Fine,' I agreed. 'I know I have to be sensible about this.'

I was back on duty fourteen hours later.

That little monkey did a lot of damage to my thumb. And, of course, my monkey episode became the talk – and amusement – of Shepherd's Bush police station. I became known as 'that bloke who got bitten by a monkey.' But that would not be the last I heard of my furry assailant. Clive was his name, according to the article that appeared in the *Hammersmith Gazette* two weeks later.

"Cheeky ape Clive nips arm of law", screamed the headline. Several copies of the *Gazette* were circulated in

the canteen, sparking more hilarity among my colleagues.
I laughed too when I read the opening lines:

Unsuspecting officers were the victims of a spot of monkey business when they tried to recapture an escapee.

Two policemen were given rough treatment when they were called to a home in Rylett Crescent, Shepherd's Bush, to catch Clive, an escapee squirrel monkey.

The diligent *Gazette* reporter had tracked down Clive's owner, a local lady who kept exotic pets. She hadn't noticed Clive was missing until the reporter chapped her door. Incredibly, after attacking me, Clive had legged it through the Jones' kitchen window then hopped home – via several gardens.

Police however deny rumours the monkey will be appearing at his local magistrate court on a charge of assaulting a police officer.

It took three months for the tissues in my thumb to heal and over a year for the nerve damage to repair. After the story broke, I asked Bob if he'd been the *Gazette's* 'anonymous source'. He gave me a wink and burst out laughing.

Unfortunately, being attacked and injured on duty is an occupational hazard for a cop.

I have the scars to prove this – including the one on my left thumb, courtesy of Clive. Over the years I would be attacked countless times at work. Sometimes, I received financial compensation for my woes. Once, I nicked a man for assaulting a police officer after he shoved me in the chest. He got convicted, heavily fined, and ordered to pay £50 to yours truly. In the late Eighties, a police Constable's take home pay was around £140 per week, so an extra fifty quid in my back pocket felt like a small windfall. A year later, a drunk woman bit my hand as I guided her into the police van. She lashed out after I arrested her for credit card fraud. I subsequently received £1,000 from the Criminal Injuries Compensation Board (CICB).

About a year after Clive assaulted me, just as I began to regain proper use of my thumb, I became the victim of another attack. It happened on a late turn, around 9pm. Only this time, my assailant was at least five feet taller than Clive – and armed with a machete some two inches longer than the animal, too.

The initial call sounded innocuous: 'Two men fighting in Adelaide Grove. Looks like a dispute between neighbours.' I was just around the corner from the address, on foot patrol, so I radioed back.

'This is PC 292FS. Just round the corner. I'll do this.'

This'll be another petty ding-dong over a broken fence, noisy music, or a barking dog. Or a drunken brawl. I thought. I jogged to the scene, wary that the pavement was frosty underfoot. It was a crisp November night, the sky a fluid indigo, occasionally embossed with glittering explosions: rockets, screamers, and fountains and such. Foot patrol could be a spectacular event this time of the year.

I neared the house, expecting, as the operator had indicated, to see two men fighting. Instead, I found one stocky man in a black hooded coat, stooped, and swaying in profile over a garden wall, silver sparks spraying around his left arm to the sounds of grunting and metal scraping brick. In the darkness, the effect looked cosmic, reminiscent of the fireworks. Then I trained my torch on the guy – and glimpsed a shimmering machete, which he was sharpening, Sweeney Todd-style, on the wall. I cleared my throat and, at once, he wheeled round, waving the blade in the air. The weapon glinted as it sliced through the torchlight. I glimpsed flashes of his face, all wet teeth and fat gums, as he lurched towards me, shouting, slurring, 'That's my fucking wife, I'll fucking kill you,' while cutting haphazard arcs over his head with the machete, which grew in size as he advanced, faster now, on thumping feet. He was so close I could smell his breath – whiskey and tobacco.

I should've backed off and radioed for armed response, but pumped with adrenaline, I charged at him, ignoring the words of our Wanstead PT instructor PC Davies that suddenly thrummed a mantra in my head: *Never start a fight you can't possibly win, never start a fight you can't possibly win, never start a fight you can't possibly win.*

In I went.

It happened in seconds. Stumbling, the guy swung the machete, aiming for my right arm. I blocked his blow, and the machete flew from his hand and skated along the frosty pavement. As the guy went to turn, I jumped on his back, wrestled him to the ground and pinned him down, a slobbering, growling mountain spewing whiskey gases. Then I reached for my handcuffs and began my spiel, resisting the urge to say, 'Never start a fight you can't possibly win.'

When my Sergeant, Tony, heard how I'd challenged, disarmed, and arrested an aggressive drunk, he submitted an excellent report recommending me for a bravery commendation. However, two weeks later, I received a letter saying this idea had been rejected by a desk-jockey senior police officer, who ruled that, machete or not, the assailant was in his late sixties, drunk, and therefore not a threat to a frontline cop acting alone. I was gutted.

I would challenge anyone to fight an aggressive, machete-wielding drunk person and feel comfortable about it. To me, this naïve decision emphasised the fundamental differences between police officers who work on the front line, and those who have nice, safe office roles. But I shrugged it off – and got on with the Job.

Night shifts were invariably more eventful than days and, as you know, I craved action – foot chases, car chases (even as a passenger), and arresting criminals. But, on the Sunday before Christmas 1988, I endured the worst shift of my career.

It started at 10pm with foot patrol, plodding the streets of Shepherd's Bush in the freezing wind and rain. I didn't mind this as I was used to patrolling in all weathers, but with nothing happening, other than tipsy festive revellers spilling out of the pubs, it was looking to be a long, cold, wet and tedious shift ahead.

I walked on, past shop windows festooned with tinsel and fairy lights and glittering signs shouting, 'Merry Christmas' and 'Ho, ho, ho'. I stopped and drooled at a picture of a cooked turkey with all the trimmings in Bejam's window, taking comfort in the knowledge that I'd be tucking into an identical dinner come 2am. As tonight was the last night shift before Christmas, my team was due to meet for a festive meal in the canteen. I rubbed my hands together and continued through the rain, thinking, *I hope they do pigs in blankets.* Two hours later, the following happened:

Chris, my patrol Sergeant, called me on the radio just after midnight and asked for my location. 'I'll pick you up in the car. I'm on my way,' he said. *Nice one*, I thought, *I'll get to spend the last two hours in a warm police car. We might get some exciting emergencies if we're lucky.*

Chris picked me up at Savoy Circus. 'There's been an attempted murder,' he explained as I warmed my hands over the air vents. 'Lovers' tiff. She's fighting for life in hospital, he's in the cells. You'll be guarding the scene overnight until the forensics team arrive in the morning.'

'Sure, no problem,' I said, again presuming this would be a warm indoor number.

The crime scene – a tower block flat on the Edward Woods Estate, on the east side of Shepherd's Bush – was a health hazard. The accused had stabbed his girlfriend multiple times with a kitchen knife. Both were heroin addicts, their flat littered with discarded needles and splattered with the victim's blood, which, according to hospital records, was infected with HIV and Hepatitis B.

My scene-guard position was outside the door to the flat, on a sixteenth-floor communal landing that smelled like a urinal. I arrived as the CID officers were leaving the flat, its front door sufficiently ajar to reveal a segment of room lit by a bare ceiling bulb. A ripped piece of grey linoleum covered part of the floor, strewn with blood, syringes, scrunched pieces of tin foil, spoons and brown-stained empty milk bottles. A mattress, also holding heroin paraphernalia and sprayed claret, lay on the floor along the back wall. A bright, vinegary smell wafted from the room to the landing as the last CID officer pulled the door shut on that tableau. *Hmm, that'll be the smell of heroin.*

The detectives left then, leaving me alone on the landing. It was an indoor landing, but there were no panes in the window frames at either end of the corridor, and the wet wind howled murderously through the empty frames as time ticked on. I was freezing – starving too. Had I known about this job in advance, I would have come prepared with a Mars Bar or two and something to drink. Two hours passed and, sadly, I missed my team's 2am slap-up Christmas dinner in the canteen. The call on the police radio went out at around 2.15am. It echoed eerily off the damp concrete with my footsteps – 'Dinner's ready' – followed by a short rendition of *Jingle Bells* to set the mood. I unclipped my radio, held it to my face and inhaled deeply. For a moment, I thought I smelled pigs in blankets and gravy through the speaker. Then a colleague's voice cut in – 'I'll be there in ten, save me a leg,' and jolted me back to my grim, vinegary, urinal reality.

Six o'clock came and went. My shift over, I expected an early turn Constable to relieve me on scene guard duty. But when nobody arrived by 8am, I radioed the control room. 'Sorry, which Constable are you and what are you doing?' said the operator. Great. While CID had worked through the night arranging the necessary resources for the forensic examination, a communication breakdown on the uniformed side of things meant there had been no handover between the night and early shifts. It took a further ninety minutes for the early shift Sergeant to send a colleague to relieve me. By which time my fingers were blue, I could not feel my feet, and my stomach was nauseous with hunger.

It was 10.30am when I finally crawled into bed – only to be woken by my screaming alarm clock two hours later ahead of my next late shift. During parade I swallowed my yawns, barely able to keep my eyes open as Sergeant Tony announced my posting for the day. 'Right, 292,' he said with a wince, 'you're back on scene guard duty at the Edward Woods Estate.'

'Thank you, Sarge,' I said.

My heart sank.

CHAPTER NINE
GOOD COPS, BAD COPS AND FINGERTIP SEARCHES

In a grimy alley at the heart of the White City Estate, a man lays foetal on the cold pavement, jerking and shrieking violently into the night. Hollow, vulpine screams that ricochet off graffitied walls and bend around the housing blocks. Blood gushes from his hand and pools around him, black and glossy in the dark. He doesn't want to scream; he's a gangster embroiled in territorial drug warfare, a known face in the area. But he's just had his right index finger hacked clean off his hand in a bloody knife fight with a rival gang, which warrants a certain amount of howling, I'd say.

Minutes earlier, residents watched from their windows as a gang of twenty-something lads, many armed with knives, fought next to the kids' play centre in nearby Canada Way. One terrified woman called 999. 'Help,' she cried down the line. 'There's a huge fight outside my front door. It's the local gangs again… they have knives… guns even…'

Sirens sounded. Blue lights flooded the estate. Amid the frantic tangle of limbs and knives, somebody shouted, 'cops, run.' The gang members bolted, scattered like ants in all directions, into the muddy shadows. The amputee gangster managed to stumble a few feet before slumping in the alley, where he was now trying to get up, get out of there, his cries subdued to low moans and gargled, blue vows of retribution.

Two coppers jump out of their car, hear the gangster's whines and charge into the alley. They assail him with torchlight that reveals a fish spine scar from jaw to cheekbone. The gangster's on his arse, still trying to stand while clasping his four-digit hand over his heart, blood saturating his grey hoodie. One copper radios-in for an ambulance while the other officer steps forward. 'Hello Grimes,' he says.

Nathan Grimes was known to police, had a rap sheet the length of Leo Tolstoy's *War and Peace*. His offences included several assaults on police officers, and two convictions for attempted murder after he had shot and seriously wounded two members of a rival gang.

Grimes swore and hit out at the paramedics through-out the ambulance ride to Hammersmith Hospital, where a junior doctor took one look at the villain's hand and told the accompanying cop: 'If you can fetch me his missing finger within the hour, the surgeons should be able to reattach it.'

The message was relayed to the control room at 11.30pm.

I wasn't at the scene when Grimes was found and ferried to hospital that Saturday night, but I heard the events unfold over the radio while responding to a burglary in nearby Oaklands Grove. To be honest, I hadn't paid too much attention to the incident; drug turf wars, gang fights, stabbings, muggings and shootings were common fare on the White City Estate. But as I left the burgled property, I too was drafted in on the job – along with every other available officer in the area. The call was probably the most unusual one I'd had thus far: 'Head to the White City Estate and join the search for a missing finger.'

Fearing revenge attacks in the area, the duty inspector had organised a finger-tip search for Grimes' digit (no pun intended). 'This is a race-against-the-clock business,' we were told on the search job. 'The victim is Nathan Grimes. A violent criminal who lost his right index finger in a knife fight. If we find his finger within the hour, surgeons will be able to reattach it,' he said.

There was no time for further discussion; as the boss had explained, we were on a meter, so to speak. There were about twelve Constables, me included, on the search, and we were each given separate areas to scour. Some officers arrived before me and were already twenty minutes into the search. I was posted to Canada Way, where the knife fight had erupted. Obviously, crawling over pavements stinking of fox piss and dog muck at midnight was not my idea of fun. But I was there to do my job, and I wanted to do my *best* job. And, as you know, I also wanted to be noticed by the bosses, so I put my heart and soul into the search. I was determined to find Grimes' finger. *If I find it, I might get fast-tracked onto the driving course,* I thought. I searched forensically, rummaging through bins, looking under parked cars, and rifling through a Chinese takeaway splattered in the gutter.

Then I got excited when my torch picked out a flesh-coloured, slender shape hugging the rear left tyre of a clapped-out Skoda parked some ten feet ahead. *Yes,* I thought, as a rat scurried into the torch beam and sniffed around the tyre. I powered forth on my hands and knees and the startled rat scurried on, but the object was still there, getting chunkier and more pinkie-like as I advanced. *Is this it? Have I found the gangster's finger?* My excitement lasted all of two seconds, until I could see clearly the 'finger' in all its up-close, torchlit glory. It was a slightly squished chip – probably from the same discarded Chinese takeaway behind me. Great, I'd found a greasy chip, not an amputated finger.

Don't you just hate it when that happens?

On the stroke of half-past midnight, the search for Nathan Grimes' finger was called off. Nobody found it – or if they did, they weren't confessing as much. Meanwhile, Grimes lay in his hospital bed and told officers, 'I'll sort out my own retribution.' And with no witnesses and little evidence, the crime remained unsolved, but…

Years later, while on foot patrol, I bumped into Tom, a retired police dog handler who'd joined the White City Estate search. He was walking across Shepherd's Bush Green one Monday afternoon. I stopped for a chat; I'd always got along well with Tom. He was a good old sweat, just like Bob. I asked Tom if he missed life in the force and a reminiscent smile flitted across his face. 'Yeah, I do sometimes, son, but, you know, I've got my pension – and time to myself. But, yeah, I had some crazy days in the Met, that's for sure.'

I laughed then, suddenly recalling the finger search. 'Hey, Tom, do you remember that night they had us all crawling over the White City Estate, looking for that gangster's finger?

Tom's mouth twitched – I could tell he was trying not to laugh. He looked right, left, right again, then leaned towards my ear. 'My dog Rex found the finger within thirty seconds,' he said. 'And it went straight down the nearest drain.'

'No way, really?' I said. I thought Tom was joking but his face turned serious.

'Absolutely. With that scumbag's rap sheet there was no way he was ever getting his trigger finger back.'

Cops don't always play it by the book. Tom was a good, respected officer who chose not to help a violent gangster. I understood his motivation, but I still wished I'd found Grimes' finger before Rex did.

There are, of course, some bad apples in the Met's 50,000-strong workforce, and I encountered my fair share of bent cops. I was shocked, however, to discover that Keith, who I'd trained with in Wanstead, had been up to no good. I hadn't seen or heard much from Keith since we'd graduated as he'd been posted to Marylebone police station. We lived in the same section house, but I could count on one hand the number of times our paths had crossed there. Then, one Sunday morning, as I flicked through the newspapers over breakfast in the canteen, I was reunited with my former classmate via an 'exclusive' spread in a red-top.

He'd been exposed as a drug dealer in an undercover sting. I almost choked on my dishwater coffee. Cocky Keith, king of the log runs. Smart arse in the classroom: busted. There was even a photo of Keith handing a parcel of crack cocaine to the undercover 'investigator' at an inner-city park. According to the report, Keith had been peddling wares with his colleague, Malcolm.

That tabloid expose marked the end of Keith's policing career. He was booted off the force and sentenced to 200 hours' community service. I heard he was spared jail because he was fitted up by a colleague, who bought drugs from Keith then sold the story.

The Met's secretive Professional Standards Department deals with complaints against officers and staff, police misconduct and corruption. And in 1989 the unit ran surveillance on a civilian staff member called Desmond, a reception officer in Shepherd's Bush police station. Desmond's colleague Sharon once told me: 'Every time I'm on late shift in the front office, I take call after call – all these different women, asking for Desmond by name. He must be a real gigolo.' However, investigators found that Desmond was an active member of a people-smuggling gang that imported female illegal immigrants into the UK from Africa. Desmond's role was to assist the trafficked women on their arrival in the UK to safe houses dotted around London. Astonishingly, Desmond landed himself a job with the Met – and gave the smuggled women his contact number at the police station. Desmond was arrested, convicted of various immigration and human trafficking offences, and jailed.

Alcohol abuse was the downfall of other officers. I once walked into the locker room to find my colleague – I'll call him Constable Adam – unconscious on the floor in full uniform. Above him stood a flushed-faced, bearded chap who I would soon discover ran The Greyhound pub, an Irish boozer round the corner from the police station. I looked at Adam, dribbling into his tunic, then looked at the bearded guy, who I did not recognise. He breathed out and his beer belly inflated in his Pringle sweater, stretching the diamond design. 'This officer has been drinking in my pub all morning," he said. 'He left about midday, then when I came outside, I found him in the gutter. I didn't know what to do so I slung him in the back of my truck and brought him here.'

'Right,' I said, 'does anybody else know about this?'

The bearded chap sighed. 'Your Sergeant is aware of the matter – says he's dealing with it.' I went to my locker, grabbed my kit, and made a swift exit. I did not want to get involved.

Although drinking on duty or in police uniform is strictly forbidden, Adam wouldn't be the first cop to sneak a cheeky pint or two in while working. But Adam had a serious problem with alcohol – one that would end his career in the Met.

A few weeks after his binge in The Greyhound, Adam, while off duty, crashed his private motor into a row of parked cars. He was arrested for drink-driving, convicted and kicked off the force.

CHAPTER TEN
DEAD ENDINGS

The market, gloomy and deserted at 4am, smelled of rotting vegetables and mildew. Or was last week's sudden death still clinging to my uniform?

I walked alongside the railway arches beneath the viaduct for the Hammersmith and City Tube line, past skeletal metal shells of empty stalls, the rubber grips on my shoes making steady gluey sounds as I plodded on. My feet and back ached; this was my last night shift of the week on foot patrol, and I was looking forward to four days off. *This shift has been so long and quiet. Deadly quiet. Boring.* Such were my thoughts when I noticed, on the pavement outside one of the market stalls, a pool of blood, soupy and russet beneath the sodium lamp light.

Crouching, I shone my torch on the circular pool – about half a metre in diameter, and noticed that the puddle gave way to thick, smeared lines of blood – trails resembling drag marks that cut eerie paths into the stall under a railway arch curtained by two tarpaulin sheets. Mindful not to step in the blood and risk contaminating the scene, I entered the archway through the gap between the two sheets, the smell of blood, ammonia and faeces now overpowering the market aromas. I angled my torch and slowly swiped the ground with light, tracing the drags of blood, to the far-left corner of the cave, where my light then caressed the splayed, camouflage-trousered legs of a man. He lay supine, his torso a heavy, unmoving shape encased in a tatty donkey jacket.

As I advanced, other parts of him emerged from the tawny shade: hands, limp and bluish, his face stark white and marked with bloody patches, eyes wide and blank. Jaw dropped open. More blood pooled his skull, which was cracked and flattened into the ground. I bent over him, shining my torch into his eyes, checking for signs of life. As expected, the man did not react. Likewise, I checked for a pulse, but his wrist was ice-cold and stiff. Rigor mortis had already set in. It was clear this man had died after suffering a serious head injury, but still, I radioed for an ambulance. (Police officers are never allowed to "assume" somebody is dead, regardless of the state of the body.)

Paramedics arrived and confirmed the death, then I sealed off the market and radioed CID. The dead man looked to be in his mid-forties and, quite possibly, homeless. While waiting for CID officers I began writing my incident report – and re-examined the blood marks connecting the pool of blood to the body. To me, those marks suggested the dead man had been moved – and I told the two detectives so when they arrived at the scene. However, they seemed uninterested in my opinion.

'We don't know the time of death,' I explained, performing a walk-through of the scene. 'The market was deserted when I stumbled across the body… nobody loitering or running away from the scene.' I pointed at the streaks of blood on the pavement. 'As you can see, it does appear the victim's body was dragged inside.' One of the detectives walked away as I spoke, while the other half-heartedly pulled a Biro from the top pocket of his blazer, bit off its cap, and said, 'OK, thanks, son, we can handle this from here.'

'Righto,' I said and retreated to finish writing my statement. After all, there was nothing left for me to do at the scene. *I'll leave matters in their good hands*, I thought, and returned to foot patrol for the last hour of my shift.

Although usually good at switching off after work, I did wonder, as I climbed into bed later that morning, whether a murder probe would be launched into the market death. I certainly expected as much, so when I returned to work on the Thursday, I nipped up to the CID offices on the first floor to enquire about the incident. I spoke with a detective called Neil, who had on a wonky, yellowy paisley print tie that had a life of its own. He leaned over his desk as he spoke, foraging through an unkempt pile of papers and files. I could smell the remains of a Big Mac wafting from the wastepaper basket beneath the desk. 'Victim's name is Michael Merriman,' said Neil. 'Forty-four, no next of kin. Homeless. Anyway, it's all done and dusted – it was an accidental death.'

'Accidental death?' I said, trying not to sound incredulous. Questions tickertaped in my mind: *What about the drag marks? There was a large pool of blood outside the railway arch – yet the victim was found several feet away from his blood. How did he move?* But, still young in service, I did not dare to quiz a seasoned detective – let alone suggest Michael Merriman had been murdered. Instead, I asked, 'So, just out of interest, what actually happened to Michael Merriman?'

Just then, another detective appeared and stubbed out his fag in the ashtray amid the clutter on Neil's desk. 'Christopher Schliach murder briefing in two minutes, mate,' he said.

'Gotcha, mate,' said Neil. He grabbed a cardboard slip folder from his desk. 'Sorry, er…'

'Matt, Matt Calveley,' I said.

'Yeah, look, son, we've kinda got our hands full right now with this Schliach case. It's a complex one. Very high profile.'

I nodded. 'Yes, indeed.'

The murder inquiry was the talk of the force and The Bush right now. A week previously, Christopher Schliach, a gay German barrister-turned-legal-magazine-sub-editor, was stabbed to death in his flat in Coverdale Road. Knifed twenty-three times, the post-mortem concluded.

Neil plucked a pen from his messy desk-tidy and stuffed it in the breast pocket of his shirt. 'Anyway, gotta run. I wouldn't lose any sleep over your man, Michael. Geezer clearly had too much to drink and fell over and banged his head. Get over it, son, it wasn't a murder.' Neil gave me a quick, twitchy smile then sauntered off to his briefing.

I headed back downstairs for parade, feeling dejected. It was clear that all police resources in F district were focusing on the Schliach case. Such murder investigations got an unlimited overtime budget; some officers would work shifts above twelve hours for twenty or thirty days in a row, which meant bumper pay packets. The Schliach investigation was proving difficult to crack. Weeks and months passed without as much as an arrest. Meanwhile, more details emerged about Christopher Schliach, who was seemingly well-known in the area. Locals described him as a well-to-do, flamboyant sort, always dapperly dressed in a mustard waistcoat adorned with a gold pocket watch. A trilby hat and monocle accessorised his eccentric-professor look. He drank in local pubs – Beaumont Arms, The Richmond, White Horse and The Bush – and read Russian literature. Before his death, Schliach was immersed in *Oblomov*, by Ivan Goncharov.

By stark contrast, I found out little more about Michael Merriman other than he was a "heavy drinker known for brawling". And while I appreciated the urgency to seek justice for Christopher Schliach, it saddened me to think Michael's death had been written off as "just another drunken tramp who fell and banged his head". Meanwhile, as the hunt for Schliach's killer(s) continued, the council paid for Michael's cremation. There were no mourners because, as Neil had explained, Michael had no next of kin.

Death: I couldn't avoid it. Murders, suicides, drug deaths, unexplained deaths, old age deaths and those who died in "accidents" like poor Michael Merriman (supposedly). I would deal with at least one of those causes of death per week – and would invariably learn a valuable lesson with every scenario I faced.

Then there are "freak accidental deaths" – the crude term to describe rare and bizarre – and often violent – tragedies.

I dealt with a few such deaths, but one devastating case remains vivid in my mind.

One Saturday evening, police received a call from A&E staff at Hammersmith Hospital. A twenty-something woman called Lucy had been ambulanced there with what appeared to be a stab wound to her thigh. Tragically, the cut had severed Lucy's femoral artery, and, despite paramedics' efforts, she died soon after she arrived at the hospital.

I was one of seven constables urgently dispatched to the victim's home, a one-bedroom flat on a local estate. Assuming this was now a murder inquiry, I ran to the address (I was on foot patrol, again). I pictured myself entering a bloodbath, then arresting a suspect and seizing a weapon before sealing the flat to preserve evidence for the forensics team.

I was on scene in five minutes, give or take a few seconds. My colleagues and I searched the deserted flat and initially, there looked to be nothing untoward. There were no signs of a break in or disturbance – until we entered the bedroom. The scene puzzled us: abutting the window stood a free-standing full-length mirror frame holding a few jagged teeth of glass. The remainder of the mirror lay in blood-splattered shards on the floor. Among the debris was a hairbrush and a scattering of cosmetics – makeup, hairspray, perfume, and the like. Blood soaked the carpet. The wardrobes and duvet were also sprayed red. A magnolia push button phone was on its belly on the floor, its bloodied receiver, howling the off-the-hook tone, abandoned nearby amid the silver splinters. But, as we would soon learn, this was not a murder scene.

A probe – which included listening to a recording of the harrowing 999 call Lucy made from her bedroom – concluded she died in a tragic million-to-one accident. Lucy, who lived alone, had been getting ready for a night out with friends when she'd tripped and crashed into the mirror, which shattered on impact. The piece of glass, recovered from her thigh at her post-mortem, was over 30cm long. In addition to severing Lucy's femoral artery, it also speared her pelvis and abdomen. The poor woman didn't stand a chance.

While death had become a vocational norm from which I'd trained myself to detach mentally and visually, I still struggled with one aspect: the smell of human decomposition. Any other police officer will tell you the same. And in early 1990, I encountered the smelliest death of my career. Like Michael Merriman, the body of this man – I'll call him Neville – was found beneath a railway arch.

When the call came in on that Monday morning, my colleague Jerry and I assumed the job would be a routine arrest, and had no idea this call would involve a gruesome death. We were patrolling the area in the police van at the time, Jerry at the wheel. The operator said Dorset Constabulary was hunting for Neville, who was on the run after throwing acid in his ex-wife's face, causing serious burns. Neville had fled three days ago in a brand-new, "nouveau red" Ford Scorpio.

Officers had raided a couple of addresses in Dorset, to no avail, but further inquiries revealed Neville owned a vehicle repair shop beneath a viaduct in Shepherd's Bush.

'Intelligence suggests the suspect could be here,' said the operator before rattling off the address. A quick U-turn followed by a sharp left, then right, and we were there.

The doors to the workshop, which looked just like Phil Mitchell's 'Arches' in *EastEnders*, were locked, but when I jumped out of the van to investigate, I could hear the low grumble of a car engine ticking over. I climbed back into the passenger seat. 'Forced entry needed, mate,' I said. Jerry parked the van with its front bumper kissing the doors, then edged the motor forwards until those wooden gates burst open, sending the broken padlock and wooden splinters spinning across the floor of the workshop. The van's front windows were down and in flew a fug of carbon monoxide and death. Beneath flickering fluorescent tubes sat a brand-new Ford Scorpio, with a hosepipe feeding fumes from the chugging exhaust to the small gap through the front passenger window. Jerry and I approached the car and, right enough, there he was: Dorset Constabulary's most wanted fugitive, not only dead but completely casseroled from a weekend of engine heat. Choking, Jerry staggered outside to ask the control room to inform the Dorset officers that we had found their man while I opened the driver's door and switched off the engine. 'No, he's [Neville] in no fit state to face criminal charges any time soon,' I heard Jerry say as I too ran outside for air.

Half an hour later, once we'd ventilated the workshop of carbon monoxide, we called for the local funeral director to remove Neville's rotting remains from the vanilla leather that no longer smelled leathery and new. Within the hour, two undertakers arrived, both immaculate in their solemn black three-piece suits and shoes you could see your face in. What followed was like a tableau from a zombie film. As the undertakers tried to pull Neville out of the car, his right arm and left leg simultaneously fell off. During their second attempt, the body completely broke in half at the waist. I stood there watching with Jerry, whose face turned a minty hue. The undertakers explained it was common for a body to disintegrate after a 'gas suicide'. But they cracked on with the grisly task, intestines and blood sluicing the back seat of the Scorpio, as well as their trousers and shoes.

The stench of faeces and cooked flesh was horrendous, so Jerry and I left the poor undertakers to their unenviable job while we stepped outside to complete our admin – and get some much-needed fresh air. I ran the Scorpio's registration number through the Police National Computer and established it belonged to a car rental company. Jerry, never one to miss a bargain, promptly phoned the company, told them the horror story of what had happened in the back seat of one of their cars, and brazenly offered to take the car off their hands for £1,000 (about a tenth of its market value). The company representative just laughed at him. 'Happens all the time, officer,' he said. 'We'll just stick a new back seat in it, give it a quick valet and rent it out again.'

And from one horror scene to the next…

Late one evening, during the August 1990 heatwave that saw the country sweltering in temperatures reaching 37C, I was sent to a house following concerns for a widower, Mr Murphy, who lived there alone. His daughter Julia raised the alarm. She lived away from the capital and was naturally worried when phone calls to her father went unanswered. Julia called the Met for help but fearing the worst, jumped in her car and drove to London.

Julia was waiting in the dark driveway when I arrived. 'I can't get in,' she said gesturing at the red brick Arts and Crafts house. 'I don't have keys. I've been ringing the doorbell and banging on the door, but he's not answering. This is not like Dad. Something's happened to him, I know it.' Julia's voice wobbled in the still, close air. It was gone 10pm, but still boiling.

I looked at the house, lonely and unlit. The front room curtains were drawn. 'I'm sorry,' I said, 'but I agree. This does not look good, I'm afraid.' I didn't know what else to say. Dealing with relatives was never my forte; that's why the Met employs Family Liaison Officers (or FLOs, as they're known) – to help bereaved relatives through police investigations. 'I might need to force entry into the property – are you OK with that?' Julia held the sides of her head.

'Yes, whatever you need to do, officer. Oh, please let Dad be OK.'

'I'll take a look around the building first.' I switched on my torch and looked first through the letterbox. A few flies escaped; one swiped my nose as it buzzed skywards. Inside the house, dozens more flies darted and swirled in the shaft of white light. I should have told Julia to wait in her car then; flies love dead bodies but, for some reason, this didn't register with me at that moment. Instead, I walked to the back of the house and let Julia stand beside me as I swept my torchlight through the living room window. On I went, swiping the beam up and down, side to side, then suddenly, Julia let out a piercing scream and collapsed to her knees, her chest heaving with hollow sobs. At the same time, I did a double-take along the torch beam. In the spotlight sat Mr Murphy, bolt upright in his armchair, facing the window, his skin, eyes, and lips had long since rotted away, leaving empty eye sockets and a grotesque toothy smile staring right at us. I stepped back. 'I'm so sorry you had to see that,' I croaked. God, I felt awful. What was I thinking?

Turned out Mr Murphy had died in his chair three weeks previously. That horrific image of Julia's father, decomposed in his chair, would no doubt haunt her forever. As for me, I learned a valuable lesson that day: *never* take a relative on a search for a potential dead body.

CHAPTER ELEVEN
GOOD OLD BOB

I stood next to Bob in the parade room, straight-backed and keen as ever as Area Commander Jeremy clacked towards us in his glossy shoes. The area commander, a chief officer, would visit the station every few months. He would praise us for our 'outstanding' policing – then scuttle upstairs and bollock the chief superintendent for our 'poor performance'.

The commander rarely spoke to constables during his visit. Today was different.

Clack-snap, clack snap, clack-snap, stop. A ceremonial silence enveloped the room as Jeremy advanced along our line then stalled in front of Bob, immaculately turned out, combover stiff with Cossack hairspray, which slightly masked his tobacco-y fragrance. The commander looked him up and down, then gave Bob a small nod of approval. 'Morning Bob, good to see you again,' said Jeremy. Most of us in the room had never met Jeremy before now – but Bob and he went way back, it would seem.

'Good morning, *sir*,' Bob replied, his tone military, professional, and laced with sarcasm.

'Surprised to see you here Bob. I thought you were a dog handler?'

'That's correct, *sir*. Worked with Red for a few years, as you know.'

'And now you're an Area Car driver?'

'That's right, *sir*.'

'So why the change?' enquired the commander.

'Dog was a twat, *sir*.' replied Bob, still standing to attention, looking straight ahead. As you can imagine, our parade burst out laughing. My ribs rattled as my stomach convulsed. Bob had explained all about Red, the German Shepherd who wasn't up to the Job. 'Don't get me wrong, Red was a lovely dog,' he'd told me. 'But the daft mutt was terrified of his own shadow. He made me look stupid.'

I glanced a sideways look at Bob. He seemed to be the only one in the room not laughing. Instead, he maintained his deadpan expression and confirmed his statement by nodding briskly at the commander.

'I see,' said Jeremy after a short pause. He looked to be on the verge of laughter too. 'Well, keep up the good work.'

Recalling Bob's 'dog was a twat' moment still makes me laugh today. Bob had an infectious personality. Always quick with a joke, he didn't take himself too seriously, either. But this never affected Bob's prowess for the job. In my opinion, Bob was one of the best constables in the Met – and a big inspiration to me, particularly in my desire to be an advanced driver. And it is with much sadness that I refer to Bob in the past tense because, unfortunately, Bob passed away in 2019.

We enjoyed great times as crewmates before Bob retired from the Met in 1997. And I can think of no better way to honour Bob's memory than to share these anecdotes with you here in this chapter. I'll begin on one wet and windy January morning, when Bob and I responded to reports of a possible suicide jumper on a railway bridge near Willesden Junction.

The call came in just after 4am: 'Young man sitting on the barrier of the Old Oak Lane road bridge over Willesden Junction. Feet dangling over tracks. Looks like a possible jumper.' Bob and I were nearby in Harlesden, driving along Park Parade in the Area Car. We responded immediately but with great caution. Screeching up at the scene on screaming twos and blues would only spook the man and could cause him to jump – if he hadn't done so already.

Bob parked the car on Station Approach, which is perpendicular to the Old Oak Lane bridge. 'Poor lad,' said Bob, switching off the engine. 'Makes you wonder what goes through their heads don't it, son. I mean, you've gotta really hit rock bottom to contemplate ending it all. But I do feel sorry for the youngsters of…'

'There he is,' I said, pointing at a shape upon the bridge through the top left corner of the rain-streaked windscreen. A still, rounded silhouette upon the bridge. Bob squinted at the glass.

'Yep, that'll be him. Let's go then. Gently does it though, son. Christ, I hate jobs like this.'

I agreed with Bob. We police officers regularly deal with suicides, attempted suicides and self-harming incidents. And while the Met has round-the-clock specialist negotiators, the fast-time nature of these events invariably means a response team constable is first on the scene, shouldering the responsibility to try and save the tormented individual from causing further harm or suicide. The pressure of knowing the wrong word, tone of voice, or body language could cost somebody their life is immense.

Bob and I crept along in the icy drizzle towards the bridge. Still dark, there was hardly any traffic on the road. The figure remained perched on the ledge and, as we neared him, I could see his legs, dangling some twenty feet above the tracks. But he was only dimly side-lit by two streetlamps positioned at either end of the bridge. 'Oh, please don't do it, son,' Bob said under his breath.

We turned left, onto Old Oak Lane, and gradually, the image of our figure sharpened. He had on a snorkel parka, its hood drenched and limp upon his hunched shoulders. Protruding in profile from his chest was a fancy, long-lense camera. A rucksack clung to his back. He heard us coming and turned to look. 'It's OK, son,' said Bob, taking another tentative step towards the man, who looked to be in his mid-forties rather than the young lad the operator had described. His shoulder-length hair, wet and stringy, was the same colour as his parka: khaki. He didn't flinch and did not seem distressed. Instead, his face was arranged in an expression that asked, 'What are you two clowns doing here?' Despite the vertical drop below him, he looked calm, bored even, like he was sitting at a bus stop waiting on a delayed service to god knows where. Something clicked in my mind then.

I stepped forward. 'Sorry, mate,' I said. 'But would you please mind returning to this side of the parapet?' I gestured at the pavement. 'It's for your own safety.' The man on the wall jutted his chin then wiped rain off his forehead with the back of his hand.

'Sure, no problem, sorry,' he said flatly, swinging a leg over the barrier. Then, once safely back on the pavement, added, 'It's not happening, anyway.'

'You're a bit keen aren't you, getting up here at 4am in this weather, just to get a photo of a train?' The guy took a deep breath and exhaled through the side of his mouth, like Popeye.

'Oh no, I've been here since ten-thirty last night,' he said. 'The train was due at eleven-fifteen. It hasn't turned up.'

'Bugger, sorry to hear that, mate,' said Bob. 'That must be some special locomotive?'

'Yeah, a 1960 British Rail Class 37. I was hoping to get a picture to share with the trainspotting fraternity, but... well I guess I'll just go home now.' And with that, our trainspotter pulled up his soggy hood, turned and shuffled away, head down.

'Good luck next time, mate,' called Bob, and the train-spotter replied with a fragile wave. I turned to Bob, who was chuckling wheezily into his chest.

'Come on,' I said, 'I'll shout you a coffee.' Bob rubbed his hands together and went, *brrr*.

'Great. Sod the expense, eh.'

'Yeah, yeah, sod the expense, Bob.' I laughed. Bob always said 'Sod the expense' when somebody else was paying.

* * *

While doing our utmost to 'truly serve the Queen in the office of constable', Bob and I did get into some scrapes, which often ended with yours truly getting injured (remember that pesky monkey Clive?) or with Bob helping me back on my feet after a tumble or two. OK, we weren't exactly Starsky and Hutch, but we were a good team, and the age difference between Bob and I worked in our favour. As the old sweat and experienced driver in our outfit, Bob's policing instincts were top-notch – and he aced at car chases too. Being in my early twenties and a good sprinter meant the foot chases were down to me. But those chases didn't always go according to plan.

One night, Bob and I were out in the Area Car when we got involved in a lengthy pursuit around The Bush with a stolen Ford Escort. The chase went on for a good twenty minutes, the car thief driving like a lunatic, jumping red lights and kamikaze-ing it through streets and roundabouts, until he lost control of the motor and smashed into bollards on the junction of Du Cane Road and Wood Lane. There was a sound of metal crushing, followed by the screech of the Area Car stopping, then a panicky thud of trainers on concrete as the driver bolted. I leapt out of the Area Car like a gazelle escaping its predator, Bob shouting after me, 'Get him, son,' as I chased the joyrider towards the spiked railings penning the Latymer Upper School Playing Fields. He was fast, vaulted the fence in one liquid movement and made off across the unlit field. I reached the railings about two seconds later, but my launch was less nimble. As I heaved myself up and over my left shoe caught on one of the spikes, and I bulleted forth before crash-landing, via a scratchy privet, in a buckled heap on the grass. My torch catapulted from my hand in transit, too, its bulb smashing when it landed hard on the ground.

Determined not to lose our escapee, I scrambled to my feet in the sooty darkness. I'd lost a shoe, but there was no time to waste; my target was at least a hundred metres ahead, sprinting diagonally across the grass. I could just make out his jolting shape. Fortunately, my torch had a spare bulb in the battery compartment and, somehow, wearing only one shoe, I managed to sprint and replace the bulb simultaneously. Breathing hard, I powered on. My truncheon, handcuffs, and notebook flew off my uniform, but still I pursued the thief – and pounced on him as he tried to hurdle the fence bordering Wood Lane. I wrestled him to the ground, panting, then read him his rights, elaborately.

The car thief was exhausted. I assisted him back over the railings, where Bob waited. He had driven the Area Car to the far side of the playing fields to head-off the chase. We bundled our detainee – a bloke called Jason who, now he'd caught his breath, demanded to know, 'Ain't you got nuffink better to do?'– into the back of the Area Car. 'This is bullshit,' he muttered. Ten minutes later, sporting a look that would give Worzel Gummidge a run for his money, I proudly escorted Jason through the doors of Shepherd's Bush police station while still wearing only one shoe. Another constable searched the playing fields for my missing kit. Alas, he found only my shoe, impaled on the railings. The metal spike had speared its sole and tongue and laces. But miraculously, my foot was fine, barely a scratch on it. And, to add a cheery footnote (see what I did there?) to this tale, over the next few days, the school grounds' staff found my notebook, truncheon, and handcuffs – and returned them intact to the police station.

A few nights, and a new pair of Marks & Spencer shoes later, Bob and I were involved in another car chase. This time the pursuit ended when the joyriders dumped the stolen Vauxhall Astra on the Becklow Gardens estate in Shepherd's Bush. Two young lads mounted the kerb in Lycett Place, a skinny lane that runs alongside the Greyhound pub and legged it from the motor. 'Got the passenger,' I shouted and flew out of the Area Car.

Bob chased the driver, who bolted in the opposite direction to his companion. I caught the passenger on Becklow Road, arrested and handcuffed him and brought him back to the Area Car. I put him in the back seat, then I got in and sat next to him. Bob was still adrift somewhere in the estate, looking for the driver. But something wasn't right. Why was the engine running? The blue lights were still flashing too. *Shit, Bob must've left the keys in the ignition in his hasty departure to catch the driver.* A few minutes passed without any sign of Bob or the driver. Irish music and laughter pumped from the pub, and my prisoner sat there sulking. 'We just gonna sit here all night?' he said. He looked no older than eighteen and had ACAB (All Cops Are Bastards) tattooed on his knuckles. I was too busy eyeballing another miscreant loitering outside the Area Car to respond to the inked one. And what happened next was unbelievable. The lad outside peered into the driver's window then, spying the keys in the ignition, opened the door, jumped in, and cranked the gear selector into 'reverse'.

'Oi,' I shouted, then threw my foot through the gap between the front seats and kicked the gear selector to 'park', jolting all three of us backwards as the rear wheels locked. My prisoner in the back started laughing, while the chancer in the front seat went, *Oh fuck,* flung the driver's door open and tried to make a run for it.

Yeah, right, not on my watch. Off I shot again – and caught him after just a few paces. I arrested him for attempting to steal a police car, dumped him in the back seat and handcuffed him to the tattooed prisoner, who was still laughing.

'Wow, that was wicked, man,' he said.

Five minutes later, Bob returned to the Area Car, out of breath and empty handed, the driver of the Astra having made good his escape. He looked in the back of the Area Car, saw not one, but two prisoners, and his face lit up. 'No,' I said, reading his mind. 'They're not both from the Astra. Take the bloody keys with you next time.'

We cops are not perfect, and mistakes like Bob's leaving the keys in the car happen to all of us from time to time. But mostly, they're minor errors that we'll later laugh about – like the time Bob and I responded to a mass brawl between rival football fans at Hammersmith Tube station one Saturday night.

Bob and I were first on the scene. We'd raced to the punch-up on twos and blues in a Ford Sierra Area Car then, swift as lightning, ran into the station and grabbed and cuffed a hooligan in a Queens Park Rangers shirt as he tried to take down a Chelsea fan. By the time we frogmarched the man, Dean was his name, out of the station, more cops had arrived, also in Ford Sierras. Blocking our path on the pavement was a cameraman and reporter, who had been filming a documentary outside Le Palais nightclub in the same street when the drama kicked off. The reporter pointed his microphone at my face, and I was momentarily blinded by the cameraman's spotlight. 'Can you tell us what's been happening here tonight?' gushed the reporter. 'What have you arrested him for? 'Anybody badly injured, anyone killed?' The questions continued, but Bob and I ignored the eager duo as we bustled past with our staggering detainee, who was now shouting, 'It's a fucking joke,' through bloodied busted lips.

The reporter followed us to the Area Car. 'Well, where are you taking him?' he said.

'Shepherd's Bush police station,' I said over my shoulder, then bundled Dean into the back of the car with me while Bob jumped in the driver's seat. All set to make a roaring Sweeney-style exit. The film crew was still there, the camera lens almost touching the backseat window, but we weren't moving. Bob hadn't even started the engine. And wait a minute, where was my kit bag? *It should be here on the backseat where I left it.* 'Hey, Bob,' I said. 'This is strange – my kit bag's vanished.' Dean, who reeked of stale beer and B.O, cursed and laughed.

'Yeah,' went Bob, 'I can't reach the pedals. And the ignition key won't turn.'

'Shit.' That was Bob and me, in unison. The camera crew was still filming, waiting to capture us speeding away on twos and blues – but we were in the wrong bloody police car, which Dean found highly amusing.

We waited a few minutes, hoping the television lot would get bored. It wasn't happening. Eventually, we had to admit defeat, get out of the car, and look for our motor amid a sea of police Ford Sierras. We tried to be discreet but our gobby prisoner had other ideas. 'Wrong car,' he shouted at the TV crew, laughing. 'Wrong police car, can you believe it? They don't even know which is their own fucking police car.'

We finally found our Area Car, and Bob screeched away. After we'd delivered Dean to the custody suite and completed the paperwork, we returned to duty. As we sat down in the Area Car, we looked at one another and burst out laughing. ''Ere, you never know,' said Bob, still chuckling away as he lit a fag, 'We might end up on the telly, lad.' My stomach cramped with laughter.

Good old Bob.

CHAPTER TWELVE
DEADLY SURPRISES

After four years on the frontline, I thought I'd become hardened to death. As you know, I'd already witnessed some horrendous sights. I'd also performed CPR a few times, albeit unsuccessfully, but nothing compares to the shocking scene I encountered at the first fatal road traffic accident I attended. The image still haunts me today.

It happened one morning around 9am, close to the former BBC Television Centre on Wood Lane. It was one of those bright spring mornings: fresh but warm and the sky clear as mouthwash. A short-sleeved-shirt day. On an early turn, I was patrolling near Shepherd's Bush Green in an unmarked Astra – I had recently passed my Standard Driving Course – when I received the call. A cyclist had undertaken a loaded lorry as it made a left turn into an industrial estate. Sadly, the lorry driver hadn't seen the cyclist, and the two collided. 'It appears the cyclist has gone under the rear axle of the lorry. Doesn't sound too good, I'm afraid,' said the operator. I flicked on the blue lights and was there in less than two minutes.

I arrived to find a small crowd of spectators huddled around the BBC security box outside the Television Centre, which overlooked the accident spot. Panicked voices mingled; I heard a snippet or two as I dashed from the car: 'It wasn't your fault.' 'You wouldn't have seen him coming.' 'I'm sure he'll be fine.' Which told me the lorry driver was among the group – a group living in hope for the victim at that. However, speaking with witnesses was not top of my list of actions at that point. Being the first officer on the scene, I now confronted what I labelled a 'conflict of priorities'. Dozens of tasks that need executing at once. My priority, especially in this scenario, would be to save a life – if possible. Although, at first glance of the accident scene, I feared the chances of this happening were slim.

The lorry nosed at an angle across the road. Behind its left back wheels trailed viscous marks composed of black rubber and human flesh – indicating the cyclist had been spun around the wheel at least four times before the lorry came to a halt. I called into my radio for an urgent ambulance, the fire brigade, a traffic sergeant, and traffic units to seal off the road and control the crowd, as I hurried around the gore to the side of the vehicle, where I dropped to my haunches, then onto my hands and knees, and crawled into the diesel-y heat beneath the lorry – and gasped, audibly, as I assimilated in a flash the view, backlit by sharp morning sun.

The cyclist lay in front of me, blood containing churned flesh and bone and tissue trailing behind him. He'd been dissected at the waist, his lower half completely shredded, with no pelvis or legs remaining. His head and torso, however, remained intact. He was face down on the tarmac with his right arm bent at a right angle on the ground, framing his head. His left arm twisted behind him, palm-up, and the sleeves of his sweatshirt were pushed up to his elbows. A fresh red graze covered his left elbow. I crawled on, nearing his head of dense black curls, a heavy sadness washing over me. Judging by what remained of the cyclist, I estimated he was in his early twenties, and in those few seconds I thought about the unbearable, all-consuming grief his family would endure. *How will the FLO break this news to his relatives?*

The poor lad was dead, mutilated, and I felt helpless that I couldn't even attempt CPR. I looked around beneath the lorry, hoping to see a wallet or bank card – any article that might identify the cyclist, but a sudden movement made me recoil in shock. I almost hit my head on the underside of the lorry. How could this be so? The cyclist was alive, moving. Slowly, he lifted his head and looked at me through heavy eyelids, like he was emerging from a sedated sleep. His eyes were dark and marbly, set deep in deathly pale, waxy skin. Blood drained fast from my face too. I felt it happening as the cyclist's lips began to move. 'My left arm hurts,' he said in a thin voice. Was I hallucinating? I watched unblinking as he winced, then continued: 'Could you move it for me?'

'Yes, of course,' I said, and, neck hunched, sat back on my heels to free my hands. The cyclist's left arm was still warm to the touch. He was still here, still alive, thinking and talking and aware that his left arm hurt. Gently, I untwisted his left arm and lay it into what I hoped would be a more comfortable position mirroring his right arm.

And my heartrate quickened painfully when again, our eyes locked, and the cyclist managed a weak smile. 'Thank you,' he whispered, then lowered his head, rested his right cheek on the tarmac, and closed his eyes. He died less than a minute later.

I remained under the lorry for a few seconds, completely stunned – until the wail of sirens brought me round and I snapped back into work mode. The ambulance arrived, followed by the fire brigade, who erected screens around the lorry and ambulance to shield the public from the gruesome scene.

I found the victim's wallet close to the rear right wheel of the lorry. It must have flown from his pocket before impact. The contents of his wallet – bank card and work photo ID – confirmed his name was Ryan, who worked at an office in Hammersmith. Ryan had been cycling to work that morning, unaware he would never make it to his desk. Further checks revealed he had just turned twenty-two.

When I told one of the paramedics how Ryan had asked me to move his arm, he explained he'd seen this happen before. Ryan had no chance of survival because most of his vital organs were obliterated in the horrific accident, but his brain had been the last of his organs to die, which explained how he'd managed to speak.

My work at the scene over, I got back in the Astra and headed back to the police station to finish my statement and for a quick wash and change (I had blood on my hands and trousers). But as I drove, I could not shake the image of Ryan's face from my mind – and while I considered it a great privilege to have been able to grant his last request,

I knew this incident would take me a long time to process in my head. I also felt sorry for the lorry driver, who was in no way to blame for Ryan's death. I didn't speak to the driver as another constable took his statement, but I can only begin to imagine how dreadful he must have felt. A twenty-two-year-old lad had lost his life after colliding with his lorry. How do you live with that?

The day continued as normal. I washed my hands and face, changed into a fresh pair of trousers, wrote my statement, and returned to duty. Although still I could not forget the sickening events of the morning. As I said, I did not envy the FLO officer tasked with explaining Ryan's death to his family. I wouldn't have known where to start because, like I've mentioned before, I was not good when it came to speaking with bereaved relatives. This was the one – and only – advantage of being at the scene of gruesome deaths: you would rarely be asked to deliver the tragic news to the victim's loved ones as, usually, you'll have the dead person's blood on your hands or face or uniform. And I don't need to explain how horrendously insensitive that would be.

Fortunately, my contact with grieving relatives was minimal. But when I was the bearer of terrible news, I often messed up the job – as I did when I accidentally lit up Mr Murphy's decaying corpse in front of his daughter. Mostly, I found the job of death-news messenger awkward – because I never quite knew what to say. Often, there were no words, other than, 'I'm very sorry.' Nothing I could say or do could bring back their loved ones. Understandably, most people break down; they'll sob and shake uncontrollably. Some scream or punch the wall, while others fall into silent shock. Denial is another common reaction. Whatever the response, I would always try my best to offer words of comfort, but when the reverse of this happened, I didn't know what to do with myself.

About two weeks before Ryan's death, I had to deliver harrowing news to a young woman called Tracy. Her boyfriend Rick, who suffered from depression, had disappeared eight days previously, leaving no message of his plans or whereabouts. Tracy had reported Rick missing to police when he failed to show up at work one day, and a search began. The hunt ended when Rick, in his mid-twenties, was found dead in a bleak hotel room in Bournemouth. He'd hanged himself with a belt tied to the bathroom door – and it was my job, on that Tuesday evening, to explain this devastating outcome to Tracy.

She was eating her dinner when I knocked on the door to the Shepherd's Bush home she'd once shared with Rick – a cosy studio flat above a pharmacy on Goldhawk Road. It was a tuna pasta bake. I can still smell it, cheesy, fishy, filling the kitchen that doubled as a living room. I can still see it; steam rising in waves from the gooey spirals. And in that moment, as Tracy urged me to 'have a seat' on the sofa, her dinner smelled worse than death to me. I felt sick as I sat down, but Tracy knew the purpose of my visit before I opened my mouth. 'It's about Rick, isn't it? You've found him, haven't you,' she said, and dropped weakly onto her chair at the table opposite me. She played nervously with a black hair scrunchie wreathing her wrist.

'I'm so sorry to have to tell you this,' I began, my voice wobbling. I cleared my throat as Tracy burst into tears.

'He's dead, isn't he,' she sobbed. 'Rick's dead.' I confirmed with a nervous nod and, in my best apologetic tone, told her how Rick had chosen to end his life in a hotel room a hundred miles away. I wanted the sofa to swallow me whole; I would have preferred to deal with a badly decomposed body than to be sitting in Tracy's flat, being the one to shatter her world in less than five sentences. 'Did he leave a note?' she asked.

'No, I'm afraid not.'

I looked at Tracy, knowing my expression was one of pure awkwardness. She responded with a shuddering intake of breath and fresh tears, then, tilting her head, said: 'I'm really sorry.'

'Erm, you don't need to apologise,' I said, again, unsure how to react.

'No, I do… I must,' added Tracy. 'I'm so sorry you had to come here today and tell me about Rick. This must be so difficult for you… I'm sorry, I'm sorry…' I felt my face redden as Tracy continued to apologise. 'Can I get you anything, a cup of tea – or something stronger?' she asked. I'd never felt so uncomfortable at work. I was supposed to be comforting Tracy but instead she was assuaging my unease.

'Really, there's no need to apologise,' I reiterated as Tracy showed me out. Walking to the car, I breathed a sigh of relief, but I also felt a bit guilty; I was getting paid to deliver the worst news Tracy could ever have imagined – and she was the one apologising? Yeah, as I said: dealing with grieving relatives was not my area of expertise.

* * *

So, how do we cops cope with the constant horrors of death every day? Even those able to switch off after a grisly shift need a coping mechanism sometimes – and that strategy comes in the form of humour: very dark humour. This is not intentional; as most emergency services workers attest, we always strive to give a hundred per cent professionalism and empathy when dealing with the deceased and their bereaved families. But we also need some outlet, if only to preserve our sanity. One incident involving humour that springs to mind was a gruesome 'one under' affair.

In police parlance, 'one-under' means a person has collided with a train. In this case, a twenty-something student had thrown himself in front of a high-speed train at Willesden Green Tube station. The train was one of those services that comes with a 'stand back from the edge of the platform' announcement before whizzing past in a torrent of air. The student jumped during the morning rush hour, in front of horrified commuters who would hold the disturbing display in their minds forever. The victim's body was mangled beyond recognition. He had a crushed head and chest, and blood and flesh and bone splattered the platform. He was missing a leg. Surveying the carnage on the tracks, I wondered, *What must have been going through this poor man's head before he jumped? Was he depressed, like Rick? Did he have money troubles? Jilted by a lover, perhaps? Or grieving the loss of a loved one?*

Again, I thought about the irreparable pain his family would bear while also dealing with the task at hand. Part of my job was to brief the British Transport Police (BTP) sergeant when he arrived at the scene. (BTP has the ultimate responsibility to deal with all incidents on the rail and underground network, though the sheer size and spread of the Met meant we often got to accidents before they did.) The sergeant arrived about ten minutes after me, pulling a face that said, 'Not another one-under.' I walked along the platform to greet him. 'Morning, Sarge,' I said, and launched into my spiel. 'Victim is a male in his twenties. Clearly deceased. Severe head and chest injuries.'

'Uh huh,' went the sergeant, writing in his notebook.

'Oh,' I added, 'He's also lost his right leg.' At which point a firefighter who'd been assessing the scene further up the platform behind me, made a noise.

'Oh no he hasn't – here it is,' he shouted. I wheeled round to see the firefighter holding aloft the victim's severed leg, encased in bloodied denim with his trainered foot still intact. He raised the limb like a trophy, then gently placed it back on the platform. I admit I chuckled a bit. The sergeant did too. Then it was back to work. There would be no more laughing. Soon, some poor officer would deliver the heartbreaking news of the victim's death to his family.

And so, the tragic cycle continues.

CHAPTER THIRTEEN
IN SICKNESS AND IN HEALTH

In January 1992 I thought all my Christmases had come at once when my inspector, Roger, called me into the station duties office one lunchtime to say I'd been offered a place on the Advanced Driving Course. 'You're down for the May slot,' he said with a grin. Roger knew how much this meant to me; I hadn't missed one opportunity to convey my enthusiasm to drive fast cars to the Met's top brass.

'Wow, thanks, sir. This is amazing news,' I said. I could not believe it. After six years' chasing criminals, pounding the streets of Shepherd's Bush, my dream of driving the force's most powerful cars was about to come true. I thanked Roger again and floated out of the office, smiling a smile so euphoric my face ached. As I said before, places on the coveted Advanced Driving Course come along only twice a year, so I felt honoured to have been chosen. All I had to do now was pass the course. How difficult could that be? I grabbed my packed lunch from my locker, then bounded, two stairs a time, up to the canteen, excited about sharing my news with my colleagues. *I'm going to put every cell and tissue and muscle and organ and fibre of my being into this course*, I thought.

Things were going well for me in both my professional and personal life. While grim news of the recession flooded in, I realised how lucky I was to have a secure job on the frontline. I'd long since moved out of the section house and got myself on the property ladder. My new home was a one-bedroom flat, occupying the ground floor of a terraced house in Stanley Road, South Harrow. When I first moved in, the flat was grotty inside, with threadbare carpets and cold walls patterned with scuffs and the occasional food stain. The place smelled of cat litter trays and leftover bubble and squeak. A spectacular tea spillage fountained a wall in the kitchen. All the rooms were adjoined around a small hallway, so there was little light indoors. What was I thinking? I hated the flat, but at sixty grand it was the best I could afford at the time. And at least it got me away from the kerosene-infused box in the sky. At last, I was a homeowner, with a landline telephone and small garden to boot. The telephone itself was a luxury; in the section house I had to run down eleven flights of stairs if I wanted to use the payphone (if it was free, that is). So, I was grateful for my lot – and blissfully unaware that I would make a £23,000 loss on the property six years later. We live and learn, eh.

I had a girlfriend now too. I'd met Laura, a civilian in the Met, at a work function. We got chatting over dinner and instantly hit it off, so I asked her out on a date, and our relationship grew from there. Petite and blonde, I warmed to Laura's kind nature and loved how she always saw the best in people. And like me, she was a hundred per cent dedicated to her job. Actually, Laura and I had been together for well over a year when I received my good news from Roger.

The Advanced Driving Course is notoriously difficult. I'd heard all manner of horror stories about cops who'd failed the course for making momentary judgement calls that turned out to be monumental fuck-ups. One cop, for example, I call him Liam, was performing a pursuit on his final drive exam, racing along a country lane at 100mph in a Rover 827 when the car in front of him slowed, so Liam moved into the right lane. 'Clear for the overtake,' he announced.

'No,' shouted the instructor, slamming his hand on the dashboard. The instructor had spotted the bonnet of a Rover nosing out of a side turning fifty metres ahead. Liam aborted the manoeuvre, pulled back, and returned to the left lane. Had he continued with the overtake, there could have been a high-speed, head-on crash. After his near miss, the instructor told the cop to pull over.

'That's it, I'm afraid,' he told him. 'You're off the course.'

The thought of my making a similar error turned my stomach maggoty with nausea. So, with dogged devotion, I threw myself into preparing for my upcoming course. I pored over *Roadcraft*, the police driving handbook, learned parrot-fashion the Highway Code and studied in detail the cars I would be driving, from Rover 827s to Ford Cosworths and Vauxhall Senators. There was no way on this earth that I was going to ruin what I considered to be my opportunity of a lifetime. Then, about a week into my studious routine – and still three months before my course was due to start – I made one absent-minded mistake that would throw the next eighteen months of my life into disarray: I forgot to take my packed lunch to work.

On that Tuesday, ahead of my late shift, I'd stood in my poky kitchen and prepared my lunch, listening to the news on the radio. More depressing bulletins about the recession and BSE (mad cow disease) which had spread through the nation's dairy herds.

As always, I made two rounds of cheese and pickle sandwiches (on white bread), cut them into neat rectangles, and placed them in my Tupperware lunchbox on the right, leaving the left side of the box free for my Tracker cereal bar and an apple. Next, I chucked in the pièce de resistance: a Peperami. All sorted, I pressed on the lid and left the box on the counter while I went for a shower. Forty minutes later, I headed out the door, minus the box of treats I'd laboured over.

I didn't realise I'd forgotten my lunch until 5.30pm, when my stomach began rumbling at a volume hinting a seismic event within. A sustained noise. My crewmate, Bernie, behind the wheel of the Astra we were patrolling the Bush in, shot me a sideways look of disbelief. 'What the fuck was that?' he said. 'Are you hungry, mate? Do I need to get you to a hospital or something?'

I laughed. 'Nah, I'm just bloody starving.'

'Yeah, now you mention it, I could really go for a burger,' said Bernie, eyeing the bright lights of a well-known fast food chain restaurant ahead. 'Let's grab dinner. There's nothing doing just now, anyway.' He pulled up outside the restaurant and I reached behind me, grabbed my bag off the back seat. I couldn't wait to get stuck into that Peperami.

'You go ahead, Bernie,' I said, foraging in my rucksack for my Tupperware. 'I've got my packed lu...'

What, wait a minute, no lunch box? Bugger it. Bernie was already out of the car so I rezipped my bag. 'Actually, yeah, wait up, Bernie, mate,' I called before he locked-up. 'I'll join you.' Ravenous, I followed Bernie into the oily mouth of the restaurant. 'Can I get a chicken burger and fries, please?' I said, handing a fiver to the bloke behind the counter.

Worst. Decision. Ever.

That chicken burger tasted great at the time. Just hit the spot. Bernie said the same about his beefburger. We sat in the Astra and tucked hungrily into our food, chatting between mouthfuls about work politics and cars, the usual. I remember laughing when Bernie quipped, 'I hope I don't get that mad cow disease,' between the last bite of his burger and switching on the engine.

I should have known better than to laugh in the face of malady.

The pain struck at midnight. A sharp, agonising pain spearing my lower abdomen. Within seconds I was doubled up in bed, groaning loud with every cramp. I'd never known pain like it; I felt like I was being repeatedly knifed in the gut, slashed from side to side. Nausea rose like liquid molten from my stomach to my throat. Crunch, bubble, twist went my bowel, until an urgent need to expel from both ends of my gastrointestinal tract forced me out of bed. Clutching my stomach, I hobbled to the bathroom via the kitchen, where my untouched lunchbox sat on the counter in a smug, I-told-you-so manner. I spied the green foil Peperami wrapper through the clear Tupperware and retched violently.

For once I'll spare you the gruesome details of what happened next, but let's just say, I was at last grateful to have a bathroom the size of a kids' shoebox. It meant I could sit on the loo and stick my head in the sink simultaneously. *Must've been that chicken burger,* I thought when I vomited for the third time. *You'll be OK, this'll pass, it's just a bout of food poisoning.* But after four hours of interminable vomiting and diarrhoea, combined with a raging fever and intensifying stabbing pains in my stomach, I began to think, *Hang on, this isn't right.* I tried to drink some water, but it left my body as soon as it went in. Eventually, around 4.30am, I managed to lever myself from the toilet and sink, crawl into the lounge and call my GP surgery's out-of-hours number from my prized landline. When the on-call doctor arrived at 6am, he took one look at me, and after the briefest palpation of my stomach, said, 'We need to get you to hospital, now. May I use your telephone?'

I don't remember much about the ambulance ride. And the next twenty-four hours passed in an agonising blur – as did the following two weeks that I remained, flat on my back in a starchy bed, hooked to a drip. Alone in a glass box in the isolation unit at Northwick Park Hospital. With the cause of my infection initially unknown, the doctors were taking no chances. They communicated with me via a telephone on the other side of the glass screen – like how you see prisoners do in American movies. And those medics who did enter the glass box – to carry out vital tests, extract samples, and pump me with saline solution and hardcore painkillers – were masked and gloved and gowned and booted. Their presence conjured images of the scene in *E.T: The Extra Terrestrial*, where men in hazmat suits and breathing apparatus storm Elliot's house. They treated me like I had Ebola, and my body was expelling fluids at an alarming rate; I lost three stone in weight in as many days. Weight I could not afford to lose. After a week in isolation, my weight dropped to just below seven stone, and test results revealed the cause of my malaise: severe salmonella poisoning, the culprit most certainly being the chicken burger I'd eaten from the fast-food chain I'll not name. Most infections are caused by eating food contaminated by animal or human faeces, said the doctor when he talked me through my test results. 'Your GP was wise to call for that ambulance,' he added. 'Another six hours and you wouldn't have made it.' I had to shunt that terrifying thought to the back of my mind. All I could think about was recovering, getting back to work, and preparing for my Advanced Driving Course. But salmonella, being a stubborn parasite, ravaged me long after I left hospital.

I was signed off sick from work for the foreseeable. I looked like a dying stick man; every day, I would wake up and think, *Right, today's the day that I keep my breakfast inside of me.* Mostly, said breakfast would end up down the toilet. Unable to eat or drink much at all, I constantly felt weak and tired. Then, as if my illness wasn't devastating enough, in late February I received news that further shattered my world.

The phone rang as I lay on the sofa, half watching the Winter Olympics while reading *Roadcraft*. It took all the little energy I had to lift the receiver and emit from my cracked lips a faint, 'Hello?'.

'Matt, it's Roger, how're you doing?'

'Yeah, good, thanks, sir. Well on the road to recovery,' I lied. 'Looking forward to getting back to work soon. Actually, I was just swotting for my Advanced Driving Course. I can't wait to get going and...'

'Er, listen, I'm going to have to stop you there I'm afraid, Matt,' said Roger. My heart dropped and died in my diseased stomach. I knew by Roger's apologetic tone that bad news followed. 'Look, after much consideration, I've decided to give your slot on the course to somebody else. Health-wise, you're not up to it just now, Matt, so I think...'

I sat up fast and the room whirled. 'No, don't. Please don't do that, sir. I'm fine. I've waited six years for this course. Please don't give it to somebody else.'

'I'm sorry, but you need to get fit first, Matt. Getting slung around and driving at 140mph is not wise in your condition.'

'But it's not until May. I've got plenty of time to get fit.'

'I made the decision based on your medical reports, Matt,' Roger went on as I stared blankly at the telly. *Great, all I need: super-strong speed-skaters flexing their ripped muscles in spandex suits.* 'But, here's the thing. I promise I will get you a slot on the next available course.' My stomach cramped again.

'With all due respect, sir, that's bullshit,' I said. I couldn't help myself. 'I'll be waiting another two years for another course. Everybody knows that's how it works.' Roger sighed loudly down the phone, breathy and hollow, like the noise you hear when you clamp a seashell over your ear.

'Trust me on this, Matt. I promise I *will* get you on the next available course. I won't let you down.' I looked down at my legs, thin and hard as drumsticks in my pyjamas. I knew Roger was right, but I didn't want to face the truth.

'OK,' I said after a long pause. 'Well, I guess I'll just have to wait to hear back from you, sir.' Roger repeated his promise and hung up. Then I rushed to the bathroom.

My dream is slipping away from me.

Seriously, I didn't expect to hear back from Roger any time soon. The weeks dragged on, and my recovery was slow. Then, true to his word, Roger called me in June, not long after I'd returned to work on restricted duties. 'Good news, Matt,' he said. 'You're on the course. You start on the twenty-seventh of July, so that gives you six weeks to get fit. Do you think you'll manage that?'

'Oh, absolutely, sir,' I beamed. I was still severely under-weight and suffering occasional salmonella symptoms, but I was adamant no obstacle would come between me and the course this time. 'I'll be fighting fit by then.' I thanked Roger, several times.

I wasn't exactly fighting fit when July 27 dawned; although I'd put on a little weight, I was still very ill. I'd had to dash to the loo a few times before leaving the flat on that sunny Monday morning – though I do believe nerves attributed to my watery stomach. While quietly confident – I'd been fortunate to spend three days on the road with a traffic sergeant in preparation for the course – the fear of failure hung over me like a cumulonimbus.

There were twenty of us on the course, based at the driving school at Hendon Police College, but the numbers would dwindle as the weeks progressed. Some students simply didn't have the potential to reach the standard required for high-speed response and pursuit driving. Others, like Liam, were booted off for making one dangerous mistake. But for Patricia, a skilled driver in our class, her downfall came when she whizzed along a country lane at 120mph – and ran over a duck. 'A duck doesn't qualify as an "animal" under the 1988 Road Traffic Act, Sir,' Patricia informed her instructor as she continued her high-speed drive. She was right about the duck. Under the Road Traffic Act 1988, there's no legal requirement for a motorist to stop and report a collision with an animal – unless the animal is a "dog, sheep, cattle, horse, mule, ass, pig, or goat". All other wildlife, including cats, foxes, rabbits, badgers, and ducks, are not covered by the legislation. Patricia's error, however, was to continue driving at over 100mph, with a smashed headlight and the end of the bumper hanging off.

I had my fair share of hairy moments, too. One afternoon on the M1, while driving an unmarked Rover 827 at 110mph in torrential rain, the car started to aquaplane. This occurs when the wheels are spinning so fast on a wet road that a wedge of water builds up under the tyres, meaning that they are no longer in contact with the tarmac. At high speed, aquaplaning can be catastrophic – and I had three passengers in the car when it began to glide out of control. Instinctively, I eased off the accelerator and dropped to around 90mph. The two constables in the back seat remained silent, but Sergeant Jeff, the grumpy, fifty-something instructor sitting beside me, went off on one. 'What the hell are you doing, Calveley?'

'Aquaplaning, Sarge,' I replied, trying not to sound too anxious amid the tsunami noises surrounding the vehicle.

'OK, fair enough,' said Jeff. Then, after a few seconds: 'Tyres got their grip back yet?'

'Er, yes, I think so, Sarge,' I said, relieved to feel the vibration of rubber on tarmac again.

'Well then, what the fuck are you waiting for?' shouted Jeff. 'Move it. Get that speed back up.' I touched the accelerator, and off we flew again, at warp speed in the monsoon weather.

Sergeant Jeff held a debrief at the end of each driving day. Usually, he'd point out all the mistakes we'd made, occasionally throwing in a positive remark or two. After my aquaplaning incident, I was terrified I'd get a bollocking or, heaven forbid, get thrown off the course for my handling of the situation. Surprisingly, Jeff was begrudgingly happy with my response to the aquaplaning event. Instead, he criticised me for another incident that happened earlier in the day when I drove through a ford during a simulated emergency call in Essex. 'How deep was that ford you crossed in Danbury, Calveley?' Jeff asked.

'I would say about six inches, Sarge,' I said tentatively.

Jeff's forehead concertinaed. 'Ha, really?' he barked. 'More like four inches, if that.' Now I was confused. I wondered, *What's his point?* 'So, why the hell did you stop at the water's edge and look both ways?' Jeff went on, and I half-shrugged. 'Stopping, when there was no need to stop, lost you vital seconds on an emergency call. What did you expect would be coming, a bloody toy canoe?' Polite laughter rippled around the classroom.

'Right, good point, Sarge,' I said.

Fortunately, my mistakes were not huge affairs and, after six weeks of challenging response and pursuit training, I faced my 'final drive', which consists of a two-part driving test, your every move judged by the examiner in the passenger seat. My examiner was Superintendent Matthews, another old sweat in his fifties. The first half of the test was a simulated emergency call, with the examiner directing you along country lanes and dual carriageways around Hertfordshire and beyond. I got through that hour – at points reaching 140mph – without major incidents (as far as I was aware). But the second part of the exam, the simulated vehicle pursuit, was trickier. This involved chasing a "bandit car" – an alleged stolen motor driven by another instructor – whose mission is to lead you into hazardous scenarios, like swerving across two lanes of a motorway at breakneck speed to make a sudden exit at the next junction. So you need to keep up. Fall behind by two cars and you'll lose the bandit driver. The bandit driver *wants* you to make a dangerous mistake. Throughout the entire pursuit you must also maintain a running commentary of your proposed actions. It's highly stressful. You're constantly thinking about your last manoeuvre, worrying that you did something wrong, while contemplating your next move. At high speeds too.

After my pursuit test, Superintendent Matthews told me to drive 'as normal' back to Hendon. That drive was possibly more nerve-racking than the exam itself. Thoughts skittered like ball bearings in my head. *Was I too tight on that overtake? Should I have performed that overtake on the dual carriageway? Should I have stopped at that zebra crossing? Will I pass?*

Please let me pass. I pulled into the college, parked the car, and switched off the engine. I didn't know whether my thin legs would carry me into the building, where I would learn my fate in a debriefing with Matthews. But as I went to get out of the car, Matthews stopped me. 'Just one moment, Calveley,' he said. I looked at him and he gave me a smile. 'So, you're in F District. Where are you based?'

Shepherd's Bush, sir,' I said, my heart pumping.

'Oh, I see,' he added, his face almost conspiratorial now. A game show host holding back on the big reveal. Could he hear my heart? Then, finally: 'So that means you'll be driving Foxtrot Three when you go back.' I made a fist and pulled my elbow into my ribs.

'Yes,' I went. Foxtrot Three is the call sign for the Area Car for Shepherd's Bush. I couldn't believe my ears. Minutes later, during my debrief, Matthews formally told me I'd passed the Advanced Driving Course. I was over the moon. The last eight months had been tumultuous, so this news was exactly what the doctor ordered – if you'll pardon the cheesy expression.

After being so ill – and almost losing my life over a chicken burger – I took nothing for granted. My illness made me appreciate life more. As I said previously, so often I worried about getting killed on duty, but I hadn't stopped to think that sickness might finish me off. This appreciation for life was further enforced when, in October 1992, I encountered another brush with death.

During the early Nineties, the Provisional IRA intensified its campaign of terror in England – and I narrowly missed being involved in an explosion that rocked the city. I was driving a police personnel carrier with six of my colleagues to the police station after we'd finished policing a demonstration in central London. The route took us past a coach parked outside the Novotel, in Shortlands, Hammersmith. Four minutes after I drove past that coach, it was bombed by the IRA.

CHAPTER FOURTEEN
TWOS & BLUES

'MP [Metropolitan Police] from Bravo Two. Chasing white van involved in a smash and grab. Following vehicle on Kensington High Street. Bandit's heading southwest towards Hammersmith, over.' Sebastian's voice, short, sharp and accompanied by the wail of sirens, hammered over the radio. I jolted forwards in my seat as though electrocuted. *This is it. It's actually happening.* 'Suspects raided a jewellers, over.'

'Foxtrot Three, copied that. Responding. Heading to Shepherd's Bush Green, over.' I flicked on the sirens, slammed my foot to the floor of the two-litre Ford Sierra Area Car, and scudded along Wood Lane to the Green, my innards turning to barbed wire with nerves. It was my first week as an advanced driver, starting on a run of night turns. Bravo Two – Kensington's Area Car – was requesting back up. And if my thinking proved correct, the bandit, with Bravo Two in hot pursuit, would hit the Green in a matter of minutes. Then I would join the chase.

More noise flooded the radio en route to the Green. Hammersmith's Foxtrot Two this time, an old sweat called Bruce at the wheel. 'Responding. Heading from Hammersmith Broadway. Foxtrot Three, just stay back, son. Stay in third position.' I screeched to a stop at the Green.

'Copy that, Foxtrot Two,' I said reluctantly. Bruce's 'stay back' comment was code for: 'You're newly qualified, son. Let the experienced drivers handle this – and don't fuck up the chase.'

'Yes, hold back Foxtrot Three, don't get too close,' parroted Sebastian, then it was over to him, as passenger in Bravo Two, to lead the commentary throughout the pursuit.

'They're telling you to hold back, Matt.' That was Badger, my crewmate for the night, pushing back the passenger seat with a deep yawn, getting comfy for the imminent ride. I couldn't help but laugh. Badger – nicknamed for the stripe of white interrupting his heavy thatch of black hair – was the most laid-back officer I knew. Nothing fazed Badger so far as I could tell.

'That's right, Badger,' I said, looking all around – through the windscreen, side windows, in the rear-view mirror – for the first glimpse of blue lights. Poised to respond. Ready to "hold back". A few minutes before 3am, all was pretty quiet, but for a shape lumbering between trees on the green, shouting obscenities and throwing drunken punches: Danny. Not my concern tonight though.

Sebastian in Bravo Two continued his commentary. He'd be the only one speaking throughout the job; everybody else listening would need to stay off the radio so we other Area Car responders could hear Bravo Two's location as he chased the bandit. They were close now. On Holland Road.

'Approaching Holland Park roundabout,' Sebastian announced. Already I could hear the sirens crescendoing. I saw first the van in the rear-view mirror, bombing along at alarming alacrity, then whoosh, the van flew past us in an iridescent white stripe to rival the one on Badger's head.

Bravo Two tailed the van in a fanfare of blue lights and banshee screams, followed by Bruce and his partner in Foxtrot Two. I gave it a couple of seconds, then pulled away, accelerating fast on twos and blues while maintaining a fifty-metre distance behind Foxtrot Two. Fifty, sixty, seventy mph, jolting Shepherd's Bush awake. Buildings streaked past. The van led us on to Uxbridge Road. 'Turning right in East Acton Lane, bandit heading towards Acton,' said Sebastian. I was now doing 80mph but wary about getting too close after being warned to "hold back". My palms were slimy with sweat. This was my first "real-life" pursuit in the Area Car and I was terrified of screwing up the chase by going too fast. At the same time, I didn't *want* to hold back; I wanted to be in Bravo Two's position.

'Taking first exit at the roundabout. Heading westbound on East Churchfield Road.'

I zoomed through the roundabout, hitting East Churchfield Road, a straight, narrow, residential street, at 90mph. From my position I could clearly see the bandit, hurtling towards a level crossing. The barriers were up, so the van zipped on, its taillights jerking into the distance as, crunch, Bravo Two tackled the crossing – and grounded the car's engine on the tracks. The vehicle swerved before coming to a halt at an angle about 100 metres ahead on the other side of the crossing. Bruce slowed down. I did too. But it was too late for Bruce, who hit a glistening oil slick left behind by Bravo Two. His Sierra skidded and spun several times then smashed into a parked car – as I came to a screeching stop just shy of the rail crossing. Sirens still sounded but the radio commentary died. Badger leaned forwards and sucked his breath through his teeth as he squinted at the wreckage. 'Well, that's gonna leave a mark, eh?' he said.

I nodded. 'Oh yes, Foxtrot Two's a write-off. And Bravo Two's not looking too healthy, either.' But I wasn't surprised. The underside of the engine on a two-litre Ford Sierra is very low and perilously close to the road surface. No wonder Bravo Two ripped off the sump when he hit the rails at almost 100mph.

'Good job you held back, Matt,' Badger added.

Fortunately, all four occupants of the two crashed cars were uninjured, but the drivers subsequently got a good ribbing for unwittingly performing two spectacular polcolls. I admit, although annoyed that the job ended in carnage and our bandit escaped, I did feel a little smug. I was the newbie driver, ordered to "hold back" – yet I was the only driver who didn't crash. Funny, that.

A few days after the bandit chase, I was driving on twos and blues to a pub fight on Chiswick High Road when the radio cut in: 'Foxtrot Three. Urgently diverting you to King Street, Hammersmith. There's been a shooting at a newsagents.' I spun the wheel hard, performed a screeching U-turn while my colleague Adrian spoke to the caller. I pulled up at the scene twenty seconds later. Adrian and I ran into the shop, not even contemplating that the gunman could still be on the premises, and were immediately hit by the severity of the emergency.

The shooting victim was a man who looked to be in his thirties. He was sprawled on his back on the floor between two aisles, his shirt and jacket soaked with blood. More blood pooled around him, and his eyes were slipping into his brow as he tried to mumble something. He was fading fast, but he was alive. There was no time to lose. The shopkeeper stood over the shot man, body and voice trembling with fear. 'He went that way, he went that way,' he cried, throwing a shaking arm towards the door. 'He's got a shotgun. Another police officer chased him. Over there, into the park. He's got a shotgun. It just happened. He shot him and ran. I didn't know what to do. I didn't know what to do.'

I radioed for an urgent ambulance. 'Man with gunshot wounds in his stomach,' I said and dropped to my knees, but the victim was no longer mumbling or moving.

'No pulse,' said Adrian, feeling the man's neck. Every microsecond counted now, our priority being to save this man's life. 'I'll breathe,' Adrian instructed as I knelt over the man's lifeless body and started performing chest compressions.

'One Mississippi, two Mississippi, three Mississippi,' I began. I counted to fifteen, paused while Adrian breathed twice into the man's mouth, then continued for another fifteen counts, to no avail. As I pressed down on the victim's chest, blood spurted and gushed from the gun wounds in his stomach. It was like pumping a bag of blood. Adrian lowered his mouth again.

Fresh-faced: A training school photo in January 1986, aged 21, with big dreams of becoming a police officer in the capital

Basic: My room at Wanstead Training School wasn't luxurious

Brutal: The 'Beast Run' was always a tough challenge

Fame: Clive the squirrel monkey and I found fame in the local paper

Cheeky ape Clive nips arm of law

UNSUSPECTING officers were the victims of a spot of monkey business when they tried to recapture an escapee.

Two policemen were given rough treatment when they were called to a home in Rylett Crescent, Shepherds Bush to catch Clive, an escaped squirrel money.

The officers turned up after Clive broke out of his cage and took refuge in the home of the ██████ family.

After eating his way through a basket of eggs, Clive resorted to biting one unfortunate officer before finally being overcome.

Police however deny rumours the monkey will be appearing at his local magis-

On the

HAS TOR
Tebbit fin

Word is vative hea down in Gordon Hammer

Stash: The Essex computer burglar's kit, discovered after a chance encounter on the roads involving an illegal right turn...

Saviours: A commendation ceremony with 'Gemma' and 'Michael', two heroic members of the public who helped out when I found myself chasing a dangerous criminal while off-duty

Giving chase: A dramatic pursuit ends when a stolen Porsche crashes into the gates of a luxury hotel. The driver also had a gun, which I didn't realise at the time

Risk: Following a suicidal woman along a motorway hard shoulder

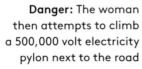

Danger: The woman then attempts to climb a 500,000 volt electricity pylon next to the road

Proof: Exposing the lies of the driver who killed six-year-old Fatima Mahmoud. CCTV shows suspect Kurunathan Ananthakumar leaving a shop with two carrier bags...

... before returning 36 seconds later, minus the bags. This was key information which helped us build our case against the driver

Caught: Ananthakumar driving in the bus lane, seconds before he hit Fatima. This footage helped demonstrate a pattern of dangerous driving and was crucial to securing his conviction in court

Honour: Receiving the Livia Award from Viscount Simon for my work on the Ananthakumar case

Injured: Assaulted at a domestic incident involving a shower screen

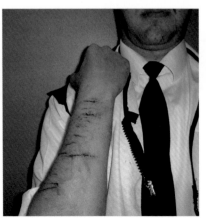

Cuts: More injuries sustained in the line of duty

Retiring: My last day at the Metropolitan Police, in January 2016...

... sporting my 'specially adapted' uniform for the occasion

'He had a shotgun. I didn't know what to do.' The shop-keeper's voice jangled above. Outside, a woman screamed. Our man was not responding to CPR, but we would not stop trying.

I pressed down again. 'One Mississippi, two Mississippi...' Between rescue breaths, Adrian radioed information from the shopkeeper out to other units. Everything blurred around me. In that moment, all I could think was, *I must do everything I can to save this man.* We continued, counting and pressing and breathing and I didn't even hear the sirens. I remember seeing flashes of high-vis jackets in my peripheral vision and moving out of the way on the bloody floor to make room for the paramedics. They stretchered the victim into the ambulance, where they would continue to administer CPR throughout the mile-long journey to Charing Cross Hospital.

As it was evening rush hour and most definitely a life-or-death situation, I chose to escort the ambulance. This involved driving the wrong way down King Street, a one-way road, on twos and blues, carving a route through choc-a-block traffic. A highly illegal move: police escorts can only be carried out by traffic cops in accordance with sanctions from the Road Traffic Act 1988. And those sanctions do not include one-way streets. But we needed to save vital minutes – and if that involved performing an illegal manoeuvre, then so be it. I'll face the consequences later, I reasoned. However, back then, our bosses accepted that officers would do everything in their power to save a life – including breaking some rules.

Despite the solid rush-hour traffic, which meant we could not drive faster than 15mph, we got the victim to hospital within twenty minutes after the shooting. Sadly, our efforts were not enough and the man, who'd only nipped into the shop for some groceries, was pronounced dead on arrival at Charing Cross Hospital. 'You did everything you possibly could do,' the consultant later confirmed to Adrian and me as we bagged up the dead man's clothing to present to CID.

Identification found in the victim's wallet named him Amaranath Bandaratilleka, a thirty-two-year-old barrister's clerk known as Nath Banda. 'He [Nath] was shot at point-blank range,' added the consultant. 'Twenty pellets went into him. That's like being stabbed twenty times in the stomach with a knitting needle. That's how it would have felt for the victim. Those twenty pellets punched holes through which blood was lost very quickly.' And with that, the consultant thanked us, then disappeared to another part of the hospital, and Adrian and I finished bagging the clothes Nath had picked to wear earlier that day.

Back at Shepherd's Bush station, we handed over our evidence to CID officers and wrote our statements. I had a wash and changed into fresh trousers as my previous pair were still wet with Nath's blood. Then Adrian and I returned to patrol duty.

In December 1993, a jury found Eyjolfur Andrews guilty of Nath's murder. The court heard Andrews, a junkie, was just sixteen when he stormed the King Street store armed with a sawn-off shotgun. He burst into the shop demanding cash – then opened fire when customer Nath handed him just twenty-six pence.

I was not called to give evidence in court, but I followed the trial via the news. It transpired Andrews' actor dad, Barry, who appeared in ITV series *The Bill*, persuaded his son to give himself up to police. The teenager told his father that the gun went off by accident, would you believe? Thankfully, judge and jury didn't buy that absurd claim and Andrews was jailed for a minimum of twelve years. His sentence was later reduced to nine years – for making "exemplary progress" in prison. It sickened me to hear this.

I did, at times, wonder whether I did enough for Nath. When interviewed, Andrews told police he'd pulled the trigger in panic when he saw me approaching in the Area Car with twos and blues activated. This played on my mind for some time. *Was I responsible for a robbery ending in murder? What if I hadn't switched on the lights and sirens – would Nath still be alive?* But such is the nature of this job. You cannot predict what's going to happen. And besides, I was on an emergency call to a pub fight in Chiswick, twos and blues already screaming, when the control room diverted me to the robbery.

At the time, I did everything I thought was right and necessary.

CHAPTER FIFTEEN
MOVING ON

Sergeant Michael looked at me over the brim of his "Number One Dad" mug.

'Your arrest figures are too high, Matt. Ease off, stop nicking so many criminals,' he said, then knocked back a few gulps of tea and returned his novelty cup to the desk with a ceramic thud. For a moment I thought Sergeant Michael was pulling my leg, but his face was deadly serious. 'Listen,' he added, 'some of the old sweats are complaining. Your figures are reflecting badly on their efforts. D'you see where I'm coming from here, Matt?' I couldn't believe what I was hearing. It took me a moment to process Michael's words. This was my annual appraisal; you'd think he'd be over the moon with my high arrest figures. I leaned forward in my chair and threw Michael an incredulous look. I mean, what was this, a bollocking for being a good cop?

'So, what are you saying, Sarge? That I'm getting marked down for arresting lots of villains and responding to loads of emergencies? With all respect, Sarge, I'm just doing my *job*,' I told him.

Michael put his head on one side, a slight squirm quivering on his face. 'Well, er, no. No, not really, I mean…' He took another sip of tea. 'Look, your enthusiasm is commendable. I'm not disputing that. But you're kind of out on a limb here, Matt. And you know, the older officers, they're a bit… Well, you know what I'm trying to say. Just wind it down a bit. Take it easy.' He raised his hands and bounced them palms-down a few times in a shh, calm down gesture.

I liked Sergeant Michael. He'd taken over when Sergeant Tony retired a few months back. But he was young for a skipper, around twenty-eight, and it infuriated me that Michael had chosen to act on the old sweats' concerns about my making them look bad. *Why doesn't he tell them to up their game instead?* I wanted to ask Michael but instead bit my tongue. Besides, there was no way I would jeopardise public safety by ignoring emergencies to massage the egos of a few old sweats. If anything, Michael's comments inspired me to further escalate my efforts. 'But you're a great cop, Matt – a real asset to the force,' added Michael, reaching for his mug again. *Yeah, cheers, thanks mate.* 'Well, that's about it, Matt – unless you have any questions or issues you want to discuss?' I shook my head.

'No, I think you've covered everything, Sarge,' I said. I think Michael detected the sarcasm in my voice.

I left Michael's office feeling utterly pissed off. I stomped up the stairs to the canteen, my sergeant's comments pulsing in my head: *Ease off, stop nicking so many criminals. Some of the old sweats are complaining. Wind it down a bit.* But as I walked into the steamy heat of the canteen and assimilated the view, I had what you might call an epiphany. There was Bob and a few other old sweats, laughing and joking and smoking over their habitual morning teas and coffees, at their usual table. A group of lads, all probies, thronged the dated arcade machines, and the same hair-netted woman shovelled bacon and sausages onto plates. East 17's *Stay Another Day* floated from the radio. Bits of tinsel everywhere, a drunk-looking plastic Christmas tree. Another Christmas at Shepherd's Bush. *This is my ninth Christmas at Shepherd's Bush,* I thought, as I made a beeline for the coffee machine. And it was at that moment, about halfway through *Stay Another Day,* that I thought, *I need to leave The Bush. It's time for me to move on.*

Once I'd decided to leave, I didn't hang around; I got straight on to personnel and asked for a transfer to Harrow. 'I've been a PC for nine years,' I said. 'I'm an advanced driver and I want to move from inner to outer London.' A month later, in January 1995, I waved goodbye to the Bush and headed north-west to Harrow on a career development transfer. A new year, new colleagues, and different geography were just what I needed. My move coincided with a significant event in my personal life too. We'd not long found out Laura was pregnant with our first child, so it was new beginnings all round for us.

Harrow, at five times the size of Shepherd's Bush, had a completely different dynamic to any inner-city patch. The area is more rural, villagey, and, back then, had four police stations covering Harrow, Wealdstone, Pinner and Edgware. I was based at Harrow on the Hill's West Street station – a charming, listed Victorian red brick building that had served as the region's police base since 1873. The four stations worked as two teams: Harrow and Pinner, and Wealdstone paired with Edgware.

What I loved most about my new patch – aside from my workmates, who were a great bunch – was the quiet rural roads, which paved the way for longer and faster runs in the Area Car. My new call sign was Quebec Three and the vehicle, a two-litre Vauxhall Cavalier, was a death trap. Its engine would regularly cut out, which was extremely dangerous when driving the motor close to its performance limits. One poor constable had a near-catastrophic-miss in the Cavalier. He was on an emergency call, negotiating a left bend at high speed when the engine again died, and the car spun out of control. Thankfully, no collision occurred but the scary incident did prompt the constable to write, 'THIS CAR IS DANGEROUS' in the faults section of the maintenance record.

Top brass finally got the hint and replaced the Cavalier with a three-litre Vauxhall Omega, an impressive response and pursuit vehicle and a world apart from its under-powered and unreliable predecessor. Wow, the Omega was a dream to drive – extremely fast and held the road well. And with every emergency call I attended, my confidence as an advanced driver mushroomed. The longer drives enabled me to get my speed up when blatting (high speed driving on twos and blues).

There was a certain amount of rivalry among us Area Car drivers regarding who would be first on the scene of an incident. Be it an odd disturbance, burglary, an activated alarm, road accident murder, or, dare I say, a smelly, sudden death, we all wanted to beat our colleagues to the job. I noticed this competitive streak more in Harrow because we would occasionally share calls with Wealdstone and Edgware, whose call sign was Quebec Five. On my first week of nights in Harrow, for example, I kept taking calls on Wealdstone and Edgware's patch – and I was the first officer on the scene to every incident, much to the bemusement of Quebec Five, aka Constable Clive. 'What are you driving, a bloody time machine?' he said after the third or fourth time he rocked up at the scene after me. By night four, when Clive arrived at the scene of a burglary some five minutes after me, he rolled his eyes and laughed.

'Unbelievable. Matt the Blatt's done it again.' Truth was, I hadn't necessarily driven faster than Clive – I was probably just closer, geographically, to the incidents when the calls came in. Luck of the draw, right place, right time, and all that. Either way, after that week, Matt the Blatt became my new nickname in the Met, the "Blatt" part being a nod towards my blatting skills. I thought, *Hmm, Matt the Blatt, not quite Starsky or Hutch but, yeah, it's cool, I'll take that.*

I adapted well to my new surroundings. The air was cleaner, and it was a refreshing change to be among fields and trees and wildlife after nine years policing the grimy city centre. Often on twenty-four-seven response duty, the work was varied and fast–paced, and our team sergeant, Ron, seemed like a decent bloke. In his late thirties, he was laidback and enjoyed a good laugh while also running a tight ship. Plus, he never pulled me up for making too many arrests. And I was nicking folk right, left and centre.

Once, I nicked a driver en route to another emergency. When I switched on the sirens and put my foot down, a

Mondeo ahead also accelerated, so I chased the car. The driver turned into a dead end at speed and smashed into concrete bollards. His motor was a write-off; I had to drag him out of the driver's window because the subframe had crushed on impact. Incredibly, the driver, identified as Jim Tetley, was surprisingly amenable when I arrested him. 'I didn't know why you were chasing me,' he said, his expression a mixture of pain and confusion as he eyed his mangled Mondeo. 'That'll have to be crushed now. It's a write-off.' I deduced from that comment Tetley was hoping I wouldn't search the wreckage of his car. Yeah, right. Of course I searched it – and found in the boot a few hundred quids' worth of clothing nicked from a retail park ten minutes earlier.

'I wasn't even looking for you,' I told Tetley. 'I just wanted you to get out of my way.' Tetley's face crumpled like the chassis of his Mondeo. No wonder – I'd feel the same in his shoes. Tetley's car was wrecked, and he couldn't make an insurance claim because he would later be convicted of theft and dangerous driving and jailed for eight months. All because he didn't read my signal and move out of the way.

Months whizzed by in images. Gaunt trees suddenly frilled with confetti and leaves. Grass baked yellow in the sweltering August heatwave. My right arm a crabstick through the rolled-down window of the police car. Concurrent with this evolving backdrop, one job blurred into the next, and the next, and the next, from mundane false alarm calls to dramatic, quirky, or tragic incidents. Sirens in my head when I turned in at night. As you'll expect, death or near-death remained a common denominator on the Job. One period at work that remains vivid in my mind happened when the landscape berried and glowed crown gold. That was a busy couple of weeks.

Monday morning and my heart sank when I found out my partner for the day would be a nineteen-year-old special constable, fresh out of the box from training school. I wouldn't mind usually but today I was feeling a little tired. Our son, Daniel, had arrived a month ago, bringing us an abundance of joy – and a few sleepless nights. The previous night had been no exception.

Special constables, as you'll know, are volunteer police officers who work between sixteen and twenty hours per month. They receive training – then they're given a uniform and radio and full police powers. Specials tend to fall into one of three categories. First, they want to become regular cops. Secondly, they want to give back to the community, or thirdly, they're bullies who enjoy throwing their weight around in uniform. Hazel, my special teammate for the day, seemed to fall into the first group. She looked like a regular WPC with her neat, low bun hairdo and straight-backed posture. Big, inquisitive eyes. After parade, Hazel helped me load the response car, then, with no immediate incidents or emergencies on the go, we grabbed a cuppa and chat in the canteen before heading out (this was my usual routine). Hazel told me about her full-time job as a supervisor in Tesco. 'It's just a means to an end until I can properly join the Met,' she said. 'I've always wanted to be a cop.'

Hazel was extremely keen and personable, I must say.

Heading out on patrol in the drizzly rain in the response car, she turned to me and said, 'What's been the highlight of your career so far, Matt?' I took a left into Lower Road off West Street, trying to think of a good answer.

'Well, I once got my thumb bitten by a spider monkey called Clive,' I joked. 'Oh, and I once tackled, disarmed and arrested an aggressive drunk who came at me wielding a machete.' Hazel inhaled sharply, audibly. Right onto Shaftesbury Avenue, then left onto Dudley Road, lined by pebble-dashed semis and hunched bungalows. All quiet so far. 'Yeah, I got recommended for a bravery commen- dation – for the machete business, not Clive,' I added with a laugh, taking the first exit off the roundabout into Roxeth Green Avenue. 'But you'll never guess what happened?'

'Stop, look, there's a body on the pavement.' My eyes followed the flick of Hazel's right wrist towards the windscreen as I braked hard. There on the damp pavement, face down, lay an elderly woman, groceries spilling from her dropped carrier bags. Hazel radioed for an urgent ambulance and suddenly, a small crowd gathered around the woman. I darted out of the car, as did Hazel. A voice came from the spectators. 'She just keeled over and fell face down on the pavement.'

I rushed over to the woman, crouched, and gently turned her over. A few gasps and screams issued from the crowd. Somebody cried, 'Will she be OK?' Another started praying. The poor woman's face, encircled by a plastic rain bonnet, was covered with blood and completely flattened, her nose embedded. She had no pulse. I quickly began CPR while Hazel dealt with the crowd. 'Everybody stand back, move away, please,' she instructed. Then I heard her questioning people and taking down names and addresses of potential eyewitnesses. I continued CPR, thirty compressions to four breaths, even though I knew, in my heart, that the woman was beyond resuscitation. Drizzle turned to fast rain, drenching the woman's powder blue winter coat as I pressed on and on, until the ambulance arrived five minutes later.

Regrettably the woman, Ruby, an eighty-five-year-old widow, was pronounced dead at the scene by paramedics. She had suffered a massive heart attack on her feet, just walking home from the shops. I had done all that I could, but as the ambulance crew stretchered Ruby's body into the ambulance, my chest filled with heavy disappointment. 'I'm sorry you had to see that,' I said to Hazel when we got back into the car, expecting her to be distraught at seeing a dead body five minutes into her first tour of duty. I thought a debrief and counselling might be needed. But Hazel appeared remarkably resilient – and she'd shown sharp initiative when dealing with the crowd.

'Oh, no, it's fine,' she shrugged. 'I didn't know what to do so I thought I'd just get an ambulance, push the crowd back and take down some details from witnesses.' She started flicking through her notebook.

'Well, I'd say that's a pretty good start,' I said. I was impressed. Hazel showed great promise as a cop, and, even then, as we drove away to the music of swishing windscreen wipers, I thought, *She's going to go far in the Met.* Although Hazel did not become a full-time cop due to a childhood injury, she enjoyed a highly successful career in the force as a civilian. We remain good friends today.

Ruby's death was not the first one I dealt with that

week. The next day, I found myself delivering tragic news to the parents of a lad called Keiron Peterson, who had been found dead behind a sofa late that morning following an all-night house party in Harrow. Keiron's death struck a chord with me, as when I'd identified him, I noticed he had the same birthday as me, making Keiron just thirty. Walking up the path to Keiron's parents' home, a large Edwardian mid-terraced house in an affluent suburb, I felt the familiar flutter of nerves in my stomach. This part of the Job would never get any easier for me. I rang the bell and heard the shuffle of feet behind the door. *Oh God, here we go.*

Keiron's parents answered the door together. Mrs Peterson was in her dressing gown, I remember, adding to the awkwardness of the situation. I cleared my throat and identified myself. 'Please, may I come in,' I said apologetically, then Mrs Peterson tugged hard on the ends of her dressing gown belt and gave me a dirty look.

'I don't think so officer, if you've got something to tell us I'd rather you just spit it out,' she said. I stood there for a few seconds, speechless. Mrs Peterson's hostility meant that I would now have to announce her son's death on the doorstep, which wasn't ideal.

'Well, I'm really sorry,' I began, my throat tightening. 'But I'm afraid I have some very bad news… regarding your son, Keiron. I'm extremely sorry, but he was found dead early this morning… at a house in Harrow where he'd attended a party last night.' I paused, expecting the couple to fall into one other's arms, to sob, crumple to the floor even. But there was no apparent outpouring of grief from Mr *or* Mrs Peterson, who exchanged brief nonchalant looks. Then Mrs Peterson plunged her hands into her dressing gown pockets and let out a long sigh.

'I see,' she said, regarding me through rimless, magnifying specs that made her green eyes look amphibious. 'Drugs, I suppose?' I didn't know what to say. I too suspected Keiron died of a drug overdose, but this had not yet been confirmed.

'Possibly,' I said finally. 'But too early to tell, I'm afraid. There will need to be a post-mortem, which should give you some answers.' Mrs Peterson chewed the corner of her lip and shrugged. 'Oh well, it's sad but, what can I say... boys will be boys.' Her husband nodded slowly and patted his wife's shoulder, like he was consoling her over a disappointing football result. 'Oh well, never mind. Thanks officer. Bye for now.' Mrs Peterson shut the door, and, for a moment, I was too shocked to move. Had I misheard Mrs Peterson? *Boys will be boys... really?* I was stunned. I walked to the car, shaking my head, wondering how the couple were now processing their tragic news behind closed doors. Then a bizarre call came in: 'Woman believes she has a grenade in her garden. Her fourteen-year-old son found it. Could be live.'

'292, copying that,' I said into my radio.

When I arrived at the address Gwen Sampson led me to the bottom of her back garden. 'My boy Charlie and his friends found it in an alleyway,' she said, nodding nervously at the rusty pineapple-shaped object nested in the grass. 'They didn't know what it was, so they were chucking it around, playing catch with it. Then my son brought the thing home. As soon as I saw it I thought, oh my god that looks like a grenade, a bomb, so I placed it here, away from the house, and called the police. I didn't know what else to do.'

'It does indeed look like a grenade,' I said, bending to get a closer look. The pineapple had what looked to be a keyring attached to its head. Now I'm no expert on military hardware, but the item looked like the grenades I'd seen in numerous war films. 'Chances are it's a dummy, possibly a toy, but we won't take any chances.' I called Scotland Yard's bomb squad, Expo, and spent the next fifteen minutes running from door to door along the street, evacuating six houses – three on each side of the Sampsons' home. Just as I'd evacuated the last house and cordoned off the road, an Expo guy arrived on twos and blues. I directed him to the garden and, a few minutes later, he returned to the cordon, holding the device.

'Yep,' he said, holding the pineapple at arm's length. 'This is a World War Two surplus grenade – and it's live. If the pin had come out, that would've gone bang and obliterated everything and everyone within a ten-metre radius. Without a doubt.'

I crossed my brows. 'How can you be so sure?'

'See this model number?' he said, gently rotating the cartridge to reveal a series of numbers embossed on its base. I nodded. 'Well, when they made this particular grenade, they didn't make any dummies or training models. Every single one that's ever been made is live and fully armed.' A rush of heat coursed through me. Visions of Charlie and his mates chucking a live bomb around in the alley flashed in my mind.

'So, the lad and his mates throwing it around could have set it off?' I said.

'Oh yes, definitely. All they needed to do was dislodge

or break the rusty old pin at the top and it would have been game over five seconds later.'

'Wow,' I said. I didn't even want to contemplate that outcome. Charlie and his mates had had a lucky escape, that was for sure. The Expo guy then placed the grenade in a reinforced box in his vehicle and shot off to a military base in Kent, where he would blow it up in a "controlled explosion". Naturally, Gwen was horrified to learn how her son and his mates came close to death in an alleyway. I left her house thinking, *Blimey, whatever next?*

Well, the final significant event of that hectic period of duty happened on a busy nightshift. A car crash, the details of which still bring tears to my eyes today.

The call came in at 3am: a twenty-three-year-old lad in a VW Golf had hurtled into a roundabout at high speed, lost control, skidded off to the side, and crashed into some pedestrian railings. I raced to the roundabout, on the junction of Uxbridge Road and Clamp Hill, to find that Clive, in Quebec Five, had beaten me to it for once. My role as the second officer on the scene was to assist Clive. The ambulance and fire brigade crews had already arrived, and several hi-vis jacketed people were at work around and on top of the crashed car. I parked up behind Quebec Five and opened the door to be assailed by the most haunting of sounds. A man, screaming and wailing, 'Oh my god, get me out of here. Help me, help me.' The noise echoed interminably in the stillness of the early hours. A soundtrack for a horror film. But this was a positive sign. Screaming is good; seriously injured casualties are rarely the noisiest. I joined Clive on the pavement. He gave me a wide-eyed look, his face baby sick white. 'Alright mate,' I said, my voice raised amid the howls of the trapped driver. 'What do you need me to do?'

Clive blew out his cheeks. 'Mate, I need you *not* to see this one.'

'Right, worse than a fatal?' I said and Clive's face paled some more.

'Much worse. See those railings he crashed into?' Clive tilted his head towards the Golf. 'Well, one of those two-inch-wide spikes speared the windscreen and came out on the underside of the driver's seat – via the lad's genitals. The railing skewered his parts. Firefighters are cutting him out just now.' I inhaled sharply, every inch of my skin prickling just thinking about the excruciating pain that poor lad must be suffering.

'Ouch,' I said. I had no other words.

For once I was pleased not to have been first on the scene. While the fire and ambulance crew battled to free the driver, I blocked the road by positioning the police car, blue lights blazing, at ninety degrees across the carriageway. Then I put down some cones, stuck on my high vis jacket and stood and listened to the continuous wails of the VW driver while dealing with irate motorists. 'But my house is just on the other side of the roundabout,' one disgruntled driver told me. 'Why the fuck must I go on a ten-minute diversion to get home? Can't you let me through?' I resisted the urge to give him a detailed description of the victim's injuries.

The driver was still screaming when he entered the ambulance – with a six-inch-long railing skewered through his nether regions. Although free from the wreckage, the railing would need to be removed by a surgeon. I did not find out what happened to the victim, but I hope he survived – and healed – after his nightmare ordeal.

In early December 1995, I volunteered for jury protection, providing round the clock guard for a juror in a major trial at the Old Bailey. I cannot reveal details of the trial for legal reasons, but the defendants had links to notorious underworld figures – hence the need for jury protection.

Six constables were allocated for each of the twelve jurors, with each team split into three pairs working extended shifts. I couldn't wait to get started. After nearly ten years working on response, I relished the opportunity to do something different. There were other perks too: plenty of overtime to be had – plus several days off. I would be in plain clothes, using my own car, and spending weeks away from the continuous screech of sirens and tragedy. It seemed, to me, a win-win situation – until I met Daryl, my partner on this mission.

Daryl was nearing retirement and had obviously opted for jury protection on the premise it would be a cushy little number. He showed no interest in the job and I had little in common with him, which was not ideal considering we'd be spending long hours alone in a car together.

Our juror – I'll call her Ann – was a married mum who lived in a leafy London suburb. The brief was straightforward: follow Ann wherever she goes, all day, every day (with our only downtime being when the jury was in court) and to watch her house in the unmarked car overnight. Under no circumstances must we speak to Ann. All communication should be via handwritten notes only, all of which should be dated, timed, signed, then retained. Which proved tricky one freezing December morning when following Ann to the Tube station.

Daryl and I were about ten metres behind Ann when she slipped on a patch of ice and hit the ground. We rushed forwards, silently helped her to her feet, checked she was OK, with looks, not words, then backed off. I can only imagine how creepy that must have been for the poor woman.

But being out and about on foot was more bearable than watching Ann's house for long hours. Daryl would bring along his miniature military figures, which he'd paint in the car while we were supposed to be "protecting" Ann. He'd sit there, tray on his lap, loaded with small soldiers and brushes and paint pots and scalpels, tinkering away, grunting with concentration. Now and then he'd burst into dialogue about whatever infantry he was working on while I watched for movement at Ann's house and choked on enamel paint fumes. I thought, *If it all kicks off here, and we need to swing into action, you'll need to put your paints away, mate.*

We spent many long days and nights watching Ann's semi, waiting for other family members to deliver notes to us outlining her movements. On the Saturday afternoon before Christmas, we were informed Ann would be dining at a posh restaurant the following evening with her husband and ten friends. Which meant Daryl and I would need to book a table at the same restaurant. So, leaving Daryl and his soldiers on guard duty outside Ann's, I drove out to the restaurant – the kind of place where you get more drizzles and garnish on your plate than food – to scope it out and make a reservation.

'Sorry, we're fully booked. It's Christmas,' said the waiter at the front desk, eyeing my undercover kit of jeans, trainers and bomber jacket with a look that said, 'This is an upmarket establishment and you ain't got a pot to piss in. Folk like you are not welcome here.' Or something like that. I asked to speak to the manager and a bit of a ding-dong ensued before the waiter sloped off then returned with his boss, a cheery chap with a smile too big for his narrow face. The smile of a ventriloquist's puppet.

'Frank Murray,' he said with another big smile. 'How may I help you?'

I flashed my warrant card. 'Constable Matt Calveley,' I said, and Frank's features dropped an inch. 'You've got a booking for a dozen people for tomorrow at 7.30pm. One of the diners is under round the clock police protection. There's absolutely no risk to the restaurant, but I need you to be able to accommodate me and another police bodyguard.' Bang, Frank's smile was back. Even wider than before.

'Oh, no problem at all, officer,' he said. 'Consider it done. Please, pick whichever table you want.' He drew his arm in a generous circle.

I pulled a confused look. 'But your staff claim you're fully booked tomorrow night.'

Frank laughed. 'We *are* fully booked, but so what. We will make room for officers of the law.'

'Great,' I said, then sensing Frank's excitement, added: 'Just one more thing, sir. In the interests of national security, there must be absolute discretion. Not a word to anybody.

Understand?' Frank nodded so hard I thought his head might fall off.

As it turned out, the Sunday night meal passed without incident. Frank flashed me exaggerated winks across the restaurant, and Daryl and I enjoyed a slap-up meal for £162.50 (courtesy of the Metropolitan Police). Nice one.

Despite our best efforts to be covert, the whole neighbourhood soon knew there were two plain clothes cops parked outside Ann's house. On Christmas Day, Ann and her family stayed at home, which made for a long, boring shift for us. I think Daryl painted an entire French army that day, but the generous people of the area brought good tidings our way. Around 3pm, an elderly couple approached us with a tray laden with food – turkey and all the trimmings, Christmas pudding with brandy sauce, mince pies, the full festive works. 'We thought you could do with a bit of Christmas dinner,' said the woman. I thanked her, accepting the tray.

'Merry Christmas,' Daryl and I said in unison. Although I regret to say, we couldn't eat the couple's offerings – because this was the fifth Christmas dinner of the day donated to us. I was so stuffed I feared an episode analogous to Mr Creosote's vomiting scene in Monty Python's *The Meaning of Life*.

The next morning, while back on watch at the house again, a family member delivered a note saying Ann would shortly be leaving the house to go shopping – at the Boxing Day sales. I groaned inwardly as I read the note. I mean, elbowing your way through crowds of animated shoppers is every bloke's worst nightmare at the best of times, right? But the Boxing Day sales? That's a form of torture. 'This is going to be challenging,' I said to Daryl as we followed Ann to the Tube station. I was right, of course. Ann led us on a blistering fourteen-mile-round tour incorporating London's busiest thoroughfare, Oxford Street. The place was rammed with bargain-hunters. We did Debenhams four times, Selfridges twice. Went up and down and round and round in Liberty, moving at a slug's pace. Next, we did Regent Street, then Ann led us all the way to the Whiteleys shopping centre in Bayswater. Daryl and I were exhausted when we returned to the car that evening, watching Ann bundle through her front door, both arms loaded with bags. But, hey ho, it had to be done.

My jury protection stint finally ended after six weeks and, paint fumes aside, it hadn't been a bad gig. Several defendants received lengthy jail sentences. I quadrupled my take-home pay in overtime, so I treated myself to a new conservatory. When my mate Chris came to visit from Lytham, he said, 'Constables don't earn much. How the hell did you stump up the cash for a big conservatory?'

I just looked at him and laughed. 'Proceeds of crime, mate, innit.'

CHAPTER SIXTEEN
JINGLE CELLS

Harrow, 2am, Christmas Day, 1997

'Ha, there goes Santa Claus,' I said to Constable Pete, my wingman on this blustery Christmas morning. I caught a fleeting glimpse of white frothy beard and fur-trimmed red hat as the Mercedes stretch limousine cruised past us beneath a streetlight. The man who looked like Santa was behind the wheel of the flashy motor. 'Hmm, sleigh must be in for a service – or...'

'That limo's nicked,' said Pete, finger stubbing his list of "hot" vehicles taped to the dashboard. Pete, a probationer in his early twenties, reminded me of myself at his age. Super keen, he'd trawl police databases for registrations of dodgy or stolen automobiles – then print off his list before each shift.

'Right then,' I said. No time to laugh at my sleigh joke, I slammed on the brakes and swished the Area Car into a white-knuckle U-turn on the narrow country lane, then floored it on twos and blues. But lights and sirens did not deter the limo driver, who also put his foot down. He flew around a sharp bend, out of sight for a couple of seconds until I hit the same corner at 60mph. Pete also sprang into action, excitement palpable in his voice as he briefed Scotland Yard and Traffic Patrol over the radio.

'This is Quebec Three, pursuing limousine on Old Redding, Harrow. Heading west towards Oxhey Lane.' Pete proudly rattled off the registration from his list. 'Vehicle is stolen. Driver has failed to stop.'

I was at a safe distance behind the polar white limo now, flashing my headlights for him to pull over. Although it was clear he had no intention of doing so; he boosted along the winding road which, at 2am, was fortunately quiet. Santa's driving was maniacal, swerving onto the other side of the road at every twist and turn and accelerating wildly on straighter stretches. He pushed the limo to its maximum speed, around 70mph, but that was no match for our three-litre Vauxhall Omega, capable of 150mph. *This is going to end in carnage*, I thought as the limo bombed on. Into Oxhey Lane, fishtailing through a roundabout.

'Bandit heading north into Watford,' Pete announced. Minutes later: 'Pursuing bandit on Watford ring road.' That ring road became Santa's racetrack. We chased him around it a few times before he led us on a death-defying spin through Bushey, then back through Harrow, skidding into Hanger Lane, bulleting across Hanger Lane Gyratory. Santa jumped red lights at 70mph, went the wrong way around roundabouts and mounted pavements. The chase went on for at least forty minutes – until the limo hit yet another roundabout on Uxbridge Road at crazed speed, and the following montage, bathed in cool blue light, filled the Omega's windscreen like an action scene in a movie: the limo barrelled diagonally into the heart of the roundabout, mowed a long, glossy streak through its grass verge, skidded back onto the road, veered off the road, then crashed up a kerb and into a bush. The scene slowed before us as I hit the brakes, stopping the car about five metres before the stalled limo. 'Bandit crashed near roundabout on Uxbridge Road,' gushed Pete and flung open the passenger door, ready to burst forth and nick the limo driver. Or maybe not?

Suddenly, chuckle, chuckle, vroom, the limo's engine splutters to life. The car moves forward, sleek as it slices through foliage. Shit, Santa's on the move again. *'Hold on, Pete,' I shout and boot the accelerator, powering us towards the limo. Pete's still clinging to the open door, feet on its threshold, poised to jump out. I've heard of officers being killed performing such stunts. Santa's getaway is too slow. He inches along the pavement for a second or two as I speed ahead. And I'm not stopping until, crunch, I ram the Omega into the back door of the limo, shunting it forwards a few feet, then, smack-bang, into a lamppost. 'I've got him,' says Pete as he leaps out of the car.*

The limo driver had on a full Santa suit. 'Alright, alright, you've got me, I'm nicked,' he said as Pete assisted him out of the car. I stood aside, trying not to laugh while Pete cuffed our festive offender and read him his rights. The pom-pom on his hat joggled about his head in the high wind, and his nylon beard was all skew-whiff, but Santa appeared uninjured after the crash. And fortunately, he had not been carrying any passengers. At this stage, we had no idea why the bloke had dressed up as Santa to cruise the streets in a stolen limo. Not the most covert disguise going, if you ask me.

Soon after Santa heard his rights, officers from Harrow arrived. He huffed and puffed a bit when he climbed into the cage in the rear of the station van, but, overall, Santa was compliant, which told me he'd been through this drill before. The doors banged shut, then Pete jumped in the front of the van to deliver Mr Claus to the cells at Harrow police station. I did laugh when the van pulled away. I mean, nicking Santa after a high-octane car chase on Christmas Day... you couldn't make it up.

I was delighted with the result. We had recovered a stolen car – albeit one now in need of some bodywork, arrested an active criminal (checks later revealed this wasn't Santa's first offence), and prevented him from causing death or serious injury on the road. Question was, would I get away with my polcoll? Nowadays, officers can use "tactical contact", better known as "ramming", to end pursuits. Back then, however, ramming was deemed a blatant breach of policy. But still, I was confident I'd taken necessary action and my crash could be justified as "reasonable use of force" under Section 3 of the Criminal Law Act 1977. My traffic patrol sergeant, Mark, would have the final say.

'Well, this doesn't look very, fucking "vicinity-only" to me,' he said when he arrived to inspect the wreckage of our Santa chase. Mark walked around the two vehicles, shining his torch over the crumpled nose of the Omega, shards of headlight plastic crunching underfoot.

'I never said it was vicinity-only, Sarge,' I said. 'The control room just assumed it was. I did what I thought to be right.' I went on to describe the whole chase saga to Mark. 'Constable Pete could've been killed,' I stressed. 'Santa was driving like a lunatic – I had to bring the pursuit to an end before he killed somebody.' Mark swiped his light along the length of the limo's battered flank, then made a hmm-hmm sound.

'Yes, I agree,' he said. 'I would say reasonable force was necessary. You did the right thing, Calveley.' Relief washed over me. 'But why was this guy dressed as Santa?'

I shrugged. 'Good question.'

Later, when interviewed at the police station, Santa told us that in a "moment of creativity and innovation", he had bought a Santa Claus fancy dress outfit, broken into a prestige car showroom, stolen the car keys from the office then driven off in the stretch limo. He then drove around London touting for hire as a novelty Christmas minicab driver. The four-hundred quid we found on him suggested his enterprise had been lucrative, too – until the nasty old police put a stop to it.

Santa was kept in the cells overnight, still in his fancy dress. On Boxing Day, he appeared in the same outfit before magistrates. He pleaded guilty to burglary and aggravated vehicle taking. Likewise, our Santa, who turned out to be a notorious car thief, was in full Christmas regalia when the prison van deposited him at Wormwood Scrubs nick (oh, what I wouldn't have given to be a cockroach on the prison wall). Santa's moment of "creativity and innovation" earned him eight months behind bars.

Ho, ho, ho.

Meanwhile, back on normal response duty days after our Santa chase, I stumbled across what you might call a lucky arrest while patrolling Harrow in the Area Car. It happened during the morning rush hour. Driving along The Bridge, I spotted a silver Ford Mondeo making an illegal right turn at the George Gange Way junction. Only buses and bicycles are allowed to make this turn, so I pulled the Mondeo over. The driver, who called himself Danny Bond, was a cocky so-and-so in his early thirties. Dressed in a designer suit with a glittering gold watch that looked like a Rolex wreathing his arm. 'I can't believe you're stopping me for a wrong turn,' he said, reluctantly getting out of the Mondeo. 'This is fucking ridiculous.'

'The sign clearly states this is a no right turn for cars,' I said, gesturing at the sign at the traffic lights behind us. Danny sniggered then.

'Really? This is a joke. What sign? Look, I'm in a hurry. I'm running late for the office. My business will suffer because of this.'

I took my time writing the penalty ticket and Danny became increasingly agitated. He started backing away from me, avoiding eye contact, like he had something to hide. Next, he fumbled in the inside pocket of his suit jacket then stuffed something into his mouth, trying to be discreet. I caught a whiff of spearmint: chewing gum. Now I knew why he was being so shifty – he'd obviously had a skinful the night before and was worried about still being over the drink-drive limit. I finished writing the ticket then grabbed my breathalyser from the car (chewing gum, mints or sucking copper coins do not trick a breath test, by the way).

'If you could blow into this for me, Danny,' I said, proffering the device to his mouth. He gave me a cold, evil stare and clamped his lips around the tube. *There's something not right about this bloke*, I thought as I watched Danny empty his lungs. He failed the test – and subsequently declared it was "rigged". 'You're setting me up,' he insisted when I arrested him for failing the breath test. 'Why don't you do something useful and catch rapists or burglars?'

Another constable arrived and parked the Mondeo in a side road while I took Danny to the police station and booked him into custody. 'This is bang out of order,' he continuously complained throughout routine procedures – DNA swab, fingerprints, and mugshot. 'I told you, you should be out catching rapists or burglars,' he again sneered after two more breath samples came back negative on the Evidential Breath Machine (EBM). The readings showed Danny had thirty-two micrograms of alcohol in his system, which is just shy of the thirty-five-microgram drink-drive limit. 'You gonna let me go now? You can't keep me here for an accidental right turn,' he added, smiling.

'After the paperwork's completed, you'll be free to go,' I said and went to process his documents. I felt a little jaded. Danny was right; aside from his illegal right turn he hadn't broken any laws. Or so I thought. When I looked at Danny's electronic fingerprint scan, I did a double take. Danny Bond was not Danny Bond – because Danny Bond was a fake name. According to the paperwork, the driver I'd nicked for making an illegal turn was Darren Johnson, then the most prolific commercial burglar in Essex. The list was incredible; Darren Johnson was wanted by Essex Police for dozens of break-ins at commercial buildings. You should've seen Johnson's face when I arrested him for the string of burglaries. He actually looked shocked that I'd found out his real name. I stuck Johnson in a cell and arranged for his Mondeo to be brought to the station for a full search. And low and behold, there in the boot were the tools of Johnson's criminal trade. An Aladdin's cave of professional burglary equipment: balaclava, grappling hook, torches, surgical gloves, bolt croppers and a baseball cap. Stolen computer parts accompanied the gear. I reported my findings to Essex Police, who sent two officers to Harrow to collect Johnson. They were delighted – and solved numerous outstanding burglaries in the process.

In the eyes of the law, that wrong, right turn in front of my police car was the best thing Johnson could have done. Cocky till the end, though, Johnson denied all charges, despite the damning evidence against him. However, his innocent act didn't wash with the jury; at the end of his trial Johnson was convicted of more than twenty burglaries and jailed for four years.

It's strange. I knew from the moment I'd pulled Johnson over there was something not right about him. Perhaps it was that cocky remark he made: 'Why don't you do something useful and catch rapists or burglars?'

You said it, Darren Johnson.

CHAPTER SEVENTEEN
UNARMED RESPONSE

January 1998

My voice, jagged and low, flooded the airwaves. 'Send armed response, ASAP!' The steering wheel was an eel in my hands. There I was, in a police car – bright white with orange stripes on its flanks, lights on its roof and "POLICE" emblazoned on the bonnet – and right up the backside of a Ford Focus that had fled the scene of a fatal shooting six hours earlier. Intelligence suggested the suspect was inside the Focus. Armed with a shotgun. Now I was following the car after recognising its registration plate while responding to another routine call.

We stood still at a red light, no more than one foot separating my front bumper from the back of the getaway car. It was dark, around 5.30pm, but I glimpsed three heads behind the rear windscreen of the Focus, the person in the back seat fidgeting, turning. I tried not to look. I didn't *want* to look, conscious of the fact that, any second now, the alleged gunman could fly out of that car and shoot me point blank through the windscreen. And today, for the first time, I wasn't wearing my bullet-proof vest.

The lights took an age to change. Long, tense seconds, punctuated by the thud-thudding of my heart in my unarmed chest and warped thoughts splicing in my head. *Please god, don't let them shoot me. Don't let my son grow up without a dad. How will they tell Daniel, 'Daddy's not coming home again?' He's only two.* Such was my fear on the Job of late; becoming a dad had made me more aware of my mortality. *Is that person in the back seat looking at me? Can they see my face? Did they see my lips moving when I radioed the control room for backup?*

Amber, green. The Focus pulled away at regular speed, and in that split second, I could've made a turn and ditched the chase. But no, I followed the getaway driver. 'Suspect's heading west into Eastcote,' I announced, trying to conceal the dread in my voice. 'Best get that armed response to me sharp – I'm right up behind them… in a marked vehicle.'

Where the fuck is my backup?

The irony of my predicament was this: I wasn't even supposed to be on duty that day, hence my not wearing a Metvest (the official name for the stab and bullet-proof vest worn by Metropolitan Police officers). While I risked my life following the Focus, my Metvest remained at home, hanging in the kitchen where I'd left it drying after a much-needed wash.

Until now, I'd always, *always*, been meticulous about wearing body armour. Keeping the Metvest in the boot of the police car and only donning it when there was some known threat, as many officers did, wasn't an option for me. Back in 1994, I was one of ten constables chosen to take part in the Metvest trial. The project invited ten private companies to bid for the contract to supply thousands of sets of body armour to the Met. During the course a firearms instructor told us: 'An average bullet travels at just over three hundred metres per seconds. But your Metvest will prevent any pellets entering your body.'

The importance of wearing body armour on duty had been tragically highlighted only three months ago following the death of PC Nina Mackay. The twenty-five-year-old officer was stabbed to death by paranoid schizophrenic Magdi Elgizouli as she attempted to arrest him in a bedsit in east London. Nina had removed her Metvest for ease of movement when she used a battering ram to force her way into the property. Elgizouli knifed her once in the stomach with a seven-and-a-half-inch blade.

Driving behind the Focus, still waiting for armed response to arrive, Nina crossed my mind. I didn't know her, but her death devastated the entire force and remained a poignant talking point among officers. Undoubtedly, Nina would have survived had she been wearing her Metvest. I felt naked without mine, like a skinned animal, awaiting slaughter. Vulnerable. *Would I suffer the same fate as Nina?* I'd been chasing the Focus for only a few minutes, but it felt like hours. Along Northolt Road. Bright lights from takeaway shops blurring in my peripheral vision. Buses ferrying commuters. Normality passing by, while I sat in my police car, on the precipice of possible death. *An average bullet travels at just over three hundred metres per second.*

The Focus stopped at another red light, turning my limbs to straws. If the gunman were to strike now, I wouldn't escape. I had the 395 bus up my arse, slow moving traffic in the opposite lane and pedestrians on the pavement on the other side. *There's possibly a gunman in that car and I'm not wearing my Metvest. How did this happen on my day off?*

At that point, the events that led to me chasing the Focus were insignificant. My chief concern was getting out of this mess alive. But to recap, here's what happened earlier:

In the morning, I attended court regarding a trivial traffic matter. (I was happy to do so too as we cops were then paid a minimum of six hours' overtime for stepping into the witness box.) As it happened, my work in court was over quickly and, come 11.30am, I was back at the station, filling in my overtime sheet at the duty stage in the control room when it all kicked off. A burst of 999 calls, first from witnesses. A panicked woman, sobbing through her account. 'There's been a shooting... I heard the gunfire... There's a man running in the street... he's bleeding heavily...'

Next came calls from officers, swift on the scene:

Shooting at a house in Kenton (address given).

One confirmed death. Male, early twenties. Gunshot wound in head.

Another male stabbed in the chest.

Ford Focus fled the scene (registration number recited).

Suspect thought to be armed with a shotgun.

This was huge, and I knew we were thin on the ground for officers. I thought, *I'm here, in uniform, I'll get stuck in.* I won't lie, I also thought, *Ka-ching, I could earn some decent overtime money.* I approached Stan, the inspector in charge who would soon head out to the house in Kenton as scene commander. I said, 'I'm on a rest day at court. Do you want me to stay on?'

'Yes. Grab a car and get up to the scene,' was Stan's reply. So, I zipped over to Kenton in the marked Astra, but there were already several police cars at the scene. The officers there seemed to have everything under control. After half an hour, I radioed Stan and suggested I deal with the backlog of routine jobs that had stacked up.

'Good shout,' he said. 'Crack on.' And for the next four to five hours, I whizzed around the area, responding to burglaries, shoplifting incidents and various other jobs that get shunted to the back of the queue when there's a big emergency on the go. I was en route to another burglary when I spotted the Ford Focus. Heart walloping, I called it in.

'Yes, that's the car,' said the operator.

'Focus now in Eastcote Lane, heading towards Ruislip,' I croaked, my mouth bone dry. I was about fifty metres behind the getaway vehicle. *Three hundred metres per second. No Metvest. Daddy's not coming home.* 'Suspect approaching Wickes superstore. Victoria Road junct…'

And then, hallelujah, an explosion of sapphire light in the rear-view mirror. Sirens screamed. A chorus of angels after the longest, most agonising ten minutes of my life. I slowed down and pulled over to make way for the two Armed Response Vehicles (ARVs), then followed them and the Ford Focus, into the car park of Wickes.

A screech of brakes. Rapid thump of military boots as the armed cops burst from the ARVs. Mutant stag beetles with guns. I jump out of the car and take cover, crouch by the engine block and watch. Officers surround the Focus. 'Armed police,' they shout, submachine guns, Heckler & Koch MP5s, trained on the car. Four cops lunge at the Focus, fling open its four doors and drag from it three figures. The light is grainy, but a high-pitched scream tells me one of those figures is a woman. In seconds the Focus occupants are face down on the ground, hands cuffed behind their backs. I take a deep breath and notice, for the first time, that Wickes is still open. Daddy's coming home.

Actually, it wasn't quite home time for me. I worked until the end of the late shift. Once CID arrived at Wickes I wrote my statement about the chase, then headed to the next job. I subsequently heard that the three people dragged from the Focus were the suspected gunman, another man, and a woman, all three in their twenties. I also heard that CID cops found a sawn-off shotgun in the car. The shooting followed a drugs war, and the accused was later cleared of murder but convicted of grievous bodily harm against his victim.

Being at work took my mind off my terrifying follow earlier. Only when I arrived home, just before 11pm, did I fully comprehend the gravitas of what could have been. The house was asleep, Daniel tucked in his cot. I made a cuppa and sat down at the kitchen table, staring at my Metvest slung over the chair opposite, its breath thick with Fairy Non-Bio. Sturdy and bold yet helpless in its current location. Today, I had put my life – and family – on the line and earned just over three hundred quid in overtime dosh. Had it been worth it? No, absolutely not. Flashbacks of the chase played in my mind. When I shut my eyes briefly, I saw the taillights of the Focus, along with its number plate. I sipped my tea and felt all the muscles in my body soften and relax, then said to myself, 'Bloody hell, that was a close call today.'

* * *

Days after the Kenton shooting, I got seconded to join an ongoing undercover mission for the Met's Counter-Terrorism Command. The assignment, Operation Heath, focussed on a vile character known only at that point as the "Mardi Gra Bomber".

In December 1994, the bomber launched a terrifying blackmail and extortion campaign against Barclays Bank, sending handmade explosives, wrapped in Christmas paper and decorated with gold stick-on stars, to six branches in north and west London. The devices comprised shotgun cartridges and rifle bullets fitted with springs, metal tubes and timers packed into video boxes and books – all activated to explode when opened. Meanwhile, Mardi Gra penned letters to Barclays, demanding credit cards with special PINs that would allow him to withdraw £10,000 a day, anonymously and for an unlimited period from automatic cash machines. The blackmailer signed off with the phrase, 'Welcome to the Mardi Gra experience.' Two of the extortionist's bombs exploded at Barclays branches in Hampstead and Ladbroke Grove, injuring two staff members. In 1996, another device, planted near a Barclays cash machine in west London, exploded and injured three passers-by. Now, after seventeen months of inactivity, Mardi Gra was back with a vengeance, the bomber's target company this time being Sainsbury's.

Several of the supermarket chain's stores were targeted, the suspect sending live bombs in the hope of obtaining money from them. Operation Heath was one of the biggest police surveillance operations ever mounted, involving up to a thousand officers from Scotland Yard and the National

Crime Squad. I would join a team of sixteen officers keeping twenty-four-seven watch of the Sainsbury's store in Harrow for a month. The purpose of the mission was simple: to identify and catch the bomber. Which was easier said than done. According to prior intelligence, the suspect was a "white male in his sixties", but, description-wise, this was all we had to go on.

Working in two teams of eight, our Sainsbury's stake-out got underway. I had high hopes of us catching the bomber, despite it being a needle-in-a-haystack kind of number. For the first two weeks, my team watched the Northolt Road Sainsbury's from the Observation Point (OP) while the other eight officers worked undercover instore, acting as staff and customers. The OP was a derelict flat opposite the supermarket. My god it was grotty. It reminded me of the filthy flat shared by students Rick, Vyvyan, Neil and Mike in the eighties' sitcom *The Young Ones*. Worse, even: bare floors, mouldy, graffitied walls and mouse droppings everywhere. The toilet had broken and there was no heating. The place was freezing – as cold as the sub-zero January weather outside. Four of us watched through gaps in the iced windows, relaying information over a private radio system to the remainder of our team on foot outside. They would receive our tips via covert earpieces. We did this for ten hours a day, seven days a week. Staring at Sainsbury's, looking for a shady bloke in his sixties. Occasionally we'd spot a likely candidate, then the guys outside would follow, stop, and search him. But none of those men were unmasked as our bomber.

After two weeks, the two teams switched roles. Now it was our turn to work in the store. This exercise required a separate briefing. 'It's a big supermarket and you'll witness other stuff going on,' explained the detective chief inspector. 'Shoplifting, pickpocketing, maybe even robbery. Ignore all that stuff. We're specifically looking for a terrorist, a bomber, so stay focused.'

Store duty was infinitely more comfortable than being inside that arctic, damp-ridden flat. Equally tedious and frustrating, granted, but quite funny at times. My colleague, Aiden, who was also based at Harrow, put his heart and soul into his job of posing as an assistant manager. Aiden, known for his jokey demeanour, had never looked so serious, parading the aisles with his clipboard, his name badge proudly displayed on the breast pocket of his blazer, flaunting his new faux name and title: 'Ernie, Assistant Manager.'

My role was to pretend to be a shopper. I would pick up a basket and fill it with packet and tinned food (fresh food was off limits) while surreptitiously scanning the aisles for our would-be bomber. After a while, I'd slip through the back doors into the staff area, where I'd dump my full basket. A worker would later return my haul to the shelves, hence why we weren't allowed to basket fresh food – it would just get binned at the end of the day. I would repeat this process while trying not to look too conspicuous. I wouldn't want to spook the real bomber if he was watching us from a secret spot. But, guaranteed, every time I turned an aisle, I'd encounter Ernie, Assistant Manager, and I'd have to turn around for fear of laughing. When he wasn't greeting passing customers with cheery songs of 'have a good day,' and 'thank you for shopping at Sainsbury's', he'd be engrossed in rearranging the shelves or making sure every item matched its price ticket.

Once, I rounded the crisps, snacks, and confectionary aisle to find "Ernie" lecturing a young recruit on the virtues of successful merchandising. 'The popular brands should be displayed in the middle of the aisle,' I overheard him saying. 'That way, the customer will pass by lesser-known brands before, ta-da, they arrive at the desired product. Merchandising really is an art form, you know.'

I walked past Aiden-as-Ernie, gulping back laughter. This time I couldn't turn away as there was a bloke ahead who looked to be in his sixties from behind: flat tweed cap, anorak, slightly hunched shoulders. I slung a multipack of Monster Munch into my basket and advanced along the aisle, slowly, watching the man while also feigning interest in a marked-down tin of Quality Street. He turned right, then right again, into the lane that stocked bog rolls and bleach. I followed, excitement rising inside. *What if that's him? What if I catch the Mardi Gra Bomber? Imagine?* Softly, softly, past washing-up liquid and bin bags. Then tins of Whiskers and Pedigree Chum. I held back for a moment, grabbed a tin, just as the man in the tweed cap pivoted towards me. Our eyes met and my heart sank. The bloke was in his late thirties at most.

By the end of my stint on Operation Heath, I was itching to return to normal duty. Unfortunately, our team didn't catch the bomber, who planted eleven devices near Sainsbury's stores between November 1997 and March 1998. I did feel a little deflated – and sick of traipsing supermarket aisles.

It had been a long, slow and intense month, but somebody walked away from Heath a happy man.

Days after our surveillance operation ended, Aiden got a call from the boss at Harrow Sainsbury's, offering him a full time, real-life job as assistant manager. Aiden was chuffed, and tempted by the offer, but politely declined. He returned to the frontline, but kept his Ernie, Assistant Manager badge as a memento of his turn on the shopfloor.

CHAPTER EIGHTEEN
LIFE IN THE FAST LANE

One Saturday evening in summer 1998, as a riotous thunderstorm walloped in the London sky, our sergeant Ron disappeared. Vanished off the airwaves during a late-late shift (6pm till 2am).

Ron had been in a chipper mood at parade that evening when he'd announced our postings and allocated vehicles, making a few quips here and there. Partnered with Aiden, my Mardi Gra stake-out buddy, we headed out in the Area Car into a busy shift in the muggy, stormy weather. The night, filled with one RTA after the other on the hazardous wet roads, whizzed by – with no word from Ron. We called him several times on the radio. No answer. Aiden and I phoned the station a few times (I'd recently got myself one of those mobile phones), but nobody had seen Ron since parade. 'He must be out on a job,' various workers told us. Which seemed plausible. Probably dealing with a big arrest somewhere, Aiden and I concurred. But when clocking-off time arrived at 1.30am, Ron was still at large. What the hell was happening? We were waiting for Ron's voice over the radio, telling us to 'knock it on the head for the night'. Nothing. Without Ron's say so, we could not be dismissed from duty.

'Fuck this,' said Aiden. 'Let's radio Wealdstone and Edgware. I need to get home. I can't wait to get the wife's knickers off – they're bloody killing me.' I laughed, even though I'd heard Aiden's joke more times than I'd seen dead bodies, then radioed Sergeant Phil at Wealdstone.

'Yeah, sorry chaps,' he said. 'Ron's very busy just now. You're all dismissed. Thanks very much. See you tomorrow.'

To be honest, I didn't give the matter much more thought. Like Aiden, I was keen to get home after a hectic night. But when Ron failed to turn up for work the next evening – and the one after that – people started talking, the Met's gossip mill spinning with cyclonic force. And if the rumour doing the rounds was true, then it stacked up with Sergeant Phil's 'Ron's very busy' comment on the night of our skipper's disappearance.

The story morphed in detail as it rippled through the force from officer to officer, but the main narrative went like this:

After last Saturday's parade, once we response cops had dispersed into the night, Ron slunk out of Harrow police station, got into his black Golf GTI, in full uniform, and drove fourteen and a half miles east along the A40 to King's Cross. Ron (allegedly) stopped in a street close to King's Cross station, and picked up a twenty-something brunette woman decked in a lime PVC, arse-skimming dress. The woman's name was Donna, a prostitute who advertised her services on the walls of red payphone boxes throughout London.

Eyeing Donna's bare legs as she climbed into Ron's motor, he didn't spot the two men in jeans and lightweight jackets approaching. Nor did Ron see the other two blokes watching the scene from their car parked ten metres behind him. All four men were plainclothes officers on a mission titled Operation Welwyn. Ironically, the undercover police initiative, run in conjunction with Camden and Islington councils, was a highly publicised crackdown on drug crime and prostitution in the King's Cross red light district area.

Busted.

When the two cops on foot knocked on Ron's window, he wheel-spun it off with his lady of the night. The undercover guys in the car followed and a chase ensued around the backstreets of King's Cross, ceasing some twenty minutes later when Ron led his pursuers into a dead-end road. The undercover cops dragged Ron out of his car, bundled him to the ground and handcuffed him, while Donna fled the scene, running and screaming in her six-inch heels.

The story above was confirmed to me by my inspector, Oliver, when he called me into his office later that week. 'Have a seat, Calveley,' he said, motioning at a blue upholstered conference chair on the other side of his desk. I sat down, feeling a tad on edge. Had I done something wrong? Oliver leaned forwards and placed his forearms on the desk, hands clasped.

'So, as you've no doubt heard, your skipper, Ron, is in the shit,' he said with a half-smile. He then reiterated what I'd already heard about my boss. 'I mean, what was he thinking, picking up a hooker, while on shift, in uniform?' I gave Oliver a 'search me' look. 'Anyway, Ron's suspended. There'll be a misconduct inquiry, but, yeah, put it this way, you'll not be seeing Ron again.'

I nodded. 'I agree. I don't much fancy Ron's chances.' Oliver straightened in his chair, his expression flitting from amused to business-like.

'Anyway, you're now acting sergeant. Go and collect your stripes and away you go.'

'Right, great. Thanks, sir,' I said. I was shocked. I'd recently thought about going for promotion, but I hadn't seen this coming. *Acting Sergeant? Me? Where do I start?* I thanked Oliver again and went upstairs to collect my stripes. Two silver chevrons as opposed to the usual three worn by a sergeant – because I was 'acting'. I felt nervous and chuffed in equal measure.

So, I took on the role of supervising the constables on our response team. Then, a few weeks later I was put in charge of a ten-week street duties course at Harrow, preparing seven fresh–faced probies for twenty-four-seven response team action. Initially, I doubted my teaching ability, but I did a good job, if I do say so myself.

There were seven probies, all fresh-faced and eager, just like me twelve years ago. Teaching them brought back fond memories of my street duties days and made me realise, *I'm an old sweat now. When did that happen?* I threw myself into the role, determined to give the probationers the best start possible in the Metropolitan Police. I arranged for them to attend a post-mortem and took them to watch cases at the local magistrate's court. I invited experienced officers from the force to give talks – detectives, a Scenes of Crime

(SOC) cop, a dog-handler and a traffic cop. I found myself learning a lot too.

One Saturday night, I arranged a drink-drive checkpoint. It was eventful; the new constables took six drivers off the road for being over the limit, including one on a warrant for attempted murder. They were a great bunch of probies. One guy struggled a little, but I managed to get him up to speed, and all seven of them passed the course.

By December, I had settled well into my new position. I enjoyed the extra responsibility – and the pay rise that came with my promotion. "Acting Sergeant" looked good on my C.V., too. At that time, I was keen to move on. I fancied my chances as a traffic cop next, so my new title would surely add weight to my application should a vacancy arise.

A week before Christmas, our response team held its annual Christmas do. This year, the venue for our festivities was a Tudor pub in Pinner. A lovely, olde-worlde boozer with wood-panelled walls, log fire and leaded light windows. It was a Friday, late afternoon, and while we tucked into our turkey dinners, pulled crackers, and sang along to songs like Slade's *Merry Xmas Everybody*, Ron was learning his fate at his misconduct hearing held at London's imposing Empress State Building. Naturally, as the wine flowed and inhibitions subsided, our former skipper became the subject of conversation. Jokes flew around the table.

'I always knew he was a wrong 'un,' piped one colleague.

'I bet Ron's ears are burning just now,' added another cop as Christmas pudding was served. Then suddenly, like a slowing record, the volume around the table dropped. Conversations dwindled. Jaws dropped and heads turned to look at the figure, waifish and weaselly in a suit too big for him, cutting a wonky path to the bar. He bought a drink then turned and headed shakily towards our table, beer slopping from his pint glass. It was Ron. A very shit-faced Ron.

'Hello everyone,' he slurred. Ron's suit jacket swallowed him as he dropped like a broken string puppet into an empty chair at the head of the table. Big drunken grin on his face. 'I lost my fucking job today.' Ron raised his glass, eyes swirling. 'Merry fucking Christmas, all.' The table went deadly quiet, awkward looks exchanged.

Constable Annette broke the silence. 'Well, I think I'm going to make a move now,' she said, removing her tissue party hat as she rose. Ron drained his pint. A few more cops mumbled excuses and made for the door. I sat for a few more minutes, the only sober one at the table. As Ron's informal replacement I felt especially discomfited.

'I'd better get going too,' I said, standing. 'Early start tomorrow.' I wished everyone a happy Christmas and left the party, still wearing my paper crown.

That was the last time I saw Ron.

In the late Nineties, the Metropolitan Police was labelled "institutionally racist" following a public inquiry into the force's handling of the Stephen Lawrence murder case. The eighteen-year-old schoolboy was stabbed to death in an unprovoked attack by a group of white youths at a bus stop in Eltham, south-east London on April 22, 1993. The MacPherson Report – written by retired high court judge and former soldier, Sir William MacPherson – concluded that the Met's probe into the killing had been "marred by a combination of professional incompetence, institutional racism and a failure of leadership". Specific officers in the Metropolitan Police were named and the entire force criticised. Sir Paul Condon, then commissioner of the Met, accepted the report's findings and promised new reforms to make the force "an anti-racist police service".

Many of us cops felt sold out by Sir Paul. Tarring all officers with the same bigoted brush seemed grossly unfair. Most of the cops I knew and worked with weren't racist. Far from it. But unfortunately, there were the occasional few who would stoop to depraved levels of racism – and I had to deal with one such sickening episode as acting sergeant. It happened at the worst of times, too.

Mid-April 1999 and two big stories topped news bulletins: the Mardi Gra bomber, Edgar Pearce, was jailed for twenty-one years following his four-year extortion campaign. Pearce, a sixty-one-year-old Londoner had finally been caught the previous year after falling into a police sting when withdrawing money from a cash machine. Pearce's capture and subsequent jail sentence should have been a cause of celebration for the Met. But the story was soon superseded with news that Stephen Lawrence's parents were suing the Metropolitan Police Service for bungling the investigation into their son's death. Around this time, the sixth anniversary of Stephen's death, one bigoted imbecile at Harrow police station defaced a poster with a vile racist remark.

The poster, promoting the NHS's blood donor service, featured a picture of a young black lad and highlighted the need for more black donors. I'll spare you the exact words the culprit scrawled over the poster on the canteen wall. The language is far too explicit, not to mention highly offensive – basically, a suggestion that the actor had illegally entered the UK to cheat the benefits system. Amid the Stephen Lawrence inquiry scandal, police senior management (understandably) reacted with fury and launched an emergency probe to identify the racist graffitist responsible for the crime swiftly named "Postergate".

Top brass pulled out all the stops to find the culprit, knowing their jobs could depend on doing so given the political backdrop. All Harrow sergeants, including me, were summoned to the Area Complaints headquarters to examine the poster. We then had to give a written statement specifying whether we recognised the handwriting. I studied the vulgar calligraphy, crude and executed with a black felt-tipped pen. I had no idea who'd written it. I often struggled to identify my handwriting, let alone another author's text. The other sergeants couldn't match the scribbling to its perpetrator either, so, determined to root out the racist in our ranks, managers sent the vandalised poster to the forensics lab for fingerprint and DNA analysis. They also hired a forensic graphologist (handwriting expert) in the hope of comparing the graffiti with samples provided by individual officers.

An internal memo outlined the seriousness of the investigation and measures employed to catch the offender. 'If the culprit wishes to come forward, they will be dealt with very fairly,' it read, which seemingly did the trick. The man who penned the racist comment, Constable Lucas, turned himself in minutes after the memo landed in his inbox.

Like Ron, he was fast-tracked to a misconduct board and promptly sacked.

Soon after Postergate, every Met officer had to undergo two days of "Community and Race Relations" training. Our tutor, a white bloke called Mr Jenners, didn't exactly endear himself to his audience. His opening line, marked with David Brent from *The Office*-inspired mannerisms, was this: 'You can say anything – absolutely anything – within these four walls and this is where it'll stay.' He jabbed his index fingers towards the floor, nodding seriously. A long silence followed, then Jenners dropped his hands and jerked back his head, blinking like he'd just woken from a hypnotist's spell. 'But, that said, if anyone says anything that's seriously out of order, I'm duty-bound to take the matter further.' Yeah, Jenners was rewarded with a silent, disengaged audience after that remark.

Jenners talked about a "monumental change" within the Met. 'Instead of treating everybody as equal, we will now be treating citizens according to their needs,' he said. I wanted to laugh. This wasn't a new approach at all. As a serving officer, I had treated citizens "according to their needs" from day one. My colleagues had done so too. For example, a wealthy businessman losing fifty quid to a pickpocket is not "equal" to a frail pensioner getting robbed of the same amount of money. Still, I endured the training session with good grace. Onwards and upwards and all that.

The summer arrived and, after five years policing Harrow, two amazing things happened: our daughter Rachel came screaming into the world, and I landed a job as a traffic cop.

Believe it or not, the role of traffic cop is a coveted one. Vacancies are rare as few traffic officers want to move on. So, when two positions came up, I'd jumped at the chance. As expected, competition was tough, with seventy cops applying for those two vacancies, but I managed to make my application stand out – after Traffic Patrol Sergeant Mark offered sage words of advice.

I'd got along well with Mark ever since he'd classed my Christmas Day Santa chase polcoll as "Not to Count". Before the vacancies even arose, I'd asked him about joining traffic patrol.

'You need to give yourself an edge, Matt,' said Mark, a man of few words.

'Right, can you expand on that, Sarge?' I urged.

'Yep, look up stop sticks.' Mark walked away without further explanation. An internet search told me a stop stick is a tyre deflation device used to stop fast pursuits. A long, triangular stick that looked like a giant Toblerone, packed with metal teeth. The device is thrown in front of a speeding car, and when the front tyres hit the stick, the casing explodes, causing the spikes to shred the tyres. Looking at the images online, an idea sprung to mind. *Why don't we use stop sticks in the Met?* With that, I asked Inspector Oliver for some funding for a few stop sticks, explaining how they worked. 'I'd like to set up some training,' I said.

'Good idea,' said Oliver and, long story short, the Met gave me five grand to buy four devices – then I ran stop stick classes at Scotland Yard's training unit. The result of this training was twofold: Harrow became the first borough in the Met to carry stop sticks. And I was able to big-up this success in my traffic cop application. And the rest, as they say, is history.

I was thrilled to get the job. Traffic policing had long appealed to me as I had a real passion for dealing with road crashes and traffic law enforcement. Also, the Traffic Patrol department has faster cars. And, without sounding too grim and callous, there are no decomposing bodies to confront after fatal RTAs. There was just one drawback. My traffic transfer depended on my passing the police motorcycle course. Although I'd passed the standard motorcycling test years ago, and I loved pushing police cars to their highest performance speeds, I was not confident on two wheels. But needs must.

Just as I'd anticipated, the police motorcycling course was hellish. A three-week game of Russian roulette I did not want to play. The gun replaced by Honda Pan European ST1300 and BMW R1200 motorbikes. Monstrous machines, each weighing almost half a tonne and capable of speeds up to 140mph. Come off one of those beasts at top speed and you'll fly a mile in the air before you hit the ground. And we were expected to reach top speeds on those bikes too. Most days on the course were spent racing around perilous, twisty country roads in Hertfordshire, Essex, Bedfordshire or Cambridgeshire in the freezing November rain. Many cops will tell you this is an exhilarating experience. For me, it was sheer terror.

We worked in packs of four at motorcycling school, each group comprising one instructor and three students. I was the slowest in my group, always trailing behind – at 100mph – trying to pretend the bike was a car while telling myself, *You must get through this if you want to be a traffic cop.* But I felt vulnerable. The engine noise alone terrified me – it sounded like the sonic boom of Concorde played over and over. A continuous gravelly roar, combined with the force of the wind whipping past at murderous velocity. Staying on the bike and keeping the machine upright is a killer abdominal workout itself – because you're trying to keep your weight forwards while the wind is pushing you backwards. I had a few kamikaze episodes, the most memorable being when I ended up in a field – and came away looking like a scarecrow in a cop uniform who'd just won the county mud wrestling championships.

My accident happened one afternoon when my group was racing at ridiculously high speed across the flat, open lands of Cambridgeshire. As usual, I was bringing up the rear in position number four, struggling to keep up with my colleagues, accelerating into the distance. Gripping the handlebars of the Pan European for dear life, I pushed the bike close to 100mph, confident that the remote country road was straight for a considerable distance. Then, out of nowhere, the road hit a ninety-degree left bend, and I continued ahead, zooming across the road and into a farmer's field. I dropped my feet to the ground, but the bike powered on, ripping through forty-or-so metres of mud and grass and straw. Eventually, the engine stalled. The sudden silence that engulfed me felt eerie. I looked behind me at the trail of devastation made by the meaty wheels of my bike. Then I glanced left and saw three tiny flecks of high-vis yellow flickering on the horizon. My colleagues. *Fuck, I need to catch them up.* I switched on the engine, did a twenty-eight-point-turn, mud churning and jettisoning in all directions, then got back on the road.

About two miles on I saw my instructor and one of my colleagues, who had stopped to wait for me. I slowed, pulled in next to them and lifted the visor of my mud-splattered helmet. The bike was a mess, mud and grass all over it. My leather trousers too were drenched and muddy.

'What the fuck happened to you?' said my colleague, Ted.

I threw my thumb over my shoulder. 'Massive, muddy puddle back there, mate. Surprised you guys missed it.'

'Puddle?' said the instructor, laughing. 'You sure it wasn't a landslide? Now, get moving, Calveley.'

I had a lucky escape that day. Fortunately, there had been no oncoming traffic when I veered off the road at the bend. If I'd hit a vehicle, I probably wouldn't be here today to tell the tale. But my field disaster wasn't the only time I made a donkey of myself on the motorcycling course.

The next day, as we stopped at the police station in Dunstable town centre for a tea break, I fell off my bike. We'd come to a halt outside the station gates, waiting for them to open. But as I stopped, I forgot to relax my knees. They were still gripping the fuel tank and down I went, taking the 400-kilo machine with me, pinning me to the ground by my left leg. Three laughing colleagues had to rescue me. Bedfordshire police control room staff got a laugh out of my accident too – via CCTV cameras that captured the shenanigans.

Despite my two epic fails, I survived my twenty-one-day challenge on two wheels and, miraculously, passed the course. I was now a fully-fledged traffic cop, dealing with carnage on the roads, cocky motorists, speeders and drink-drivers. And sometimes, the worst offenders are not who you'd expect – as I found out just days into my new job.

I was driving on the A40, my colleague Jack next to me, when I clocked a blue Mercedes in the rear-view mirror of the patrol car. The driver was approaching at an alarming speed in torrential rain. No headlights or sidelights on, despite the weather. *Must be an unmarked police car,* I thought, *a covert fast run to a burglary perhaps? Hence no lights or twos and blues.* Seconds later, the Merc bombed past us, swerving as it did so in the fast lane of the A40 dual carriageway. *Definitely not a police vehicle.*

I slammed my foot to the floor while Jack clocked the Merc's speed on the Police Pilot. 'Shit,' he said, 'He's doing 114mph – and accelerating.' Our speedometer nudged 120mph but still I couldn't keep up with a Merc capable of 155mph. We pursued the driver for at least two miles in an inferno of blue light before the Merc finally pulled over on the hard shoulder. 'Boy racer?' said Jack as we rolled up behind the speeder.

I nodded. 'Shouldn't be allowed on the roads.'

Our 'boy racer' was a 70-year-old woman called Beryl. She – and the interior of her car – smelled like a brewery. A breath test confirmed she was more than four times over the drink-drive limit. Beryl also failed an eye test – she couldn't read a car number plate further than three metres away (the legal minimum distance is 20.5 metres). We caught Beryl shortly after she'd set off on a 100-mile journey from London to her home in Leicestershire – on an expired driving licence. Beryl was slapped with a £1,000 fine and a three-year driving ban.

No two days are the same on traffic patrol, but I routinely encountered angry, inconsiderate, or downright rude motorists. In my early days as a traffic cop, I patrolled the road closure after a double fatal accident at the Fiveways Corner junction in Barnet. The crash happened during rush hour and tailbacks stretched as far as Battersea. As I walked along my line of traffic cones, a guy in a tight t-shirt pulled up. 'What the hell's going on?' he shouted from his Audi. 'I've been in this queue for two bloody hours.'

'I'm sorry for the delay,' I said, 'There's been a serious accident. Two people killed.'

Mr Audi raked a hand through a flop of stringy highlights, biceps and neck pulsing. 'Good,' he shouted, 'I'm glad they're dead.'

Welcome to the unpredictable world of traffic patrol.

CHAPTER NINETEEN
CALL OF DUTY

Late January, 2000

Throughout my thirty years' service in the Met, I don't think there was a point in which I was ever truly off duty. Even after a long, busy shift or on days off, my crime detector radar would thrum on in my mind. Aware I could stumble across a massive bank heist, a shooting, mugging, or body parts in a ditch while nipping out for a pint of milk, I was ready to swing into action at any time. Uniformed or not.

Ideally, a chance incident will happen when one is well-rested and alert. But, as sod's law would have it, it never works out this way.

I was driving home after a night shift and listening to Heart FM when a terrifying road-rage episode exploded around me on the A40. Just before it happened, Steps' *Tragedy* jumped hyperactively through the speakers as I let out a long yawn. Not my favourite hit for a leisurely morning drive. It had been a frantic Sunday night on the roads: speeders, drink-drivers, a motorcyclist rushed to hospital after crashing into a van at a junction off the A1. Heading westbound, I hit the Greenford flyover, mentally making a list of things I'd do when I reached home. *Quick shower, bacon sarnie and a cuppa then bed. Maybe go for a walk when I…*

The Rover Saloon, blood red, fast and erratic, rocketed past me in the middle lane. Next came a tow truck, barrelling along in the outside lane until it was neck and neck with the Rover. Then, smash, the truck deliberately swung left and slammed into the Rover, sending it spinning across the carriageway in a shower of splintered glass and plastic. The frisbeeing wreckage missed my (personal) car by inches. I swerved into the middle lane, now in pursuit of the truck driver, who was speeding away and, from what I could see through his rear window, pulling on a balaclava. I turned down the radio, grabbed my mobile, dialled 999, identified myself to Scotland Yard as an off-duty police officer and jabbered details of the crash, the truck driver's registration, and direction of the pursuit. 'Urgent assistance needed,' I said, and stayed on the line while still chasing the truck for a mile up to the Target roundabout, where it flew through a succession of red lights, and almost smashed into a Tesco lorry. *Yep, the bloke in the tow truck knows I'm following him.*

Horns blasted as I too overtook the Tesco lorry. At that point I also noticed headlights very close behind in my mirror. *Is that my backup?* I looked again. *No, just an old Fiat Punto.* "Where's my backup?" I shouted into my mobile.

'That truck registration matches a Richard Gregory,' said the operator, his voice calm and measured.

'Where's my backup?' I repeated. 'Following bandit off Target roundabout, Church Road exit.'

'With you as soon as possible. Officers are still in a briefing, I'm afraid.' *Hmm, shift changeover. Not the best time for a solo, off duty chase.*

Gregory sped on, me tailing him, doing at least 50mph into a housing estate. The truck's backside and crane swung and shuddered with every sudden turn before Gregory bumped up a kerb and his vehicle veered across the pavement, into a kids' play park. I came to a skidding halt by the kerb, just as the truck crashed into a fence and stalled on impact. A second later, the driver's door flung open, and Gregory leapt out, ripping off his balaclava Scooby-Doo-style as he vaulted the crippled fence and tanked it across a vast field that backed onto the housing estate.

'Truck's crashed and suspect is out and running. I suppose I'll have to follow this twat.' I flew out of the car, quickly locked up and sprinted after Gregory, yelling, 'Stop, police,' at him, then, at the operator, 'Urgent assistance needed, now.'

Heart racing, lungs heaving, feet slip-sliding over crunchy, frosted grass, I caught up with Gregory. He was shorter than me but about three times as wide, with hefty shoulders filling a three-quarter-length leather coat, its texture sweaty in my hands when I lurched at him and dragged him to the ground. My phone propelled from my hand, somersaulted then landed in the grass somewhere. 'Get the fuck off me,' growled Gregory. I grabbed his right arm, tried to get him into a prone restraint, but Gregory was powerful, turning fast and flinging me sideways. When I did manage to pin him on his back, he lashed out, throwing punches at my head, a few connecting. One on the chin, two on my left cheekbone. A blow to my right temple. I could hear the operator's voice in the grass, but it was too faint to decipher what he was saying.

'Urgent assistance,' I hollered, struggling now to block Gregory's fists. In the dusty light on the cusp of night and sunrise, I caught flashes of his big square face. A glint of a gold tooth and shiny wet gums. Grunting, panting, swearing.

'Fucking pig, fucking pig.' I was kneeling diagonally across Gregory's left thigh while grappling with his arms. Another blow. Hard knuckles smacked my jaw and my upper and lower teeth collided. I called again and again for assistance, voice weakening. My twiggy leg shook against Gregory's solid thigh. *Where is my assistance?* Punch. In the side of my head. My vision began to blur. And just then, voices from across the field. Through Gregory's thrashing limbs I made out two running silhouettes. *Shit, Gregory's cronies?* Scenes from the movie *Reservoir Dogs* flashed in my mind. Dank warehouse. Petrol. Lighter. Blade slicing my ear. *I'm a dead man.*

And… breathe. Those figures were not Gregory's mates but a lovely young couple, Gemma and Michael. My saviours. Michael helped me to restrain Gregory while Gemma got on her mobile to my police backup and directed them to the scene.

Two cops arrived within a few minutes, ran to us shouting, 'Police.'

'Cuffs,' I shouted back and at once, one of the officers gave me his manacles. The steel bracelets shone like precious jewellery in the peachy sunrise. I read Gregory his rights. Clickety click, imprisoned his wrists. Gregory snarled as we lifted him to his feet. 'Go fuck yourself,' he spat, then he squinted at Gemma, who'd suddenly burst into tears with shock, and with an evil, gold-toothed grin, told her, 'I'll remember your face, you fucking bitch.'

Gemma gasped through sobs, then, with lightning speed, lifted her right leg and booted Gregory in the balls with such force he dropped to the ground. He rolled onto his side, knees drawn towards his chest, screaming in agony. He couldn't even cup his groin as his hands were cuffed behind his back. I tried my best not to laugh. It was priceless.

Gregory was charged with a string of offences including assault with intent to resist arrest, criminal damage, dangerous driving, driving without insurance and failing to stop after an accident. He was jailed for four months and handed a hefty fine and a six-month driving ban.

We never found out why Gregory rammed the Rover on the A40 – he refused to tell us. The Rover driver fled the scene before police arrived and was never traced, leading me to speculate that perhaps he too had something to hide. I eventually got home from my night shift six hours late – just in time for lunch, then was back on duty again at 10pm that night.

It transpired that Michael and Gemma had also witnessed the A40 crash – they were the occupants of the Fiat Punto I'd clocked in my mirror on the Target roundabout. They had been on their way to work but instead diverted to help me. I could not thank them both enough. Without Michael and Gemma's courageous act, Gregory would probably have beaten me to a pulp. My bosses were also impressed. Following an excellent report submitted by my inspector, Gemma, Michael and I were awarded commendations for our efforts. Personally, I think Gemma should've received an additional gong for kicking Gregory in the gonads – but, unfortunately, we had to keep quiet about that.

A week after the Gregory affair, I found myself at yet another RTA on the A40. A Skoda had flipped onto its roof at one of the road's busiest junctions. The male driver was unconscious and trapped in the wreckage. Fortunately, I was on a motorcycle that morning and only a mile away from the crash when the call came in, requesting my assistance. When I got there a minute later, firefighters had already cut the driver from his mangled motor.

As other police officers were already dealing with the collision, I volunteered to be "continuity officer", which involved accompanying the casualty to hospital to provide an evidential link between the crash scene and a named medic at A&E. So I got into the back of the ambulance with the casualty and the vehicle howled away.

By the time we reached the hospital, the Skoda driver had regained consciousness, albeit he was groggy and confused. He looked to be in his mid-sixties, with liver-spotted hands and occasional clumps of white hair clinging to his bald head. A long aquiline nose between wishy-washy grey eyes. While specialists examined him, I set about identifying the victim and his next of kin – a vital role for me as continuity officer. I began by searching the driver's clothing – a navy polyester winter coat and flannel trousers the shade of milky coffee. Both items smelled of cigarette smoke.

Foraging in the deep coat pockets unearthed a pack of Lambert and Butler fags, a lighter, half a packet of Polo mints, some loose change and a crumpled slip from a betting shop. I found the driver's brown leather wallet in his back trouser pocket. Flipping it open, I was pleased to see his National Insurance card. For legal reasons, I'll call the driver by his surname, Stevens (not his real name). But before I had the chance to run checks on Stevens, a feature on his wallet aroused my suspicions. I noticed the top edge on the front flap had been carefully sliced open then glued where the stitching should be. I had seized such crafted wallets before – and subsequently found illegal drugs in their secret compartments. I expected to find drugs on this occasion too. Turning the wallet in my hands I also noticed that the front pouch felt padded. *Definitely something in here*, I thought.

Very carefully, I prised open the glued pocket. Packed tightly inside was what appeared to be a stack of Polaroid photographs, which seemed odd. Slipping a finger and thumb into the sleeve, I pulled out the glossy pictures – and immediately dropped them on the table in shock. My stomach lurched at the horrific sight. There were eight photos, all depicting a naked Stevens, his creepy features arranged in an expression of twisted euphoria as he performed sex acts on a girl no older than nine. In at least two of the photos, Stevens was raping the youngster. I cupped my mouth and stepped backwards. How could he? *She's an innocent little girl, somebody's daughter.* I felt sick. I'd seen some horrendous things on duty but this… this was depraved beyond comprehension. Inconceivable.

Disgusted, I showed the photos – some of which had had their white borders cut away – to the A&E consultant. He was equally horrified and agreed that the girl in the pictures could be no more than nine. Eight even. Further checks confirmed Stevens' age as sixty-five.

I made an urgent phone call to Scotland Yard, and, within the hour, two specialist detectives from the Met's child protection unit arrived at the hospital. I wrote my statement and handed the wallet and incriminating photos to the detectives.

Stevens' injuries were not life-threatening – just a bump on his head and a bit of whiplash. After treatment, the child protection officers arrested Stevens for rape and possession of indecent images of a child. When interviewed, the sneering beast denied all knowledge of his sickening stash of Polaroids, despite his face being clearly identifiable in at least two of the photos. 'No comment,' was his response to every question.

Fortunately, and due to the diligence and tenacity of the detectives, a fingertip search of Stevens' flat revealed thin slivers of plasticky paper scattered in his underwear drawer. Scientists at the forensics lab studied those shards under a microscope – and identified them as the sections razored off Stevens' Polaroids. This was crucial evidence as it linked the photos to Stevens' home address. Now, the top priority was to identify the little girl.

After a long, disturbing investigation lasting several weeks, detectives finally found Stevens' victim. She bravely recounted her horrendous story to specially trained officers, who were astonished at the level of detail she provided. During the filmed interview, the girl, in her own words, explained how Stevens had raped her several times. I could not begin to imagine the emotional trauma suffered by that little girl and her parents – an agony they were all forced to relive at Stevens' trial at the Old Bailey months later.

As the cop who discovered the Polaroids hidden in Stevens' wallet, I was called to give evidence at the trial. And while I knew our case against Stevens was watertight, I still felt a flutter of nerves when questioned by his defence lawyer. One of the detectives who came to the hospital had told me I'd committed an offence by showing Stevens' sordid shots to the consultant. I feared the defence might raise this issue in a desperate bid to discredit our case. He didn't, thankfully.

The trial continued, fraught and highly distressing. I felt so sorry for the little girl's parents, who sobbed throughout the entire proceedings, while Stevens sat in the dock, shaking his head in disbelief as the jury learned of his unspeakable acts of depravity. The victim gave her evidence via video link. It was horrendous – difficult for me, a seasoned cop to listen to, let alone for the girl's mum and dad to hear.

One morning, as security guards escorted Stevens into the dock, the girl's father suddenly sprung from his seat in the public gallery and stormed across the courtroom, his fist pulled high, ready to hammer Stevens. 'Fucking animal, I'll kill you,' he shouted, and, my god, I wanted to let him go ahead and beat the crap out of the disgusting, warped excuse for a human being who'd raped his precious daughter. But, as a Met police officer in court, I was legally bound to respond and restore the peace. I shot to my feet and charged after the girl's distraught dad, rugby tackling him to the floor just inches from the dock.

'C'mon, mate,' I said, 'Let's get some fresh air.' Breathing hard, the man got to his feet, glowered at Stevens, then, reluctantly, allowed me to escort him out of the courtroom. We headed outside, and walked for a few minutes, to the end of the road and back.

'Look, I'm sorry about what happened in there,' the girl's dad said when he stopped to light a cigarette outside the Viaduct Tavern pub. Fresh tears pooled in his eyes. 'It's just hard, y'know. Sitting in there, watching that... nonce... that evil thing... sitting there, not giving a shit... knowing what he did to *my* daughter...' His gaunt cheeks hollowed as he took a long pull on his cigarette. This dad could only have been in his early forties, but his lined, stressed-out face put years on him. He exhaled a plume of smoke. 'Sorry,' he said again.

'No, don't apologise,' I said to my feet. 'I'm sorry I stopped you.' I looked up then, into the sad eyes of a fellow father. 'Believe me, if it wasn't for this uniform, I would have happily watched you beat seven shades of shit out of that monster. I have a daughter too. I completely get where you're coming from.'

The man took another puff, then brushed away a tear with the heel of his free hand. 'Thanks for understanding.'

'Not at all. Finish your cigarette, calm down, take a breath, then we'll go back inside, eh.'

The bereft dad nodded. 'It won't happen again,' he said.

At the end of the trial, the jury unanimously found Stevens guilty of all charges, including statutory rape of a child. Stevens was jailed for eight years, which seemed a pittance compared to the lifetime of trauma his victim and her family would suffer.

After the verdict, I walked out of the Old Bailey with the girl's parents. The dad again apologised for his behaviour in court earlier in the trial, then he and his wife both burst into tears. 'Thank you so much, Officer Calveley,' said the girl's mother, tears streaming down her face. 'Thank you for giving our little girl back to us.'

My throat hardened. I attempted a sympathetic smile, too choked to speak. Then I watched the couple walk away, until they became miniature figures, blending into the daily hustle and bustle of London life.

I hope they were the first to hear of Stevens' death in jail three years later.

CHAPTER TWENTY
RED MIST

Eastbound on the M4, November 2001

'For fuck's sake, Matt, don't kill them,' said Charlie, hands clawing the dashboard. I carried on driving the traffic patrol BMW, my colleague's warning lost amid the braying sirens. I was doing no more than 50mph after all – my sole aim being to nick the two lads on the stolen, L-plated moped ahead. At that moment nothing else mattered.

The riders were not wearing crash helmets, and mopeds are not allowed on motorways, hence my reason for activating the twos and blues ten minutes ago. A pursuit had ensued, with the moped making several attempts to leave the motorway. Now, we were only inches behind the moped and, as Charlie had observed, in danger of running the riders off the road – and killing them.

'Seriously, Matt. You're right up their arse. What the fuck are you doing?' Charlie was shouting now, and suddenly, his words resonated. I raised my foot on the accelerator and inhaled sharply.

'Self-preservation,' I replied, watching the riders make their escape, bobbing left into the slip road then disappearing round the bend at the junction for Heathrow Terminals 1, 2 & 3. Naturally, I was gutted to see them go, but also furious at myself for getting so drawn into the thrill of the chase.

I'd succumbed to "red mist" – the term to describe the state of rage and excitement some cops experience when chasing a fleeing vehicle. Red mist is treacherous, responsible for myriad deaths on the roads worldwide. I should've known better. There had been significant coverage in the press of late regarding cops being overwhelmed by red mist. Fatalities caused by the rage were on the rise, prompting the Police Complaints Authority, the independent body that oversees investigations into police pursuits, to launch a probe into the matter. The investigation revealed most fatal chases lasted three to five minutes.

The dangers of red mist had been hammered home on my advanced driving course, the phrase "time to react" being the most important three words I learned. 'You can sacrifice anything for safety, but you can't sacrifice safety for anything,' my instructor Jeff would bark. Those words came back to haunt me as we continued along the M4. Coupled with a string of "what if?" thoughts. A heat radiated from my innards. *If Charlie hadn't said anything, would I have slowed down? Would I have run those riders off the moped? I could have killed those two men – and my career.* The in-car video system had recorded the pursuit, complete with Charlie's remarks. If the chase had ended in an accident – fatal or not – then a detailed inquiry would have followed. Top brass would scrutinise the footage, note I'd ignored Charlie's chilling alert, and I would probably have faced misconduct charges. Possibly criminal charges too. Then prison. What had I been thinking?

The joyriders, who'd nicked the two-wheeler in Manchester earlier that day, dumped the moped an hour after I let them escape. They got away with their crimes. But my wake-up call was surprisingly short-lived.

A few months after the moped incident poor Charlie again found himself in the passenger seat next to me during a frenetic, forty-minute pursuit around north London and Hertfordshire. Until then, it had been a quiet Saturday morning, pootling around in the car, looking for drivers not wearing their seatbelts or those still over the limit after a Friday night bender.

The bandit was a nicked convertible Porsche 911, royal blue and capable of a heart-stopping 170mph. Charlie clocked the driver, a bloke who appeared to be in his thirties, as he crossed us down a residential street close to Elstree Film Studios. He was cruising along in the stolen Porsche, roof down, one hand on the wheel, the other holding his mobile phone to his ear. 'That's the stolen Porsche reported earlier,' said Charlie. 'Reg matches.'

I made a swift U-turn, switched on the twos and blues. The Porsche driver put his foot down, revved and wheel-spun off. I also floored it while Charlie got straight on the radio. 'Oscar Quebec One Four. Pursuing stolen Porsche. Suspect heading north-west towards Barnet. Speed increasing. Over.' The radio fuzzed, Oscar Sierra One Four, the call sign for Barnet, announced their position just ahead of the Porsche, which was now zipping past the studios on Shenley Road. Then Oscar Quebec One Six (Brent and Harrow) joined the airwaves. The chase was on.

Despite the Omega being a punchy motor, it was no match for the Porsche, and I lost the driver a few minutes into the chase when he flew over a roundabout in Borehamwood, leaving me stuck behind a motorist too slow to get out of my way. Fortunately, our Barnet colleagues spotted the speeding Porsche and picked up the chase, closely followed by Oscar Quebec One Six. I caught up again, and between the three pursuing cars, alternating chase positions every time the Porsche driver executed a lethal turn or swerved or belted through a red light, managed to keep him in our sights for twenty minutes before losing him on the Barnet bypass. The Porsche was too fast.

So it was back to the drawing board. A race against time to relocate the Porsche before the driver wiped out lives with his crazed 100mph-plus antics. Charlie grabbed the Geographia street atlas from the glove compartment and set about figuring likely routes the Porsche might have taken (car mapping was yet to be installed in police vehicles). 'I'm thinking he might head east,' said Charlie, leafing through the atlas.

I stretched back in my seat, feeling flat. I wasn't used to losing the target vehicle on a pursuit. Car chases were my thing. Colleagues now called me Buzz Lightyear – after the action figure hero in the movie *Toy Story*. We could second guess the location of the Porsche driver all we liked, but I knew the chances of finding him were slim – until the radio burst to life with a message from the control room. A cashier from a petrol station at nearby Stirling Corner had called 999 to report a man acting suspiciously on the forecourt. He was driving the Porsche we'd pursued, the operator confirmed. I took off like a missile, beacons blaring.

We arrived at the scene less than a minute later, closely followed by Oscar Sierra One and Oscar Quebec One Six, and spotted the Porsche exiting the petrol station. The driver missed an articulated lorry by millimetres as he again pulled away at breakneck speed. The chase was back on.

We didn't lose our target this time, although the Porsche led us on a highly hazardous tour. Back to Elstree, east into Bushey, along wending country roads and slim residential streets accommodating speed bumps and width restriction barriers. Returning to a country lane, Charlie next to me, calmly commentating. 'Speed increasing. Seven-zero [70mph], eight-zero, nine-zero.' Onto another twisting rural road, Old Redding towards Harrow, conjuring flashbacks of my Christmas Day limo chase with Santa a few years ago. Only now I was third position behind Oscar Quebec One Six and Oscar Sierra One respectively, but perfectly placed to see the explosion of rubber when the Porsche driver misjudged a sharp right turn at around 90mph, shredded a front tyre, and careered into an ornate brick pillar at the end of a lane leading to the Grim's Dyke Hotel.

I pulled over at the crash site as my colleagues, fired with adrenaline, shot from their cars and hauled the Porsche driver out of the scrunched-nosed motor. Despite his determination to avoid capture, he offered little resistance when handcuffed.

* * *

Back at the station a few hours later, as we six officers involved in the Porsche chase completed our paperwork, a detective working on the case showed us CCTV footage from the petrol station. In the clip, the Porsche driver got out of the car, placed a handgun on the forecourt, then got back in the vehicle and spun off in a cloud of smoke. Moments later, a guy pulled up in a Ford Transit, picked up the gun and drove away. My bones turned to ice when I viewed that footage. Again, I'd unwittingly followed an armed suspect.

The Porsche driver was subsequently sentenced to four years in jail for possessing a stolen car, dangerous driving, and firearms offences. In-car footage from all three police vehicles involved in the chase were submitted as evidence in the case. I cringed when I watched my video, which showed me racing through a width restriction at 72mph. Curious, I returned to that same width restriction the following day with a tape measure. The clearance between the steel bollards and wing mirrors of the Omega was less than three inches either side. Had I fallen prey to red mist again? In the throes of adrenaline-buzzing excitement, I hadn't noticed my speed or paid much attention to the barriers even. Had I taken my passion for fast driving too far? I wouldn't get to find out – change was on the horizon that would put an end to my fast car chases... for a while.

In late 2002, Detective Inspector Martin, who headed the Collision Investigation Unit, approached me with an offer: did I want to train as a forensic collision investigator? This specialised traffic patrol department investigates and reconstructs all fatal, life-threatening and life-changing

RTAs. Ready for a new challenge, I accepted. So, it was back to the classroom for me.

The collision investigation course at Hendon meant passing maths and physics exams – the two A-Levels I'd failed twenty years ago. Poring over textbooks and getting my head around Isaac Newton's laws of motion and gravity initially invoked a few bleak memories of sixth form at Arnold School. I fleetingly recalled the pain of my brain throbbing when squinting at quadratic equations through clouds of chalk dust, thinking, *What equals* what *over* who *times thingy plus* what *to the power of* who? And so on. Mr Joyce's condescending voice whenever I raised my hand. *Dim Calveley, dim Calveley.* Ha, not so dim now, Joyce. Put into context regarding RTAs, those equations of motion were finally beginning to make sense. I got my head down, worked hard, and passed the course.

A few months later, I also passed the advanced collision investigation course, which meant I was now qualified to execute forensic reconstructions of RTAs – but only after I'd completed ten months of on-the-job training. I was deployed as an investigating officer, responsible for interviewing witnesses to serious and fatal collisions, arresting drivers, collecting and analysing CCTV footage and liaising with outside agencies such as mortuaries, laboratories and the Crown Prosecution Service.

I attended several fatal crash scenes, the first being the death of a young Eastern European man, Jan, who, after a drunken night in a West End casino, attempted to ride a stolen motorbike at 150mph or more, through a small gap separating two vehicles on the A40. The victim lost both arms, shaved off at the shoulders by the passing vehicles. The force of impact then catapulted Jan from the bike. He landed several metres ahead on the carriageway, only to be hit by more vehicles afterwards.

As a trainee forensic collision investigator, my duties included speaking to witnesses of this ghastly accident, which happened beneath the eyes of the tragic Grenfell Tower. While investigators worked at the accident scene, I visited the tower block. Every time I passed Grenfell, I'd noticed a man at the window on the fourteenth floor. He was always there, day and night, staring through his window that overlooked the spot where Jan was killed. *He must've seen something*, I thought. Alas, when I approached the man in the window, he shook his head. 'Didn't see the accident. Went to bed early last night. What happened?' Unfortunately, my search for further eyewitnesses proved fruitless too.

Investigators worked for twelve hours at the crash scene and a subsequent post-mortem on Jan's mutilated body found high levels of alcohol and cannabis in his blood. Another young life destroyed.

One aspect of my new role that I came to dread was the job I'd tried to dodge since joining the Met in 1986: confronting grieving families. In most cases, a FLO is assigned to deal directly with the victim's relatives, but I would often need to accompany said FLO. As I did when a twenty-five-year-old woman died after being hit by a VW Passatt on the A406 – the same stretch of road where a fifteen-year-old boy was killed playing chicken with cars a week earlier.

The accident happened one Saturday at midnight. Dressed head to toe in black, the woman, Tina, had attempted to run across the six-lane dual carriageway. A thorough investigation – including a reconstruction – concluded the driver had not been speeding. Plus, he had stopped at the scene, called 999, and attempted first aid on the victim. Tina's father Sami, however, claimed he had found a witness who could confirm the Passatt was speeding. Assuming the role of investigating officer on this job, I went with the FLO, Sergeant Cliff, to Sami's home to hear his claims.

'I want the driver prosecuted for manslaughter,' Sami said when he answered the front door to Cliff and me. Sami looked to have the weight of the world on his shoulders, thin as drumsticks beneath a black corduroy shirt. His eyes, empurpled with bags, desperately searched my face for a reply.

I gestured into Sami's hall. 'Shall we chat?'

Sami led us through to his living room, where framed pictures of Tina occupied the mantlepiece, window ledge and coffee table. 'I've made some inquiries,' added Sami as we sat down – he on a hard dining chair, Cliff and me on the two-seater sofa. 'I've found a witness… to the accident. The witness, Azfaar, told me that he saw the Passat driver speeding. He told me, "That maniac deliberately drove at your daughter."'

Sami then pulled from his pocket a folded piece of paper. 'Here's Azfaar's details.' I leaned forward, accepted the note.

'Speak to Azfaar. He'll tell you everything you need to know. That maniac killed my daughter – and I want you to charge him with manslaughter.' I nodded gravely.

'I'll speak to the witness and report back to you,' I said.

As promised, I invited Azfaar to the traffic base the next day. My first impression was that he did not seem credible. A nervous lad in his late teens, he appeared to be reciting from a memorised script. 'I saw the Passat driver. I was standing by the road and saw him deliberately drive into Tina,' he said, adding the Passat registration plate. 'He was speeding. Definitely.'

'I see,' I said, then showed him a map of west London. 'Can you point out exactly where you were standing when you saw the speeding vehicle at midnight?' I said, proffering the map to Azfaar, who hesitated before pointing a shaky finger at a junction, located a good half mile away from the collision scene and not even in the line of sight.

'Erm, I think it was here.'

Knowing Azfaar was lying, I asked him to tell me in detail the events he'd witnessed.

'Look, I'm sorry,' he said to the floor. 'I don't really remember much. Can I go now?'

I realised then that Sami had embarked on a very dangerous criminal path – one that could land him up to seven years behind bars for attempting to pervert the course of justice.

I declined to take a statement from Azfaar and sent him on his way. Cliff and another colleague paid Sami another visit and, unsurprisingly, no more "witnesses" were mentioned. The driver of the VW Passat wasn't charged with any offences and the case was closed and written off as a tragic accidental death.

Azfaar, I later discovered, was the victim's cousin.

CHAPTER TWENTY-ONE
THE FIFTY-SIX-HOUR SHIFT

When my line manager, Sergeant Michael Cheeseman, approached me one dark December morning and asked if I fancied 'doing a bit of overtime', I jumped at the chance. It was the nine days before Christmas, and I'd just spent a fortune on toys for the kids. The extra cash couldn't come at a better time.

'Sickness. Flu bug. They're dropping like flies,' said Cheeseman, rolling his eyes. Built like a riot cop, you wouldn't mess with him. Coupled with his gruff, south London accent, Cheeseman could pass as a gangster to the untrained eye. A great boss though. 'I've got no late person today or tomorrow. Fancy two double shifts?'

A few coughs and stifled sniggers jiggled around the office. 'Yeah, go on then,' I said, thinking, *Eight hours extra, two days running... I can do that.* Now a fully qualified forensic collision officer, I figured I'd catch up on my mountain of paperwork if the two shifts proved quiet.

'Nice one, thanks,' said Michael as he left the office. Then Curtis, a bigoted old sweat known for his rants about asylum seekers, pushed back in his swivel chair, grinning while holding his bottom lip between his teeth. The look was cast in my direction.

I lifted my eyebrows at Curtis. 'What's so amusing?'

'You're a mug, Calveley. You've just signed up to two extra late shifts. That means you'll also be on call overnight. Both nights. You might not see your bed for forty-eight hours or more, mate.' That toothy grin again, smug and mocking at once.

'Oh well,' I said. 'Nothing I can't handle.' I returned to my paperwork, a reconstruction of another fatal crash on the A40, my heart a plunging weight. Curtis was right. I had not considered the on-call factor of working nights.

'I don't envy you, mate. That's all I'm saying.' *Oh, shut up, Curtis.*

I got up and headed for the door. 'Who's for a coffee?'

Coffee would become my best friend over the next couple of days. Although I didn't know this when I walked into the canteen just after 6am on Tuesday, December 16, 2003. Shaking a sachet of Coffee-mate into my mug, I had no idea of the traumas that awaited me on the longest shift of my policing career. Looking back, I don't know how I stayed awake. But I did – and I later diarised the events that happened in those fifty-six hours from my notebook statements. It makes for uncomfortable reading now, but here goes.

Tuesday, December 16, 2003, 6.30am:
I return to the office with the coffees and Curtis gives me another smug look as I sit down. So far, all is quiet so I crack on with my crash diagram for the A40 accident. I'm grateful for the downtime amid the

usual chaos — the constant calls to crashes. It's toasty in the office too, and the radio's on, playing The Pogues' Fairytale of New York. I like that one. *I try not to think about the long hours ahead and push to the back of my mind the prospect of not sleeping for two consecutive nights.* It's okay, I'll catch up on my sleep afterwards. I've got Christmas off too. Plenty of time to rest then.

The morning passes without incident and I finish my recon-struction. I get a few more bits of paperwork done too. I've not known it to be this quiet in a long while, until…

Tuesday, December 16, 2003, 12.30pm:
I'm out on patrol on the North Circular when the call comes in. Another motorcyclist, an eighteen-year-old boy called Lee, killed on the M4 near the Stockley bypass. The lad was flung from his bike earlier that morning — then struck by several other passing vehicles, tearing his body into at least half a dozen pieces. I'm not needed at the accident scene as the investigation is already well underway. My job is to take Sergeant Cliff, the FLO, to Hillingdon Hospital, where he'll meet Lee's bereaved relatives. I don't envy Cliff of that task. Especially just before Christmas. *'Cliff will meet you at the traffic base,' says the caller.*

I wait in the hospital car park while Cliff goes inside to meet Lee's parents. I can't even begin to imagine their heart-shattering grief and shock at losing a child. How do you ever recover from such a tragedy?

Half an hour later, Cliff returns to the car. He looks pale, his eyes wide with shock. 'How did that go?' I say, although Cliff's face tells me all I need to know. He holds his temples, lets out a deep sigh and slowly allows his hands to slide down his face and drop into his lap. Sirens sound. Another ambulance delivering another casualty to A&E.

'Argh, Matt, that was horrendous. The worst scenario ever.'
Cliff shakes his head, blinking. 'I've just spent half an hour in
a room with Lee's hysterical mum, his distraught dad, the boy's
fifteen-year-old sister and two extremely traumatised younger
brothers… and the dead lad's body parts, displayed before them on
a metal trolley. Half a skull, a full set of intestines, two severed legs
and a torso.'

'Oh my god,' is my response.

'The mum said, "I just want to spend some last, precious time
with our boy." It was heartbreaking.'

Cliff is quiet on the drive back to the traffic base. Even though he's
used to dealing with grieving relatives, I can see he's still processing
the devastating hospital scene.

Tuesday, December 16, 2003, 7pm:
Still on patrol and I'm called to another fatal accident. This time, a
man has crashed his brand new, high performance four-litre BMW
into a tree in Uxbridge Road in Hayes. The BMW registration
belongs to Jagvir, a twenty-one-year-old university graduate. I'm just
a few streets away from the scene so I'm there in less than two minutes
on twos and blues.

I park short of the cordon so as not to drive over any vital
evidence needed for my reconstruction. Then I get out of the car
and speak to Brent, the scene sergeant who briefs me by the cordon.
There were three passengers in the car who survived the crash with
minor injuries. All occupants but Jagvir were wearing seatbelts.
'The victim and his passengers were on their way back from their
graduation ceremony, by all accounts,' said Brent. 'Seems they'd
been boozing all day – then Jagvir decided he was fine to drive.
Looks like he hit the central reservation, then the tree before rolling

the car. It's grim – the victim was decapitated. The car was a graduation present from his parents.' I make some notes then walk the scene. Another young life destroyed.

The first thing I notice, aside from the black BMW, on its roof like an overturned turtle, is the sharp aroma of alcohol. It smells like somebody has doused the car in whiskey and beer. Walking around the wreckage I shine my torch on the driver's side – illuminating Jagvir's headless torso hanging out of the door's smashed window. Swiping the beam down the car and across the carriageway, I see Jagvir's head, unrecognisable in several bloody pieces – some splattered over the central reservation. The alcohol smell grows heavier in the air with metallic notes. The spirit fumes must be coming from Jagvir's blood. *It saddens me to think that a day of celebration could end so tragically. But my role here is to establish the exact chain of events, work out what had caused the collision and present my findings to the coroner*

Hours pass. Eight o'clock, nine o'clock, ten and eleven. Still, I'm at the devastating crash site, one hour after my late shift ended. I've taken photographs to 'freeze' the scene and now I'm on my hands and knees with my torch, locating and marking miniscule tyre marks and scratches on the tarmac, which I'll then plot with a laser scanner. I do some sums – and later, I'll use my measurements and calculations to print a scale plan and work out the speed of the BMW using a 'critical speed' mathematical formula.

Midnight comes and goes like a ghost. The temperature plummets below freezing. When I leave the scene at 4am, life around me sleeps on behind curtained windows. I drive home, creep into the house, have a quick shower and change my shirt. Then I throw back a quick cuppa and bowl of cereal and head out the door again – ready to start my regular early shift at 6am.

Wednesday, December 17, 2003, 8am
I've spent the first two hours working through my findings from the BMW crash scene. My calculations and observations regarding the tyre marks reveal Jagvir was driving at 68mph, in a 40mph limit. As Jagvir pulled onto the carriageway from a side road, he floored the accelerator, causing the car to fishtail then crash into the central reservation. As Brent had predicted, the BMW ricocheted off the reservation then hit the tree and flipped over.

But my reconstruction will need to wait. Another call has come in. An elderly man has been hit by a car in Greenford, west London. His injuries are described as 'life-threatening', possibly fatal, and the driver has fled the scene.

I race to Greenford Broadway to find the man lying in the road. The top of the poor chap's skull is missing, exposing his brain, and his legs are shredded to the bone. He's still breathing... just. One, two weak breaths – then nothing. Paramedics arrive, but sadly, it's clear there's nothing they can do for this pensioner. I get to work, determined to find the callous driver who ran over an elderly gentleman and left him to die in the street.

Wednesday, December 17, 2003, 12.30pm
A wave of tiredness overwhelms me as I watch the pathologist remove Jagvir's remaining organs one by one. It's hard to believe those jellied meaty sacks, redundant in a steel bowl, are all that remains of an otherwise vibrant lad who was partying with his mates twenty-four hours ago.

The pathologist will send blood samples and Jagvir's stomach contents to the lab for examination. He is also looking for signs of heart disease or aneurysms that might have caused Jagvir to black out and collapse at the wheel. Although, when the lab results come back in a few weeks' time, we will learn that Jagvir was four times over the drink-drive limit.

I hear the second hand drum around the clock face on the wall and it's somehow comforting, lulling.

Coffee, I need coffee.

Wednesday, December 17, 2003, 2.45pm
Driving through Hertfordshire on the M1, Brent at the wheel, I'm now on my way to interview two potential witnesses to Jagvir's crash. But such is the unpredictable nature of policing, a call comes in. 'Sighting of a woman walking along the northbound hard shoulder of the M1 near Kinsbourne Green. Spotted on CCTV. She's walking slowly, arms crossed over her chest.'

Alarm bells ring. There are several known cases of people committing suicide on motorways by standing on the carriageway in such a pose – like a corpse in a coffin. We're just approaching Kinsbourne Green and, right enough, we spot the woman, dressed all in black, walking slowly along the hard shoulder. Head bent.

I radio for all available police cars to close the M1 immediately. Brent pulls into the hard shoulder and drives cautiously behind the woman. This is not a twos and blues affair. Tricky though; we do not want to spook the woman, but we need to creep close enough for Brent to intercept – in case she runs onto the carriageway where cars are still hurtling along at 70mph. We crawl behind her, watching, waiting, then a sudden movement makes me jump. The woman's arms drop to her sides. Blood pours from her left wrist. Her right hand grips a kitchen knife. Cars fly by, noisily. I call the police control room: 'Where are we with that full closure. Call Hertfordshire. Get them to assist in closing the M1.'

The woman walks then stops, walks then stops. Slow and solemn. We follow for another ten minutes, until other police cars manage to close the road in both directions. An eerie silence as the traffic subsides causes the woman to stop and turn. She stares at us with gaunt eyes, knife twitching in her hand. Then she wheels round, climbs over the barrier, and starts walking up the embankment, heading straight towards a 500,000-volt electricity pylon. Time for me to act.

Baton in one hand, CS spray in the other, I leap out of the car, vault the barrier and race towards the pylon, which the woman is now climbing. I call after her, 'Get down from there. Drop the knife and just come down.' And, unexpectedly, she drops from the frame and falls to her knees in the long grass, sobbing. 'Show me your hands,' I say. 'Do you have any other weapons?' Over her shoulder, Brent comes into view. Good, I have backup.

The woman drops the knife and wipes her eyes with her injured hand, smudging blood on her cheekbones. 'Yes, a razor blade in my back pocket.'

'Put your hands on your head and interlock your fingers,' I shout. 'Do it now.' I can't take any chances — she might have another knife on her. But before she can raise her hands, Brent pounces from behind, grabs her arms and handcuffs the woman. 'Right, you're going to be OK,' I say after recovering both blades from the motorway walker. Then Brent and I gently lead her back down to the hard shoulder and into the waiting ambulance. Fortunately, our captive's slashed wrist looks worse than it is. Paramedics patch up her wound and take her to hospital. Then Brent and I continue our journey.

Wednesday, December 17, 2003, 11pm
I walk through the front door to my house, bleary eyed and hollow. My shift finished at 10pm but I'm still on call. Hopefully all will be quiet, and I can squeeze in a few hours' sleep before my next shift

starts at 6am… *Yeah, right. I've not even taken one shoe off when the control room calls. 'A lorry has crashed into a house in Ealing.'*

'On my way,' I say, and note down the address. Sod the coffee this time – there's a can of Red Bull in the fridge. I head back out with my energy drink. Am I safe to be driving even?

The lorry is a thirteen-tonne vehicle, spearing the front of a mock Tudor detached house. My jaw drops when I absorb the view. Am I hallucinating? *The vehicle appears lodged in the building's throat. Yet miraculously, the lorry driver is uninjured and the house still standing. Its occupants, an elderly couple, are whisked away in an ambulance shortly after I arrive. Luckily, they were in a back room when the lorry barrelled through their property of forty years.*

Working with a colleague, Constable Kev, I again find myself in a race against the clock scenario. Aside from the wrecked lorry, we also have an extremely unsafe building on our hands. We close the road, evacuate surrounding houses and I arrange for a heavy-duty recovery truck to extract the lorry. I then call the council's out-of-hours number, requesting they urgently send out the borough surveyor. Both arrive within the hour and this heated argument kicks off:

Surveyor: Pull the lorry out then my boys'll prop up the building with scaffolding.

Recovery driver: You need to put the scaffolding in before I pull the lorry out.

Surveyor: No, mate, that won't be necessary. Let's get the lorry out first.

Recovery driver: The lorry is supporting the weight of the upper floor. If I pull it out first there's a very good chance the house will collapse.

Surveyor: That's my call to make, not yours. Now pull the damn lorry out so we can get busy with the scaffolding.

Recovery driver: OK, you're in charge.

I stand on the side-lines with Kev, watching the recovery driver attaching a hook and chain to the rear end of the lorry. Industrial clinks and clangs fill the air, followed by the slam of the truck door and chesty cough of its engine. The driver powers the vehicle towards the road, pulling the lorry clean out of the house. And there's a moment of stillness before the building shudders in delayed shock. Then the mock-Tudor façade peels away from the building in one piece, falls forward like an axed tree, and crashes to the ground. Next, a thunderous roar enveloped in clouds of dust as the couple's home and memories come tumbling down.

'Jesus,' goes Kev.

It's another late one, getting on for five in the morning by the time I finish up at the scene and write my statements. No time to sleep (again). I nip home, shower and change then it's back to the traffic base for the final leg of this interminable shift.

Thursday, December 18, 2003, 1.45pm
OK, I can barely keep my eyes open now. Brent plonks a mug of coffee on my desk, but I don't see him at first. My reaction times are delayed. 'You knocking it on the head now, mate?' he says.

In slow motion, I reach for my coffee, heart rattling. That'll be the two Red Bulls I had earlier. 'Yeah, just fifteen more minutes to go.'

Brent laughs as he goes back to his desk. 'You'll sleep for a week after that stint, mate.'

I try to focus for the last ten minutes. It's been a day spent at the base, working on my reconstructions and reports for Jagvir and the poor chap killed in Greenford. I'm yet to trace the hit-and-run driver and his vehicle. I must also write up my notes on the collapsed house, but that can wait until my next shift. Words and figures are blurring on the page. The two o'clock news bulletin comes on the radio. Never have I been so relieved for a shift to end. I float out of the building – fifty-six hours after my shift started.

A week later, rested and enjoying a rare Christmas Day off duty and family walk in Richmond Park, my colleague Ken called from the scene of an accident on Southall Broadway. 'I can't get hold of the on-call sergeant,' he said. 'There's been a hit-and-run. Nasty one. Victim is a girl, aged around five or six. It's doubtful she'll survive.'

I looked at Rachel, now aged four and laughing as her brother gave her a piggy-back.

'Do you want me to come in?' I said.

CHAPTER TWENTY-TWO
A FIGHT FOR JUSTICE

The hit-and-run victim, six-year-old Fatima Mahmoud, was thrown onto the bonnet of a car in front of her horrified mum, Maka, who had taken her daughter out to buy toys on Christmas Day.

A driver had stopped to let them cross Southall Broadway, but Fatima ran ahead, then into a bus lane – just as a maroon Toyota Carina swerved into it to undertake stationary traffic. The Carina driver fled the scene, leaving Fatima lying unconscious in the road as her traumatised mum screamed for help. Fatima suffered serious head injuries and died in Great Ormond Street Children's Hospital on New Year's Day having never regained consciousness.

When I spoke to Ken on Christmas Day, he said there was no need for me to go into the office. 'I'll leave the file on your desk,' he said. 'You can pick it up in the morning. Enjoy the rest of the day.'

So, I followed up the case on Boxing Day morning – and immediately became absorbed. As promised, Ken had left the case file on my desk – a twenty-page page dossier including sketches of the accident scene, the victim's name and address and details of her next of kin, a computer printout of the incident and details of potential witnesses. I noted Fatima's family had arrived in the UK as asylum seekers from Somalia. But two key pieces of information contained in the folder screamed out to me.

First, a young witness, fourteen-year-old Amanpreet Gill, had noted the hit-and-run driver's car registration. Secondly, forty minutes after the accident, the owner of that same registration number, Mr Kurunathan Ananthakumar, called 999. 'Somebody's stolen my car,' he'd told the operator. Bells pealed when I read this. I'd dealt with countless cases in which motorists report their vehicle stolen after a collision – or other traffic offences. 'It couldn't possibly have been me driving, officer – must've been the person who nicked my car. I reported it stolen, y'know.' Hear it all the time. I encountered such a scenario earlier in the week when I returned to work after my marathon shift. We found the car that struck and killed the poor elderly chap in Greenford. The Ford Escort was parked in a side road close to the accident scene. Gruesome but vital evidence – a piece of the victim's skull wedged in the broken windscreen – forensically linked the motor to the crash. Coincidentally, the owner, a guy called Sean, had fled the country, while his father rang the Old Bill to say, 'Somebody's nicked my son's car.' Thanks to some excellent detective work, Sean had since been traced and would soon be extradited to the UK to face charges.

I thought about Sean's case as I studied Fatima's file. Sean's father had also reported the car stolen within an hour after the fatal accident in Greenford. Ananthakumar was arrested on Christmas evening following his 999 call. He was held overnight in the cells but released on bail the following morning after questioning.

I scanned the list of witnesses again. Amanpreet Gill was the only witness who'd noted the registration of the Carina. I wondered, *Will she also recognise the driver in a line-up?*

Amanpreet Gill was an absolute star from day one. I interviewed her at Northwood police station – a video interview with her mum present. Amanpreet was brave and articulate, describing the accident in detail. 'I heard screaming, and when I turned, I saw the little girl lying in the road next to the car,' she said. 'The driver stopped, but only for a few seconds and he didn't get out of the car. I made a note of his number plate in my mind as he drove away.'

'Your quick thinking could prove to be the most essential piece of evidence in this case, Amanpreet,' I said. 'Do you think you would recognise the driver if you saw him again?'

Amanpreet nodded. 'Yes, I think so. I remember his face.'

I continued my investigations over the next few days, determined to find the key evidence that proved Kurunathan Ananthakumar was the hit-and-run driver. My resolve to crack the case escalated further when I heard of Fatima's tragic death on New Year's Day. As a dad with a daughter of similar age to Fatima, I could not conceive of the abject grief her parents must be enduring, compounded by the possibility that the man who caused Fatima's death might never be prosecuted. I could not let that happen. A burning urge told me, *I must fight for justice for Fatima and her family.* But how would I find time to do this case amid my hectic workload? Around this time, The Northwest Collision Investigation Unit dealt with approximately six road deaths per month alone. The only solution would be for Michael Cheeseman to relieve me of my other duties, so, I approached him after our weekly progress meeting and told him outright: 'Listen, Sarge, I'm working hard on the Ananthakumar case, but I'm not getting anywhere. We've got nothing on it and I'm swamped with other work just now. But if you could take the rest of my workload off me, I'll solve this case, I promise.'

Cheeseman didn't even flinch. 'OK, that's fine by me. Just focus on Ananthakumar,' he said.

'Thanks, Sarge. I will crack this.' I walked back to the office, my stomach aflutter with anticipation and a hint of nerves. Cheeseman giving me carte blanche on the Ananthakumar case was another incentive for me to solve this crime.

My colleagues were mostly supportive of my mission. Except Curtis, who was quick to slam the case with vile language.

'Why are you even bothering with that Southall hit-and-run, Matt?' he said, loud enough for everyone in the office to hear.

I looked at Curtis, across the plan desks, nibbling thoughtfully on the blunt end of his Biro. 'Erm, because a young girl has died – and her parents deserve justice.'

Curtis pulled back his chin, forehead creased. He took the pen out of his mouth. 'But it's just another dead asylum seeker case. Just write it off as an unexplained accident and move on.'

I shot Curtis a filthy look. How could he say such a thing? 'So do you think that makes her less entitled to an investigation? And regardless, Fatima was actually born in Hammersmith.' I was furious. I didn't know whether Curtis had kids but, if he did, how would he feel if *his* child had been killed?

'No, you know, I was just saying...' Curtis swung right, left, right in his chair, casting questioning looks at colleagues, hoping for a voice of solidarity. They replied with silence.

Working with my investigating partner, Brian Devereux, we began the long journey of gathering evidence to build what we hoped would be a watertight case. There were still more witnesses to approach, starting with Fatima's grief-stricken mum Maka.

Despite being accompanied by the Mahmouds' family liaison officer, Melanie, and Anna, our interpreter (the Mahmouds spoke little English), fear still gnawed at me as I stepped into their home.

Maka and her husband Abuukar were visibly distraught. Huddled on their sofa, they both looked at me with suspicion through streaming eyes. Maka balled her hands in her lap as she spoke, her voice, between gasps, laced with fury and grief. 'We came to this country for a safer life,' repeated Anna. 'And our daughter has been killed. Somebody killed our daughter. How could they?' The room darkened and chilled. My throat tightened as I cleared it.

'I promise I will do everything in my power to achieve justice for your daughter.' I looked directly at Maka and

Abuukar as Anna repeated my words in Somali. 'Absolutely everything,' I added.

Making this promise a reality would prove trickier than I envisaged.

My first two breakthroughs came a few weeks into the inquiry and were both thanks to technology – mobile phone tracking and CCTV footage.

When interviewed by arresting officers, Ananthakumar claimed he was in Hayes when he'd reported his 'stolen' motor. But data from his mobile phone provider told us his 999 call connected via a cell tower next to the Hanger Lane Gyratory, six miles east of Hayes. This evidence confirmed Ananthakumar had lied to police but did not prove he was at the wheel on the day of the hit-and-run.

The next crucial piece of evidence came from some excellent quality CCTV footage from a grocery shop. (With the population of Southall predominantly Muslim, Sikh and Hindu, most shops had remained open on Christmas Day.) This footage was dynamite as it clearly showed bearded Ananthakumar, in a blue jacket and beige trousers, lumbering into the shop, paying for his goods, then leaving minutes later carrying two full shopping bags. This grocery jaunt was caught on camera just six minutes before Fatima hurtled over the bonnet of the Carina that Ananthakumar would later report stolen. With these two vital strands of evidence now in place, we could re-arrest Ananthakumar – and this time, *I* would interview him.

* * *

Ananthakumar, in his mid-thirties, sat expressionless throughout the interview, his solicitor next to him, straight-backed and cufflinked. I first quizzed Ananthakumar about his mobile phone. This was a tactical method to pre-empt and shut down possible defences or alibis he might employ later. I began by reciting the mobile phone number from which the 999 call was made. 'Is this your number?' I asked.

Ananthakumar sunk in his chair, arms folded. 'Yes.'

'Does anybody else use this number?'

'No.'

'Not even your wife? Other family members or friends?'

'No, nobody.' I sensed a scratch of irritation in Ananthakumar's voice.

'And how long have you owned this phone?'

'Don't know, but over a year.'

'Have you ever lost this phone or had it stolen?'

'No.'

'Do you ever leave the house without your phone.'

A heavy sigh, then, 'No.'

'Did you use this same mobile number on Christmas Day to phone 999 to report your car stolen?'

'Yes.'

'Thank you, now, moving on.'

I showed Ananthakumar the CCTV footage from the grocery shop, and he confirmed the man in the images was him. 'That's me there in the blue jacket,' he said, pointing at himself on the television screen. I ran the footage until the point where Ananthakumar left the shop, then I hit pause, freeze-framing his back as he stepped into the street.

'Now, tell me what happened next.'

'I left the shop and saw that my car wasn't where I'd left it. So, I walked about 300 metres left, then 300 metres right... in case I'd forgotten where I'd parked it. I couldn't find it, so I caught a bus home instead.'

'Right, and did you go back into the shop at all?'

'No.'

'Are you sure?'

'Yes, absolutely. I caught a bus home.'

Gotcha. 'Take a look at this,' I said. I pressed play and watched Anathankumar's face plummet when, thirty-seven seconds later in the footage, he walked back into the shop without his shopping bags. 'That's you, the same man, coming back into the shop less than a minute later.'

'No, I didn't.'

'But that's you.' I pointed the remote at the screen.

'Yes, that's me – but I didn't go back into the shop.' The solicitor's suit crumpled like a crisp packet as he dropped his face into his hands.

Ananthakumar was again released on bail. A subsequent statement from London Buses confirmed no services operated on Christmas Day.

A few days later, I called our suspect back to Northwood police station to attend an identity parade. Amanpreet, and two other witnesses, identified Ananthakumar as the man they'd seen driving the Carina on Christmas day. Alas, this alone was not the smoking gun. A clever barrister can easily convince a jury that a witness has mistaken a suspect he or she glimpsed fleetingly for another person. I'd seen this happen. Also, we were yet to find the maroon Carina.

One frustrating week bled into the next. I worked day and night, chasing new lines that led me to dead ends. One day I drove to Southampton on a tip that turned out to be false. For years, I'd been able to detach from work at the end of a shift, but this case consumed me. I knew Ananthakumar was the driver. He *saw* Fatima fly over the bonnet of his Carina. Just as he saw her run out in front of him seconds earlier. Ananthakumar, a dad himself. *Why won't he tell the truth? If only for the sake of a fellow father?*

I must *win justice for Fatima's family.*

I worked late, often until the early hours of the morning. Poring over statements, diagrams, footage, studying routes and mobile phone records, desperate to find just one indisputable piece of evidence that proved Ananthakumar was behind the wheel on Southall Broadway when his car hit Fatima Mahmoud. Then one Friday, just after midnight while alone in the office, I noticed something in Ananthakumar's phone records that didn't add up. Scanning the spreadsheet listing all incoming and outgoing calls, I spotted an outgoing call from his mobile at 4am on Boxing Day. This didn't make sense as Ananthakumar was still in custody at that time. His phone would have been confiscated for safe keeping by the custody detention officer, who should have retained that device to send to forensics following Ananthakumar's release.

Excitement exploded in my chest. I visualised my heart, a bloody fist, caffeinated, clenching, thumping, clenching, thumping. I turned to my computer, fingers rapid over the keyboard, and pulled up Ananthakumar's custody record. Information flashed on the screen. I scrolled down the list: time of arrest, time of detention, reason for arrest, names of the police officers who arrested Ananthakumar, details of a risk assessment, then, bingo, the golden data. According to the log, Ananthakumar was released from custody at 3.53am on Boxing Day. All personal belongings, including a mobile phone, were returned to the suspect, the report said.

I smiled at the screen. *Who would Ananthakumar be calling at four in the morning?* I ran the mobile number through my case notes – and there it was. The number belonged to Mr Pereira, an independent witness. A passing van driver who had seen the collision, allegedly. Pereira's statement included a vague description of the driver and offending vehicle. I paused a moment to take stock. Why would Ananthakumar call a witness, somebody who should be a stranger to him, on his release from custody?

Six hours later, I paid Pereira a little visit. He answered the door in his boxers, eyes half open, scratching the back of his head. A Portuguese fella in his mid-thirties. When he clicked I wasn't there for a cuppa and a natter, he went to shut the door in my face, so I forced my way into the flat and arrested Pereira for perverting the course of justice. He burst into tears and convulsions, wailing, 'Please, no. Please don't do that. Please…'

'You do not have to say anything,' I continued.

'Please, no, I'll tell you everything. Don't arrest me.

'But it may harm your defence if you do not mention when questioned something which you later…'

Pereira's face gleamed with tears. 'I haven't done anything wrong. Please, I'll tell you everything. *Everything…*'

'... Rely on in court. Anything you do say may be given in evidence.'

Later that morning, during a recorded interview, Pereira sang like a canary. True to his earlier vow, he told me 'everything'. Pereira said he was a friend of Ananthakumar and had agreed to provide a false witness statement for him. On the day of the accident, he'd been in the passenger seat of his mate's Carina. 'We'd been to a shop in Hayes,' explained Pereira. 'Kurunathan was driving. After the shop, he drove us through Southall. Along the Broadway, he raced into the bus lane. And that's when he hit the girl. She went over the bonnet of his car and then...' Pereira broke down again then. I let him cry for a bit, to let it all out. After all, he'd already told me everything I needed to hear.

'OK, here's your options,' I said finally. 'You can stick to your original story and get around seven years in prison for perverting the course of justice, or you can give me a statement, agree to be a prosecution witness, then get on with your life.' Unsurprisingly, Pereira went with the latter option. The Crown Prosecution Service (CPS) subsequently agreed not to charge Pereira and, just like that, I had my key witness in the case against Ananthakumar.

Now the geography of the investigation had shifted, I organised another search for Ananthakumar's car. Officers located the Carina within an hour – parked in a street two blocks east of Pereira's flat. The vehicle underwent forensic tests which revealed it had hit Fatima. As expected, Ananthakumar's fingerprints were found on the steering wheel, which didn't add much to the investigation – he owned the vehicle, so his fingerprints *would* be present. I got Ananthakumar back in for a third interview. After a lengthy chat with his solicitor, he gave 'no comment' responses to all questions and instead handed me a prepared statement. In this account Ananthakumar continued to deny he had been driving on the day of Fatima's accident. Likewise, he maintained his car had been stolen. And finally, he denied any knowledge of Pereira. Ananthakumar was again released on bail.

Incredible.

But my fight for justice was far from over. Still, I needed to prove Ananthakumar was the driver who hit Fatima. And even if I did establish this, I would then need to prove his standard of driving at the time of the accident fell 'far' below competent. I'll explain why.

Back then, the only two potential charges applicable to this case were causing death by dangerous driving or driving without due care and attention. The former carries a hefty jail sentence, whereas a conviction for driving without due care and attention is punishable by a fine, penalty points and a possible driving ban. There were no in-between offences. According to the law at that time, if the offender's driving was deemed 'below' careful and competent, the motorist would be guilty of 'careless driving'. Prove the offender's driving fell 'far' below careful and competent, then you're looking at a conviction for 'dangerous driving'. Since 2004, several new offences have been introduced to the statute books to plug this loophole – causing death by careless driving, and causing serious injury by dangerous driving, for example.

So it was back to the drawing board (again) for me. The CPS rarely authorised a charge for causing death by dangerous driving if the collision was due to a single lapse of concentration or moment of madness. Instead, they looked for a 'pattern of bad driving'. Therefore, I needed more evidence of Ananthakumar's driving manner. And I hit the jackpot with another CCTV clip that showed Ananthakumar's car in the bus lane on Southall Broadway on Christmas Day.

The footage depicted two lanes side by side, the outer route bumper to bumper with traffic, the inner bus lane empty. In the clip, Ananthakumar's car ploughed from the outer to inner lane. He drove through a huge puddle pooling the inner lane, drenching pedestrians while under-taking stationary traffic in the outer lane. The car passed the camera, disappeared out of sight, and three hundred metres later, struck Fatima, who died one week later. The bus lane evidence was my final piece in this jigsaw because it established a pattern of poor driving. I also discovered Ananthakumar had submitted a false insurance claim for the 'theft' of his car, which further proved his deceit.

After three months' hard graft and sleepless nights, a CPS lawyer gave me clearance to charge Ananthakumar with four offences – causing death by dangerous driving, failing to stop after an accident, perverting the course of justice and fraud. 'You'll never get a conviction for death by dangerous driving, though,' the lawyer warned. We'll see about that, I thought. I successfully opposed bail, and Ananthakumar was remanded in custody ahead of his crown court trial.

The next few months were nail-bitingly tense as I prepared my case file, which included a dozen jury bundles containing photographs and documents, and a timeline binder of events from Ananthakumar's shopping trip to Pereira rolling over many weeks later.

My biggest worry was that the jury would be swayed by the defence's attempts to prove Ananthakumar was not the driver on the day of the accident – or that the accident was Fatima's fault for running into the bus lane in front of his car.

Ananthakumar's trial got underway at Isleworth Crown Court in October 2004. Maka and Abuukar sat in the public gallery, sobbing as they looked at Ananthakumar, blank-faced and seemingly nonplussed in the dock when details of Fatima's accident and subsequent death emerged.

Ananthakumar gave a ludicrous performance in the witness box. 'They didn't see me driving,' he said of the witnesses who'd recognised him as the driver at the identity parade. 'They just picked me out [in the parade] because they all know somebody whom they don't like who happens to look like me.' Yeah, Ananthakumar's barrister requested a short adjournment to 'speak with my client' at that point. When the trial reconvened fifteen minutes later, the barrister announced to the jury that Ananthakumar had now admitted he *had* been driving at the time of the fatal collision but would contend there was nothing wrong with the standard of his driving. I was delighted – I had overcome the most monumental hurdle in this case. Then I faced a terrifying hitch.

Part of my preparation for the trial was to line up the CCTV footage for the jury to watch. But Isleworth Crown Court only had VHS players – and my vital bus lane evidence was on DVD. A technician at the Met's video lab said a DVD to VHS transfer would take between six to eight weeks. I panicked when I heard this. What would I do now? I'd put my heart and soul into this case. I'd made a promise to Fatima's parents: *I promise I will do everything in my power to achieve justice for your daughter.* I couldn't exactly approach the judge and say, 'Sorry mate, you'll need to halt the trial for six weeks… got a bit of a technical issue – you know how it is.'

OK, Matt, calm down. Improvise, adapt and overcome. Everything in my power, everything *in my power.* That night, I took the DVD home, played it on my television and recorded the footage on my VHS camcorder. Job done, or so I thought.

Ananthakumar's lawyer got wind of my DVD to VHS creativity and tried to challenge me – in the absence of jurors – for circumventing protocol. Not only was he trying to discredit the video, but also me as a witness. If successful, he could get the case reduced to the much lesser charge of driving without due care and attention. Or he could get the whole case dismissed. I felt like I was the one on trial as I stood in the witness box on bendy-straw legs.

'Your honour, this is a clear breach of correct protocol for video evidence,' the defence barrister said to Judge Richard McGregor-Johnson. 'I ask that this video evidence be declared unreliable and excluded from the evidence.' I swear, my heart stopped. An agonising pause filled the courtroom. People coughing, throat-clearing, sniffing. I clenched my sweaty fists at my thighs, then…

'Request denied. The footage *will* be shown to the jury.' *Oh, thank you, Judge Richard McGregor-Johnson. Allow me to buy you a pint, or three.*

Ananthakumar's defence team made several attempts to thwart the prosecution case. His barrister even tried to intimidate Amanpreet Gill, who, as a child witness under eighteen, was due to give her evidence from behind a screen. Under the Youth Justice and Criminal Evidence Act 1999, Amanpreet was classed as a vulnerable witness. The screen is to protect underage witnesses – yet the defence barrister objected to this set-up and asked the judge for permission to cross-examine Amanpreet in open court. Judge Richard McGregor-Johnson tilted his wigged head at the lawyer, gave him an incredulous look. 'Do you have a copy of the Youth Justice and Criminal Evidence Act 1999?' he said.

'Yes, I do,' said the barrister.

'Then I suggest you spend your lunch break reading the damn thing. Request denied. Court adjourned.'

Oh, I wanted to laugh my head off.

Another move by Ananthakumar's lawyer was to call to the stand an independent collision investigator, whose reconstruction of the hit-and-run crash calculated the Carina was travelling at 30mph on impact. Our investigations estimated the crash speed as 40mph. However, the expert then shot himself in the foot by confidently declaring, 'When a child is struck by a car, they never go over the bonnet. They always go under the vehicle.' The prosecution barrister proceeded to cite half a dozen cases to discredit the expert's claim.

Another expert called by the defence team was a consultant trauma surgeon who suggested the Carina would have been doing no more than 20mph when it struck Fatima. The surgeon was brought before the judge in the absence of the jury. When challenged, however, the doctor admitted he had had no training in vehicle dynamics or collision reconstruction, had been involved with fewer than half a dozen cases of child victims of fatal accidents, and had never visited a collision scene. The judge dismissed the surgeon's evidence as unreliable and ruled he should not be called in front of the jury.

At last, the defence case ended and the jury retired to consider its verdict. Not wanting to miss this, I remained in the court building for the duration. The jury returned about half an hour later, its foreman confirming a 'unanimous verdict' had been reached. My stomach turned to water. I sat in the public gallery, every muscle in my body clenched. In the row in front of me, Fatima's parents held hands, Anna sitting nervously beside them, poised to translate the verdict. Seconds passed like long minutes. 'Will the defendant please rise,' said Judge Richard McGregor-Johnson. Ananthakumar stood up, expressionless as ever. Then the judge looked at the foreman. 'On the charge of causing death by dangerous driving, how does the jury find the defendant?' I swallowed hard, closed my eyes for a second.

'Guilty.'

My eyes pinged open. Did I hear that correctly? Three more guilty verdicts followed for the remaining charges. I wanted to punch the air but instead whispered, 'Yes!' Maka and Abuukar wept and hugged one another as Anna relayed the news in Somali. *We did it*, I thought. *We won justice for Fatima Mahmoud.* I had a tear in my eye.

The following month, I returned to Isleworth for Ananthakumar's sentencing. Jailing Ananthakumar for three years for causing death by dangerous driving – and a further nine months for perverting the course of justice – Judge Richard McGregor-Johnson told him: 'Nothing I can say or do can alter the facts. I cannot bring Fatima back. I accept that you have shown remorse in recent months but the effect of this accident on you is far outweighed by the permanent effect it has had and will continue to have on Fatima's family.'

The judge's comments resonated with me. Nothing could bring Fatima back, but at least Maka and Abuukar could now grieve knowing that justice had been served. Personally, I thought Ananthakumar got off lightly, but the Mahmouds were happy with his sentence. Outside the court, they thanked me profusely in English, then, via Anna, added, 'Thank you, officer, for doing everything in your power to fight for justice for our daughter.'

I smiled and gulped back the lump in my throat. 'You're very welcome.'

Later that day, I discovered I'd been nominated for the Livia Award, a prestigious annual gong for Metropolitan Police crash investigators. The award is named in memory of sixteen-year-old Livia Galli-Atkinson, who tragically died after being struck by a car that mounted the pavement in Enfield in 1998. My nomination by Cheeseman was for my work on the Ananthakumar case and I felt extremely honoured, a few months later, to accept the Livia Award for

Professionalism and Services to Justice during a reception at the Houses of Parliament. I also received a letter from the then Prime Minister, Tony Blair. Oh, and I appeared on ITV London, too.

I did wonder, as I stepped forward to receive my trophy and silver tie pin from Livia's mum Giulietta. *Had the custody detention officer not have made the error of giving Ananthakumar his phone back, would I be here, even? Would we have achieved justice for Fatima and her parents without that chance breakthrough?* I pushed those thoughts to the back of my mind as I accepted my trophy. 'Thank you,' I said.

That was the proudest moment of my policing career.

CHAPTER TWENTY-THREE
PREPARING FOR TRAGEDY

The Ananthakumar case was to be my last fatal accident investigation. Shortly after his conviction, and the Livia Award ceremony, I received another promotion. Much as I was in my element as a collision investigator, police regulations at that time prohibited in-house promotions, so as well as receiving a tidy pay-rise, I needed to transfer out of the unit. In late November 2004, I walked into Uxbridge police station wearing three silver chevrons as Sergeant Matt Calveley. No 'acting' necessary this time.

My day-to-day duty would be a world away from investigating and reconstructing road deaths. As custody sergeant, I would be responsible for the welfare of those arrested and held in the cells. All prisoners must leave my custody intact, whichever their onward destination, be it a road trip to court, homeward bound on bail, or, in some cases, hospital. But a custody sergeant's biggest fear is for a prisoner to die on your watch. The thought of that happening terrified me to the core.

Uxbridge, a suburban town in west London, is one of the leafier parts of the capital that radiates a vibrant, smart vibe – home to Brunel University and steeped in military history with the Battle of Britain bunker at its heart. The River Pinn also flows through it. As expected, the custody suite at Uxbridge police station did not hold the same charm as its exterior surroundings.

Like most station custody suites, the one at Uxbridge was at the rear of the station on the ground floor. (The ground floor location is key as it saves marching up and down a load of stairs with prisoners – especially the violent ones.) Inside, the suite was typically grim: hospital green walls, hard floors and nine steel-doored cells, each furnished with a wooden bench topped with a slither of a mattress, a CCTV camera, and a steel toilet in the corner. There were also two detention rooms, slightly gentler in appearance, for the younger custody inmates. The suite had a unique aroma, too, a heady blend of sweat and piss and shit mixed with microwave meals and astringent twang of cleaning fluids. I could think of better places to spend the next six months.

Just as it is with all other areas of policing, no two days are the same in the custody suite, as I discovered during my first couple of weeks at Uxbridge. Friday and Saturday nights were the worst; drunk detainees kicking off, shouting, swearing, and occasionally splattering the cells with vomit and urine. But, as I said, the welfare of those prisoners is paramount.

One evening, on my first week of late shifts as custody sergeant, we took delivery of a fourteen-year-old shoplifter, Sarah, arrested when fleeing an off-licence with a 700ml bottle of WKD Blue stuffed beneath her bomber jacket – while bunking off from school. She'd clearly been on the WKD before her failed shoplifting stunt. Her lips and tongue held a bluish hue and she reeked of fruity alcohol and cigarettes. Sarah's speech was slurred, and she stumbled against the female officer who walked her into the interview room. An hour later, as Sarah slept off her WKD Blue binge in the detention room, I faced the uncomfortable task of dealing with her mother Yvonne.

Dressed in low-rise jeans and midriff-baring top, Yvonne clacked into the suite in her spiky heels, face arranged in a can't-be-arsed-with-this expression. She walked up to the counter, where I waited, ready to greet Yvonne with sympathy and patience. *Learning of her teenage daughter's arrest will come as a huge shock to Sarah's family*, I thought.

Yvonne slammed her handbag on the counter, hoiked the waistband of her jeans with a wriggle of her hips and exhaled a long sigh.

'Good evening, Mrs…' I began.

'You do know she's pregnant, don't you,' barked Yvonne.

'Excuse me?'

'Sarah, my daughter. The one you've locked up. She's fackin' pregnant.'

'Actually, no, I didn't,' I replied. 'All I know is that she's bunking off school, getting drunk and robbing shops.' S*od the magnanimous approach.*

Yvonne leaned over the counter, lips curled in a frosty pink snarl that bared tobacco-stained teeth. 'I don't care about any of that.' She raised her arm, daggered a pointy finger towards my face. 'And if you lot harm her or that baby, I'll have your fackin' jobs.'

'Sarah is fine. She has been interviewed and is now in the detention room, sleeping off the alcohol she drank.

Sarah is being closely monitored in accordance with our regulations. Her fate is now in the hands of the CPS, who will decide whether or not to prosecute your daughter.'

'Oh, for fack's sake. How long is all that gonna take? I'm supposed to be going out tonight.' Yvonne then picked up her bag, pulled from it a twenty-pack of Marlboro Lights and slid the box across the counter. 'And you make fackin' sure you give her these.' And with that, Yvonne clicked out of the station. Her attitude saddened me. *Where is the much-needed support for teenagers like Sarah?*

Sarah was released from the detention room two hours later. Yvonne waited for her daughter outside the station this time.

The CPS chose not to prosecute Sarah on this occasion.

Sadly, I saw many youngsters like Sarah enter the custody suite throughout my term at Uxbridge. Again, mainly shoplifters or teenagers arrested for drug offences or GBH. But my worst-case-scenario-possible episode in custody didn't occur until the final week of my six-month stint.

It happened one Tuesday morning. I'd just taken over the responsibility of half a dozen detainees from the night shift custody sergeant at 6am. One of those prisoners was a middle-aged woman, Lucy, arrested the previous night for assaulting her landlord. Although Lucy's fingerprints, taken when she arrived at the suite, revealed a false identity, her real name being Lena, a Polish woman wanted for deportation by the Borders Agency.

Around mid-morning, the gaoler (a female constable), during a routine check, found Lena collapsed on the floor of the cell. The police doctor just happened to be at the station. He assisted within minutes and swiftly established that Lena had feigned illness. She returned to the bench in her cell, seemingly fine, he told us, and my shift continued. An uneventful shift thereon, until 2pm arrived and I handed over to the late shift sergeant, Ewan.

After checking the paperwork for each detainee, Ewan did a walk around to check all the detainees in their respective cells – a routine task before signing to accept responsibility for the inmates. I was just about to head for the door when Ewan's voice flooded the suite. Loud and urgent. 'Matt, come quick. Lena's collapsed.'

I dropped my rucksack and ran along the green corridor, up to the female cells, hoping Lena was faking it again. Skidding as I rounded the corner into her cell, however, a sinister scene greeted me: Ewan, kneeling on the floor over Lena. I joined Ewan on the floor. Lena's face had turned a worrying greyish blue. Buried in folds of skin at her neck was a ligature fashioned from a strip of fabric torn from her skirt, tightly knotted around her throat. 'She's not breathing,' said Ewan, feeling Lena's neck for a pulse. And what happened next happened fast.

While one constable called 999 for an ambulance, I ran back to the custody area, grabbed a first aid kit and a special knife called a ligature cutter, then darted back to the cell and sliced the fabric noose away from Lena's throat. Paramedics arrived then – and managed to revive Lena before rushing her to hospital. But, despite our efforts, Lena died a few hours later.

As is standard practice following a death in custody, the Independent Police Complaints Commission (now the

Independent Office for Police Conduct), launched a full investigation into Lena's case. This would be my first, and fortunately my last, encounter with the IPCC.

The gaoler and I got hauled before investigators and quizzed over the events of that fateful Tuesday. I was confident in my actions and had no issues speaking to them openly and honestly. But, a few weeks later, I received a call from one of the investigators. 'You'll need to come in for a further interview,' he said. When I asked why, he said he'd studied the CCTV from the custody suite and noticed a discrepancy between what I'd written in my report and what the cameras had revealed.

'No problem,' I told him. 'Show me the CCTV and I'll comment on it.'

'Sorry, I can't show you the footage,' he snapped.

'Well, *I'm* also sorry,' I said. 'Thank you, but I will not be attending a second interview.'

I felt outraged at the investigator's tactic; surely the primary purpose of any inquiry was to establish the truth? And besides, I was under no obligation to attend a second interview.

Only months down the line did I discover the nature of that so-called 'discrepancy'.

In my notes, I wrote that after running out of the cell, I collected the first aid kit, then the ligature knife, before sprinting back to Lena. The CCTV showed that I first picked up the knife, followed by the first aid kit. When writing notes immediately after a traumatic incident, it is easy to make such minor and inconsequential errors. Looking back on the investigation, I can think of only one reason why the IPCC refused to show me the CCTV footage – to discredit me and lure me into a dishonesty trap.

A subsequent inquest into Lena's demise returned a death by suicide verdict. The jury foreman added that they could find no fault in the actions of any police officer. No criminal action was taken against the Met.

May 2005, and again, I was on the move, posted to supervise a response team at Ruislip police station. They were a great bunch of constables, some of whom remain personal friends to this day. Two months into my new job, I said a brief farewell to those constables and headed off on a well-deserved family holiday to Greece, unaware of the atrocities soon to rock London.

I was sitting in the hotel lobby, waiting for Laura and the kids to come back from the pool, when the news broke on the wall-mounted television screen showing Sky News. The tickertape told of 'reports of an explosion outside London's Liverpool Street station'. Cut to a scene depicting an eyewitness, stood amid a sea of screaming emergency vehicles near Aldgate Station, recalling hearing a 'huge bang'. Next, reports of three bombs exploding within a minute on London Underground trains. I stood up, joined the crowd of people forming around the screen. Cries of, 'Oh my god,' and 'Oh no.' More news in of an explosion on a bus in Tavistock Square. Events that would later become known as the 7/7 bombings were unfolding before me with alarming rapidity – and suddenly, Greece lost its appeal. I wanted to be back in London, back at work, policing the aftermath of these atrocities.

I remained glued to the news over the next few days, horrified as details of the worst single terror attack on British soil emerged. On that day, July 7, 2005, four Islamic terrorists – Mohammad Sidique Khan, Shehzad Tanweer, Germaine Lindsay and Hasib Hussain – targeted innocent commuters during the morning rush hour, detonating four homemade bombs on London's transport network, killing fifty-two people. A further 700 victims were also injured in the blasts. I arrived back in the UK to a changed London – a city in mourning, fragile yet defiant amid fears of repeat attacks.

The police response to the 7/7 bombings was inevitably massive, with almost every officer in the Met involved in some capacity. Due to my new position, my policing involvement was restricted to managing a team of constables on cordon enforcement and guarding the temporary mortuary housed in huge white tents in the gardens of the Honourable Artillery Company in central London. It was heartbreaking to watch forensic-suited workers carrying body bag after body bag into the marquees. But standing for hours on end outside the mortuary frustrated me. I wanted to be more involved. I thought about what was happening inside those tents, where scores of dedicated officers, medics and volunteers were working round the clock to identify victims and, ultimately, bring some form of comfort and closure to their loved ones. And I thought, *I'd like to do that.* Fast forward a year and an opportunity to do that very job came my way.

The Met was seeking ten sergeants and fifty constables to train as on-call Disaster Victim Identification (DVI) officers. Almost 2,000 cops applied – and I was accepted. Intensive training at Hendon College followed. 'If you've seen one disaster movie you've seen them all,' the Chief Superintendent warned. 'But if you've seen one *disaster*, you've seen one disaster. Here in the Met, we've always been extremely good at planning for the *last* disaster.'

The weeks of training that ensued reflected that systemic failure, with an emphasis on preparing for imminent terror attacks. Intensive yet comprehensive, I could not fault the course. The training included full case studies of the Paddington rail disaster and the 2004 Indian Ocean tsunami, together with photo albums, video footage and witness accounts. We learned how to recover bodies and body parts from scenes of mass fatality in a way that preserved the item's forensic integrity, which maximises the chances of identifying the victim and obtaining evidence against the perpetrators. We set up mock temporary mortuaries, working in teams of five or six to carry out post-mortems. A team consisted of a team leader (usually a police sergeant), a pathologist, a photographer, and two or three police constables for form-filling, manual handling of the bodies and exhibits recording. Part of the ethos was that everyone must be prepared to do everything.

'If phrases like "not in my remit" or "I haven't had the training" strike a chord with you, then you may as well leave now, as this course definitely isn't for you,' the instructor warned. This was music to my ears. I was more than happy to get stuck into anything and everything.

Training complete, as a newly qualified Disaster Victim Identification officer, I was then placed on a call-out list and returned to my day job as a response team sergeant, poised for the call bringing tragic news of the next mass fatality incident.

Sadly, there wasn't one skill I learned on the course that could prepare me for the personal tragedy soon to rip my world apart.

CHAPTER TWENTY-FOUR
COPING MECHANISMS

We found out Laura's cancer was terminal on my forty-third birthday.

Laura was diagnosed with non-Hodgkins lymphoma fifteen months previously, just after I'd completed my disaster victim identification course. At the time of her diagnosis, the consultant had predicted a seventy to eighty per cent chance of recovery. And while the last fifteen months had been enduringly tough, Laura, the kids and I had remained optimistic that she would indeed fight this cruel illness. 'I'll be fine. I'm young, I'll beat this.' That was Laura's mantra. Now, sitting beside Laura in Michael Sobell Hospice, paper plates holding foamy crumbs of Victoria sponge birthday cake resting on the foot of her bed, it took all my strength not to collapse and sob as the oncologist's words polluted the disinfected air.

'I'm sorry, there's nothing more we can do.'

Five minutes ago, we'd both been chatting and laughing with a few of Laura's work colleagues, who'd come to see Laura after her latest round of radiotherapy, which she routinely underwent at the hospice. Today was my birthday, so we'd had a little celebration, guzzled Shloer from plastic cups and joked about the juice being 'fake wine'. I'd blown out the candles on my Tesco Finest cake to choruses of *Happy Birthday* and *For He's a Jolly Good Fellow*. We'd tucked into the cake, and I was halfway through my slice when Dr Taylor, Laura's oncologist, came in. 'Excuse me, may I have the room for a moment,' he'd said. The room turned foggy; every noise amplified through the mist. The polite squeak of chair glides shifting on the vinyl floor, the rustle of a Tesco carrier bag. Sticky, muffled clicks of lips on skin when Laura's friends said goodbye. My thumping heart.

Once Laura's friends had left the room, Dr Taylor sat down and, in measured tones reserved for the delivery of tragic news – a voice I'd practised myself so many times on the Job – dispensed the prognosis I'd reluctantly expected but prayed would never come true. I could not process what Dr Taylor was saying. I don't think Laura could, either. I caught only snippets. Blurred, veiny branches emerging behind the fog. There but not there.

Regarding treatment, I'm afraid we've exhausted all avenues.

Life expectancy, three months.

Macmillan nurses, hospices.

I'm sorry, there's nothing more we can do.

Silence. I reached for Laura's hand, and she smiled. A small smile, but still, a smile. 'I'll be fine. I'll beat this,' she said. I tried to return her smile. I could not speak. If I did, I would cry and that would not help Laura. Dr Taylor's grave voice chanted an elegy in my head. *I'm sorry, there's nothing more we can do. Three months.* This could not be happening. My Laura, one of life's kindest people. Quiet and polite and always sees the best in everybody. *She's only forty-three.* None of this made sense; just months before her diagnosis, Laura had been awarded a well-deserved commendation – for serving twenty years in the Metropolitan Police without ever taking a sick day.

Where do we go from here?

Laura's health deteriorated rapidly after that devastating day at Michael Sobell Hospice. Her fighting spirit was ever present, while I tried to process this heartbreaking news and cope with day-to-day life, giving it the I'm-OK-I-can-manage attitude, but crumbling inside.

Since Laura's diagnosis, we had received incredible support from friends and the Metropolitan Police – and the force's generosity continued throughout her illness. My commander Mark Toland was an absolute star. He let me choose my shifts to fit around hospital visits and gave me days off whenever I needed them. Thanks to Mark, I also had free use of police vehicles for hospital visits and regular contact from Occupational Health.

I had to remain strong for Laura, Daniel and Rachel. I *wanted* to remain strong for Laura, Daniel and Rachel. So far throughout Laura's illness I'd juggled twenty-four-seven shifts with hospital visits and school runs. I did all the house-work, shopping and cooking. Adding to this pressure, two months before Dr Taylor's shattering announcement that Laura only had three months to live, Daniel fell off a swing and fractured his right elbow. I then spent a month washing and dressing Daniel while his arm was cast in plaster. Even after learning of Laura's life expectancy, I maintained this 'coping' persona. Like a typical cop, I assumed I was super-human and could deal with everything.

I couldn't. Especially now.

Even after we learned of Laura's fate, I tried to keep as fit and healthy as possible with occasional workouts at the Denham Garden Village Fitness and Leisure Centre. And it was there, after a gym session, that the all-consuming grief I'd tried so long to subdue hit me like a freight train.

Alone in the sauna that morning, I closed my eyes and thought about the day ahead. The supermarket and school run I needed to do before visiting Laura at the hospice. *What shall I cook for dinner tonight? Did I wash Daniel's PE kit?* Sweat trickled down my face. Then Dr Taylor interrupted. *I'm sorry, there's nothing more we can do. Three months, three months, three months.* I breathed in the hot steam, and as I exhaled, a sound I'd never made issued from my mouth. A hollow, chest-crushing sob. Tears streamed, mixed with my sweat, filling my mouth with salt. I slid off the bench, crumpled to the slippery tiled floor and sobbed and sobbed, hysterically. 'I can't... cope. I can't cope with this anymore.'

I'm sorry, there's nothing more we can do.

I cried for a few minutes before a tidal wave of guilt and self-loathing washed over me. *Pull yourself together, Matt. You haven't got cancer. You're not the one in a hospice, contemplating your final days. Get a grip. Get a bloody grip.* I stood up, regained my composure, took a few deep breaths, and headed for the showers. *I can cope. I must cope.*

Three weeks after Dr Taylor's prognosis, on Friday November 2, 2007, a nurse from the hospice called me just after 11am to tell me that Laura was now gravely ill.

It was time.

I picked up Daniel and Rachel from their schools but instead of taking them home I drove to the hospice in Northwood.

'Where are we going, Daddy?' asked Dan, looking puzzled.

Deep breath. Control the emotion. Calm the voice. Here goes …

'We're going to say goodbye to Mummy,' I replied, tears streaming down my cheeks.

Laura passed away the following day.

Her death devastated all those who loved her – family, friends, and colleagues in the Metropolitan Police. The Met gave Laura a full police force funeral at Ruislip's Breakspear crematorium, complete with motorcycle outriders. And my team of police officers formed a Guard of Honour, resplendent in their best white-gloved ceremonial uniforms.

I walked slowly behind Laura's coffin, also in ceremonial uniform, Daniel holding my left hand, Rachel holding my right, into the crematorium.

Where do we go from here?

CHAPTER TWENTY-FIVE
THE FINAL RUN

Work became my saviour in the aftermath of Laura's passing. Mark Toland gave me total flexibility on my hours. I could not have asked for a more understanding boss.

Despite my grief, I still had the same passion for policing. Although one incident I attended after returning from compassionate leave was a bit too close to home: an explosion at a gas cylinder-filling firm – based at a workshop next to a petrol station a few doors along from my house on Oxford Road, New Denham.

I arrived at the scene to see a man, screaming his head off, being stretchered out of the warehouse by ambulance crew. He'd lost his leg from the knee down and the stump that remained was swathed in a bloody bandage. Inside the warehouse, Kerry Daly, an employee at the firm which today still trades as 'Mr Fizz', lay dead in a sea of shrapnel. He died after trying to refill a low-pressure cylinder with gas from a high-pressure machine, which caused the blast.

I didn't go into the warehouse as Thames Valley Police had the job in hand, so I worked on the periphery, controlling the crowds thronging the cordon. I knew most of the people; many of them were neighbours of mine, so they were an easy crowd to control.

The explosion later made local news headlines when the Health and Safety Executive ruled that Kerry Daly had not been sufficiently trained by the gas company – landing Mr Fizz with a £90,000 fine.

I threw myself into my job; being at work was a welcome distraction in the months after Laura's death. My constables were hardworking and, like me, passionate about policing. We managed to have a laugh too – even when catching villains.

As team sergeant, I would spend one shift a month supervising my constables on patrol. And there's one night-shift, with constables Patrick and Jess, that still makes me laugh to this day.

We headed out on patrol around 10.30pm in a shiny new BMW 530 estate. Patrick, an experienced Area Car driver with several years' service under his belt, was at the wheel, Jess in the passenger seat and I sat in the back, observing as Patrick drove around the southern end of West Drayton. But it was quiet, nothing doing on the radio, so Patrick swung by some crime hotspots in the area in the hope of stumbling across some nefarious activity. I kept quiet in the back, let Patrick do his thing. Then, pulling into Stockley Industrial Estate, we spotted an old Nissan Sunny, parked next to a high wire fence. Two hooded men stood in front of the car and, as we neared them, could see they were conversing with a third man in a silver Ford Focus parked sideways on the other side of the fence. Suspecting a drug deal, Patrick switched on the twos and blues, powered the Area Car straight in and blocked the Nissan. The two hooded figures wheeled round, our blue lights strobing their startled faces, while the driver in the Ford Focus switched off his lights and wheel-spun into the darkness.

We three jumped out of the car, cornered the two men, both as wiry as the fence behind them. I stood to one side as Patrick asked them, 'Can you tell us what you're doing here, lads?'

Then, gesturing through the fence. 'Who's your mate – he seemed in a hurry?'

The lad on the right spoke first, pulling his hood down to his brow, hands aquiver. 'Getting some gear, innit.'

'Yeah, but we ain't got any on us,' his mate weighed in. 'Big Alex was gonna give us some brown [heroin] then you lot showed up, innit.'

'I assume that was "Big Alex" in the Ford Focus that drove off a few minutes ago?' said Pat.

'Yeah, he's our dealer.'

I stepped in then. 'And which one of you owns this Nissan Sunny?'

'They're my wheels, man. Why you asking?' That was the lad on the right.

'Because your wheels – and you two – need to accompany us to the station for a thorough search under the Misuse of Drugs Act 1971. May I have your car keys?'

There were a few mumbles of objection from the two lads, but overall, they were compliant. The Nissan owner handed over his keys. 'As he said, we ain't got nuffink on us,' I heard him say when he and his mate got into the back of the police car. Patrick started the engine and off they went to West Drayton police station. Meanwhile, I would follow in the Nissan.

The battered Nissan was like a skip inside, the passenger footwell alive with greasy McDonald's wrappers and empty bottles. Not taking any chances, I pulled on my surgical gloves and gave the driver's seat a good pat down before I got in. Last thing I needed was a used smack needle harpooned in my arse. All good, no needles detected. I climbed into the driver's seat, just as the Nokia ringtone sang from the passenger footwell. I rummaged through the McDonald's wrappers, extracted from the debris a buzzing Nokia mobile with a scratched, illuminated screen displaying the text: 'Withheld number'. Excited, I answered the call.

'Yeah, what's happening, man?' I said, trying to emulate the vernacular of the boys now en route to the station.

'What the fuck happened back there, man?' came the caller's voice, bassy hip-hop music playing in the background. 'What's with the feds?' He had a pronounced south London accent.

'Yeah, dunno, man. Feds came from nowhere. Spooked us, man – but it's cool, we had nuffink on us.'

'So, you ain't nicked? You're cool, yeah?'

'Yeah,' I said, trying to make my voice sound jittery, 'but I'm clucking man. I can't handle this, I can't…'

'It's cool, man. Meet you at the Toby Carvery in Langley. Be there in fifteen minutes. I'll sort you out. Trust me.'

'Don't let me down, man,' I said, 'I'm…'

My man, presumably Big Alex, hung up, but no time to lose – this was a golden opportunity to nab a drug dealer red handed. I shoved the Nokia in my Metvest pocket, started the car, floored the banger to West Drayton police station, then sprinted inside and burst into the interview room, where Patrick and Jess were speaking with our two detainees, who were about to be strip-searched. 'Patrick, Jess, leave it,' I said, 'we need to go, now. Quick, back in the car. Meet you in the yard.'

My colleagues shot from their seats, legged it to the yard while I hot footed it to the front desk and rattled off details regarding our two lads to the station officer and an on-duty gaoler. 'Sort out the drug searches. I'll explain later.' I finished.

Out to the yard, into the back of the BMW. 'Toby Carvery in Langley, ASAP,' I said, 'we're gonna catch the dealer.' Patrick fired up the engine while Jess hit the twos and blues, and we screeched out of the yard. I briefed them both en-route, repeated my desperate drug-user impersonation.

'Blimey, and Big Alex bought that?' said Patrick, laughing.

'Just drive,' I said. 'Get your foot down, mate.'

Patrick drove the five miles to Langley flat out – it was vital for us to get there before Big Alex arrived. Langley is in Berkshire, outside of the Met area. Therefore, protocol dictated we should inform Thames Valley Police of our intentions. But this was a fast-time operation, so I decided that courtesy must give here.

Three minutes later, we were within a mile of our target. Jess shut off the twos and blues as we approached, then Patrick discreetly parked the BMW in a shadowy corner of the car park. We watched, waited and, after a few minutes, a silver Ford Focus rolled into the car park. The driver then spotted the Area Car, did a slow turn, and slowly drove towards the exit, trying to slope away undetected. Too late. Pat launched forwards, cut up the Focus and swerved in front of it to block the exit. Jess and I leapt out, ran to the Focus. I yanked open the driver's door. 'Get out,' I said.

'Alright, man,' said the driver, a muscular bloke, wide neck garlanded with gold chains. He stepped out of his car, shot his hands above his head, sending a plastic egg-shaped container somersaulting into the air. The vessel ricocheted off the Toby Carvery sign pledging, 'You're sure of a warm welcome,' dropped to the ground and rolled with a child-like clatter before bumping the Nike Air-trainered toe of our dealer suspect. Jess retrieved the container, cracked it open. It was a plastic Kinder Surprise Egg – stuffed with wraps of crack and heroin.

'Big Alex?' I said, unclipping my handcuffs from my belt.

'Yeah, that's me, why?' said the muscular bloke. I stepped forward, handcuffed Alex and recited his rights, arresting him under the Misuse of Drugs Act 1971.

Back at the station, as I relieved Big Alex of his possessions – wallet stashed with two-hundred quid, letter from his probation officer (this clearly wasn't his first brush with the law), house keys and a Motorola mobile phone – he asked who'd tipped us off.

'Nobody tipped us off, mate,' I said, plucking his Motorola off the counter. Fortunately, the phone was unlocked so I redialled the last number he'd called, causing my Metvest to burst into song with the iconic Nokia *Grande Valse* ringtone. I pulled the tatty old Nokia from my pocket and answered it. 'Feds came from nowhere, man,' I said. 'Don't let me down. I'm clucking, man.'

Big Alex's face fell. Suddenly, he didn't look so big. 'You fucker, that was you, innit.'

I smiled. 'See ya,' I said, then hung up.

Our Toby sting turned out to be a good hit. We charged Alex and he subsequently pleaded guilty to possessing controlled drugs with intent to supply. He got eighteen months in the slammer for that. The Nissan driver and his mate were released without charge. They had 'nuffink' on them.

It had been a few years since I'd been assaulted on duty sufficiently badly to warrant financial compensation. In November 2008, that good run ended abruptly.

One Saturday night I was on a supervisory patrol with constable Jenny when the control room directed us to a domestic disturbance in a one bedroomed flat in Hayes. The dispute was between a couple. I'll call them Mr and Mrs Wilson.

Mrs Wilson, swollen eyes swimming with tears, let us into the flat and, as per standard procedure, Jenny and I separated the parties to speak to them individually. While Jenny spoke with Mrs Wilson in the living room, I was left with the option of dealing with Mr Wilson in the kitchen, the bedroom or the bathroom. Bedrooms and kitchens are generally no-go areas for such fraught discussions. A bedroom is too personal and intimate, and kitchens contain knives. So, I directed Mr Wilson to the bathroom. He was shorter than me but stocky and muscular, with a bent nose that looked to have been broken more than once.

'Don't know why the fuck she's involved you lot in this,' he snarled, kicking open the bathroom door. The bathroom was about ten-foot square, with a glass-screened shower cubicle, sugary pink porcelain sink, and matching toilet wearing a fluffy fuchsia mat on its lid. It smelt of Lynx deodorant in there. I stood in front of the shower, Wilson facing me, and instantly regretted my choice of meeting room. *It's a bit tight in here.*

'Look,' added Mr Wilson, 'me and the missus can sort this out between us.' He was standing so close I could hear his breath pumping through his nostril hair. Veins pulsed at his temples. I held up my hands.

'OK, let's keep this calm,' I said as a crackle of static issued from my chest, followed by Jenny's voice over the radio. 'Sarge, he's got to come in.' That was code for me to arrest Wilson, but before I could speak or make a move, Wilson launched himself at me and I found myself embroiled in a fierce fistfight. Our fighting morphed to a clumsy wrestle, and it took all my strength to keep upright against the force of Wilson's meaty arms. Moving as one tangled, grunting mass, we crashed into the glass shower screen, which exploded with a painful crack, sending thousands of shards into the tray. I stumbled backwards into the shower cubicle, grappled at my belt for my CS gas canister, but Wilson caught me off guard again. A sudden pain shot through my scalp as he grabbed a fistful of my hair and, slam, rammed my head into the tiled wall.

Blood gushed from my split right cheek. 'It's my fucking missus, my argument and none of your fucking business,' he yelled, pushing my face into the cold wall, his face almost pressing my left cheekbone. Breath, hot, infused with whiskey. I tried to elbow Wilson, but his grip was vice-like.

He's going to ram my head through this wall. Glass crunched under my sliding feet, then, outside the cubicle, the sound of hurried footsteps.

'Stop!' *Jenny, thank god.* I glimpsed out of the corner of my left eye her hands around Wilson's weighty shoulders. She yanked him backwards out of the shower, then I regained my balance, powered out of the cubicle and landed a couple of hefty punches on Wilson. Down he went, falling in a meaty heap beside the fluffy-topped toilet. Jenny handcuffed Wilson while I stood over him, dazed with blood oozing from my cheek. Mrs Wilson was now in the doorframe, hands clamped to the sides of her head, screaming hysterically. Jenny had already pressed the orange 'emergency' button on her radio.

Sirens sounded behind the frosted glass window. Help had arrived.

Wilson was charged with assaulting a police officer – an offence he pleaded guilty to in court, which earned him a suspended prison sentence. The court also ordered Wilson to pay me £500 in compensation within fourteen days.

Life continued to look brighter again, both on and off duty. I was out on supervision with another of my constables, Karen, who had arrested a bloke called Dennis for criminal damage to his neighbour's car. Handcuffed, Dennis had walked calmly to the police car, but kicked off when Karen opened the back door. 'Get off me. You can't fucking arrest me,' he went, shouldering her sideways.

I stepped in and hustled Dennis into the back of the car. 'For fuck's sake,' he went. 'This is a fucking joke. Ain't you lot got anything better to do?' I shut the door then got in beside Dennis via the opposite back door. As I sat down, my mobile phone pinged. I extracted it from the pouch on my belt and a warm glow filled my chest as a message from Julie flashed on the screen: 'Can't wait to see you this evening,' she'd texted. I'd met Julie, a delightful PHD student from Slough, a couple of weeks ago after some well-meaning friends and my two children finally convinced me to sign up to an internet dating site. I hit reply, thought about what to write as Jenny switched on the engine. Dennis was rocking back and forth now. 'You fucking fuckers, fucking fuckers.'

'Hi Julie,' I texted back. 'Hi Julie, I can't wait…'

'Bunch of twats.'

I couldn't concentrate for his racket. 'Dennis, shut up, this is important.' I gestured at my mobile.

Silence. Dennis gave me a rabbit-startled-in-the-head-lights look. Then he glanced down at my phone. 'Oh, right, yeah, sorry. On you go,' he said. I nodded a polite thank you and got back to my message. '…to see you too.' Dennis was as good as gold after that, and I'm delighted to inform you that Julie and I got engaged a week later – then we married in Lytham in October 2009.

In January 2010, after a seven-week posting at the Safer Neighbourhood base, I was thrilled to return to Traffic Patrol as a garage sergeant – a job I'd always craved. With a fleet of upgraded Vauxhall Omegas, BMW 530 estates (by far my favourite police car) and several high-speed vehicle pursuits ahead, I couldn't have wished for a better way to spend my final six years in the Metropolitan Police.

At the TDQ base, I would be supervising a team of traffic patrol constables, monitoring the general standards of police driving, and performing roles such as road death scene manager and tactical pursuit adviser.

Three months into my new posting, late on a Saturday night, I was called out on a 'fast run'. Fast runs are often used to transport specialist people or equipment at emergency speed. Tonight's fast run involved racing a consultant surgeon, Dr Fowley, from his Hertfordshire home to the Royal London Hospital in Whitechapel, where he was due to perform an emergency heart operation.

The surgeon couldn't drive his own car to the hospital as he had downed a 'glass or two of port' and 'could be slightly over the drink-drive limit', I'd been told. Watching Dr Fowley stagger out of his colossal house and towards my waiting police car, however, I realised this was an understatement. It took me around twenty minutes to drive on twos and blues to the hospital, by which time Dr Fowley was slumped across the back seat of the police car, fast asleep and snoring loudly.

I got out of the car, opened the back door, and shook the surgeon's shoulder. 'Dr Fowley, wake up, we're at the hospital.' His reply was a port-fragranced snore into the lapel of his Harris Tweed blazer. He was due to perform emergency heart surgery in half an hour.

'Dr Fowley?' I repeated, shaking him harder this time. The surgeon stirred, gave me a look of confusion through squinted eyes. 'Where am I?'

'You're at the hospital,' I said.

'Oh bother,' he said. 'Take care of it for me, would you,

there's a good chap. It's just a coronary artery bypass graft. A trained monkey could do it'.

Dr Fowley closed his eyes. *What the hell do I do now? Fowley's in no fit state to stand up, let alone wield a scalpel.*

The answer to my dilemma came via a radio transmission from Scotland Yard:

'Oscar Sierra Five, are you receiving?'

'Go ahead,' I responded.

'Don't know if you're at the Royal yet, Sarge, but you can cancel. Hospital have just advised us that the patient has passed away.'

I whizzed Dr Fowley back to Hertfordshire. He snored all the way home.

My final years in the Metropolitan Police seemed to be flying past at a frenzied pace, with more varied roles – and awards – along the way.

In 2012, for the second time in my career, I was appointed the unenviable position of suicide-prevention officer. My first attempt twenty years ago had ended with a drugged girl falling from a window ledge – although she did survive. This time, my colleague Scott and I saved a lad who was threatening to throw himself off an elevated section of the M4 – a fifteen metre drop. Fortunately, in a moment of distraction, we pounced on the lad and handcuffed him – a move that earned Scott and I commendations.

I underwent extensive training, passed my lorry driving test after one lesson, and brushed-up on my two-wheel skills. But the highlight was the Tactical Pursuit and Containment course (TPAC), which involved racing up and down the UK's motorways in high-performance BMWs, almost touching wing mirrors at over 100mph with the 'stolen car' we were trying to box in and force to a halt. A pursuit commander's course followed – and I put these new skills to good use in several high adrenaline pursuits.

...And then this happened:

I was enjoying a BLT and a glass of Coke in the bar of the Strathallan Hotel, Birmingham, when I received a withheld call on my mobile. Julie was here on a business trip, so I'd taken a couple of days off and tagged along too, just for the hell of it. Now just six months away from retirement, I was beginning to relish the prospect of a more relaxed lifestyle.

I picked up the call.

'Sergeant Calveley?' came the woman's voice. 'I'm calling from CO3 department, Scotland Yard. I don't know if you've seen the news yet, but you need to grab your DVI kit and prepare for deployment.'

'What's the job?' I asked.

'Tunisia,' she said. 'Sorry I've got loads more phone calls to make. Check out Sky News.'

I flipped open my laptop and watched the rolling news online, my stomach in knots. A gunman, dressed as a tourist, later identified as ISIS-trained student Seifeddine Rezgui, had pulled a Kalashnikov from a parasol on a beach in Sousse, Tunisia, and opened fire, killing at least thirty-eight people. The victims, all holidaymakers at the five-star resort Riu Imperial Marhaba Hotel, included Brits and were slaughtered as they sunbathed or swam in the sea.

Four hours later, I received my deployment call from

the Yard. I would be team leader at Fulham Mortuary. The thirty British victims were to be flown in a military aircraft to the UK the following week, landing at RAF Brize Norton, then onwards to London in a fleet of hearses with a police escort.

The following Monday, I arrived at Fulham Mortuary to begin the most heart-wrenching job of my career – to oversee the post-mortems of those thirty innocent Brits, killed as they basked in the sun.

The briefing from the Senior Investigating Officer (SIO) was succinct. We had three clear objectives: confirm the identity of each victim, establish the cause of death, and recover evidence from the bodies. We had just a few hours to prepare, and then the body bags arrived.

Sweating profusely, dressed head to foot in a white Tyvek forensic suit, face mask, overshoes, and surgical gloves, I carefully unzipped my first black body bag. I steeled myself for what horrific sights lay within, but as I unzipped the bag, I reeled in shock. Over the years, I had seen countless injuries, fatal and non-fatal, caused by handguns, shotguns, and knives. But this was the first time I had seen devastating wounds caused by high-velocity rifle rounds. It would be insensitive of me to describe those horrific injuries, but I will say, I was appalled at the scale of the damage a single bullet could cause to human flesh and bone.

During that week we completed all thirty post-mortems diligently and professionally, balancing the need to move quickly to identify the victims and recover the evidence while showing due respect to them and their bereaved families. We worked flat out, with the only pause being for the poignant two-minute silence when the nation paid its respects to the victims. Three simultaneous post-mortems were underway at the time, but all the teams paused regardless – and bowed their heads as a mark of respect.

I remember watching the news after my last shift at the mortuary. The report featured pictures of all the British victims killed on the beach in Sousse. The photos depicted happy, vibrant people with their lives still ahead of them. It made for upsetting viewing as I recognised their faces – I'd helped to identify them. My heart went out to their loved ones.

Six months later, on January 15, 2016, after clocking up a quarter of a million miles (on foot and on wheels), and a couple of thousand arrests, the time came for me to bid farewell to the Metropolitan Police.

I remember well my last job on patrol on that drizzly Friday. At 2.30pm I cruised the BMW out through the security gates at TDQ and into Athlon Road, heading towards the A406. Constable Hannah came with me. She was supposed to be today's driver but, still a boy racer at heart, I wanted one last emergency drive. Just for old times' sake. About half an hour into the shift, my wish became a reality.

'Accident on the A40,' said Hannah, reading a message on our in-car data terminal. 'Motorcyclist down. Doesn't look too serious.' We'd just joined the anticlockwise M25 from the M1.

'Here goes then,' I said as Hannah activated the twos and blues. 'Let's see what this baby can do.' I floored the accelerator and the turbocharged engine pushed me back in my seat. We sped away like a plane along a runway, sirens screaming, blue lights illuminating road signs. My heart raced with the speedometer. The world flew past in stripes. Foot to the floor, I gripped the steering wheel, hands tingling against the vibrations, and watched the speedometer climb – and climb, and climb, nudging 100, 120, 140 then... 153mph. My fastest speed ever in a police car. Hannah sat there, rigid, and wordless – until we screeched to a halt at the crash scene off junction 16. I switched off the engine and turned to face Hannah. She was leaning forward with her head bent, gripping the dashboard. 'Oh. My. God,' she said slowly.

'How was that for a final run?' I said, still adrenalized. 'You'd pay good money for that at Alton Towers.'

Hannah unclipped her seat belt, took a couple of deep breaths, then turned to me, her head on one side. 'Oi, Buzz, now that you're retiring, do you think you'll calm down a bit?'

I looked in the rear-view mirror and laughed.

'Who knows? Maybe...'

EPILOGUE

November 7, 2019, 35,000 feet somewhere over the Atlantic Ocean

'Write it down!' said Julie, after I'd relayed yet another policing anecdote to her on this ten-hour flight home from Cuba. 'Seriously, Matt, you should write a book – you've certainly seen a lot throughout your career.'

I stretched back in my seat, contemplating my wife's remarks. Truth was, I'd never seen myself as any kind of writer. But had I been too dismissive? I began thinking back over my tales from the frontline. Perhaps Julie could be onto something? I reached into my breast pocket for my notebook and pen (old habits die hard) and began jotting a few notes. And just like that, *Cops and Horrors* was born.

Throughout my career I amassed hundreds of policing stories, from the tragic to the funny to the downright bizarre. This book contains only a selection of them.

Shortly after we got home from our trip, I received a letter from the Metropolitan Police. Would I consider pausing my retirement and returning to the Job, in either a paid or voluntary role? I gave due consideration to the terms and conditions of becoming a cop again. I thought about the financial implications and the fact I now lived many miles from London. Then I replied to the Met. 'Thanks, but no thanks,' I said. I'll leave policing the great capital city firmly in my past.

I bid my final farewell to the Metropolitan Police on January 28, 2016 when, having notched up thirty years' service, I handed in my warrant card. I received a great send-off from my colleagues, who presented me with a plaque, a cake and a remote-control toy aircraft which made me laugh. (I had recently qualified as a pilot and had taken several of my colleagues for 'Jollies' in the skies over Buckinghamshire.)

Retiring from the Met put me in what we retired officers call 'the sixth of the month club' – because our pension is paid on the sixth day of every month. I was also honoured to be awarded a Certificate of Exemplary Service from the Met Commissioner.

Life now moves at a slower pace, although 'once a cop, always a cop' perhaps? There's definitely a grain of truth in that aphorism. Despite my retirement from the Job, my 'police radar' is still serving to some degree. *Is that driver drunk? Why is that teenager loitering near that old lady? Have I got all my gadgets with me? Bugger, my back pocket's empty – where's my warrant card?* Pangs of envy as a police car hurtles past me on twos and blues at double the speed limit.

But I had my turn, and for three decades, it was an absolute blast.